1
S—
g

16/40.

Class Distinctions

Class
Distinctions

TIM HEALD

Hutchinson
London Melbourne Sydney Auckland Johannesburg

The author and publishers would like to thank John Murray (Publishers) Ltd for kind permission to reproduce lines from John Betjeman's 'In Westminster Abbey' from *Collected Poems*.

．

Hutchinson & Co. (Publishers) Ltd

An imprint of the Hutchinson Publishing Group

17–21 Conway Street, London W1P 6JD

Hutchinson Publishing Group (Australia) Pty Ltd
PO Box 496, 16–22 Church Street, Hawthorne, Melbourne,
Victoria 3122
PO Box 151, Broadway, New South Wales 2007

Hutchinson Group (NZ) Ltd
32–34 View Road, PO Box 40–086, Glenfield, Auckland 10

Hutchinson Group (SA) Pty Ltd
PO Box 337, Bergvlei 2012, South Africa

First published 1984
© Tim Heald 1984

Set in VIP Baskerville by
D. P. Media Limited, Hitchin, Hertfordshire

Printed and bound in Great Britain by
Anchor Brendon Ltd, Tiptree, Essex

ISBN 0 09 158700 X

For Randall and Grizel
but not about them

Think of what our Nation stands for,
  Books from Boots' and country lanes,
Free speech, free passes, class distinction,
  Democracy and proper drains.

John Betjeman,
'In Westminster Abbey', 1940

1

Somerset Burnam sat on the roller and waited for his boys. It
was 7.15 and he was chewing a blade of grass. The boys were
late. The boys were often late though it was difficult to see
why. Lights-out were at nine even for monitors. The
getting-up bell was at seven. Even growing twelve-year-olds
should be able to manage on ten hours' sleep. Mr Eden,
through whose drawing room the Suez Canal flowed, managed on virtually no sleep at all, though doubtless he had
needed more when little. Somerset Burnam had not listened
to the BBC news that morning, preferring to take a longer
walk than usual. The news was invariably depressing. There
was something about Eden that he did not like. An effemi-
nacy. It was true Winnie was very old and, it was rumoured,
slightly ga-ga. A parent whose cousin was the Member for
one of the Bournemouth constituencies had said as much at
the fathers' match. Even so, Winnie was Winnie and Eden
was, well, Eden. Not at all the same.

'Where are those boys, Muggins?' he asked sharply.

The dog looked up at him and pricked his ears. Irish
setter, domed head, russet coat, high-strung, a one-man dog.
They smiled at each other, the dog baring its fangs like a
Dalmatian. Burnam's smile was less emphatic, merely that
slightly quizzical stretch of the lips with a mild down-turn at
the right-hand corner. He rarely showed his teeth and boys,
as a rule, found this frightening, as, with reservations, they
usually found the man himself.

He had run the school for fifteen years. It was his, literally.
He had bought it with his inheritance a year after his parents
were killed in '49. He owned the house and the grounds and,
in a manner of speaking, he owned the staff and the boys.
They called him 'The Commanding Officer' or more often,

for short 'The CO'. It was a sobriquet he did not discourage.

He pressed a heel into the turf and watched it sink in. Although the morning was fine, with the light haze that suggested later sun, they had had a lot of rain recently and there was a heavy dew. The metal-tipped heel went in quite easily not only because the ground was soggy but because it was an unusually heavy boot. Although it was barely notice-able, one of Somerset Burnam's legs was shorter than the other – the result of a childhood riding accident. As a con-sequence he had been ruled unfit for military service, a decision which was more than usually upsetting, for the Burnams were a military family and had been since the eighteenth century. There had been a Burnam with Clive at Plassey and there had been many celebrated soldiers since, culminating, of course, in his brother Freddie. It was an absurdly bureaucratic decision for, despite that scarcely per-ceptible limp, he was as nimble and athletic as most men. His father had written to a friend at the War Office. He had protested himself, but the rules had prevailed and the near-est he got to action was firewatching during the Blitz. That had been hairy enough but there was no glamour in it and when his contemporaries returned from North Africa and Italy, Burma and northern Europe, with their campaign medals and a curious but unmistakable forced maturity, he had suffered. He suffered still, though he would never show it, not even to Clarissa.

'Where are those wretched boys?' he asked again, getting to his feet and spitting out the chewed stem of grass. He started to walk towards the gap in the yew hedge.

The experiences of 1939 to '45 had marked Burnam just as they had marked the country. England a decade after the end of the Second World War was still hung-over from it. There was a widespread and frequently expressed opinion that before too long 'things will get back to normal' and evidence could be called in support of this view. Rationing, for example, had been abolished and it was possible, once again, to buy as many chocolates or as much ice cream as you could afford. The English cricket team at last had a pair of fast bowlers as dangerous as the great men of the 1930s. At hundreds of fee-paying preparatory schools like West Hill small boys were studying Latin and leadership in order that

10

they should grow up to command ships and regiments and give orders to the other 95 per cent of the population which had not gone away to boarding school. Just like the good old days.

A visitor, returning to England after an absence of, say, twenty years, would have been reassured. Reassured, that is, if he had liked what he saw in 1936. Whatever aberrations might have occurred under the postwar Labour Government, power was now clearly back in the hands of the gentry. A correct pecking order had been re-established. The class structure was essentially intact.

Or so it seemed. But although it was difficult to put a finger on it, there was an underlying malaise which disturbed 'insiders' like Somerset Burnam. It was not just the constant disaffection in the Colonies. There had always been trouble in the Empire ever since the Mutiny. No use pretending the Queen's subjects in the pink parts of the globe were British. They were foreign. Always had been. Everyone knew that, even if they didn't say so out loud. But whereas in the past any native nonsense had been dealt with swiftly and efficiently, there now seemed a dangerous tendency to equivocate.

He would never have thought it during the war when he, like the rest of his countrymen, was, despite his problems, very proud to be British, but there was a discernible dilution in self-esteem and a worrying ill humour about the place. Chaps, in Burnam's estimation, were not pulling together as well as they might nor as well as they had. He noticed it in small ways which he nevertheless felt to be important. Boys when they came to him did not seem as well mannered as they had. They slouched. They needed to be told time and again to keep their hands out of their pockets. It had become so tiresome that he had even contemplated asking matron to sew up all pockets like they used to at the Royal Naval College, Dartmouth. Matron pointed out that if they did, the boys would have nowhere to keep their handkerchiefs. Fair point, he had to concede, and he could hardly blame the boys when public life was becoming so ill-mannered. Aneurin Bevan, the dissident Labour leader, so gratuitously churlish; and the affair the other day when George Brown had apparently lost his temper with the Russian leaders, Bulganin and

Khrushchev. It sounded as if the man had been drunk. It was deplorable.

He found the boys on the gravel outside the changing rooms playing pig-in-the-middle with Fieldhouse's felt hat. The felt hats were a hangover from the previous reign. They were floppy wide-brimmed shapeless objects, ordered by Burnam's predecessor in the thirties to protect boys from sunstroke.

Burnam would have eliminated them at once, but the school outfitters, Dickens and Jones, had protested that they had several dozen still in stock, all adorned with pink and green West Hill ribbon, and therefore of no use to anyone else. Reluctantly he had seen the force of their argument and agreed that there should be a phased withdrawal rather than a precipitate cancellation. The hats lingered on at the school, an optional and much derided extra, but still provided by the more anxious mother or handed down from one brother to the next. They were known by boys and staff as 'Soppoys' for unremembered reasons and were hardly ever worn. But they were quite useful for throwing and catching, rather like a flabby precursor of the Frisbee. This was what the boys were doing when Burnam found them.

They did not see him at first, being too engrossed in their game. For a few minutes he watched them, relishing the role of unobserved spectator, wistful, as always, at seeing how much more natural and uninhibited they were when on their own. In his presence there was always formality and deference even on those regular occasions when he tried to introduce a holiday atmosphere – the summer expedition to the beach at Weston-super-Mare, away matches, Guy Fawkes Night, the Ascension Day picnic. It was necessary. Discipline had to be enforced. There had to be a rein, however loosely held. At the Dragon School, in Oxford, boys called masters by their nicknames to their face. That would never do. Burnam acknowledged the title 'CO', but only tacitly. To *his* face he was 'Mr Burnam', 'sir' or 'headmaster'. In a way, at times, he wished it were otherwise but he knew it was impossible. This was a boarding school not a nursery. Parents paid £70 a term for their boys to be taught good manners and a sense of discipline, and, thought Burnam, quite right too.

12

So he watched them frolic for a moment, then shouted, 'Porter . . . Stack . . . Cut that right out! Give Fieldhouse back his Soppoy at once and stop fooling around. You're late for pitch rolling. You should be setting an example, not letting the side down. Now hurry along. You're monitors, for heaven's sake, not a lot of newbugs.'

They coloured, all of them. In each other's company masters and boys behaved with restraint, warily putting across the most impressive self-portrait they could manage. These were seen through by boys as often as by masters but the pretences were scrupulously preserved. Neither side enjoyed being caught out in anything truly characteristic.

'Sorry, sir,' said Porter, 'I didn't realize it was so late.'

'Well, you should,' said Burnam, 'you've got a watch.' Owning a watch was a privilege allowed only to the head of school. 'And you're supposed to set an example. They won't tolerate this sort of thing at Marlborough.'

'No, sir. Sorry, sir.'

The CO was irritated with Porter, though only mildly. He had been a favourite since first arriving five years earlier as a shy but determined eight-year-old, and Burnam had watched him mature with satisfaction. He was an above average brain, an average sport and, in Burnam's estimation, 'a thoroughly good influence' without being too much of a goody-goody. The CO was not sure where he drew the line between being a goody and a goody-goody but he knew there was one. Porter had just enough devil in him to be human, and not nearly enough to make him a pest. Sometimes Burnam was unsure about 'strength of character'. He occasionally showed signs of being 'easily led' (both phrases frequently surfaced in the headmaster's end-of-term reports) but a term as head boy should sort that out. The idea had been at the back of Burnam's mind when he made the appointment. It would give him confidence. Make a man of him. On the whole Burnam judged that the experiment was working. Certainly well enough not to worry too much about silly games with Soppoy hats.

The boys fell in beside and behind as he walked back towards the second-game pitch. He walked fast, as always, with long strides so that the boys could not quite keep up by walking themselves and had to hop, skip and half run, gambolling about like small tropical fish round something larger and more stately.

They were, thought Burnam, a rather bright year. West Hill was not a particularly academic school but this year he was hoping for at least three awards, perhaps more. In an average year one boy would win a scholarship to a recognized public school; in a good year two. Three had not been achieved since 1926, and one of the awards that year had been to a school called Leighton Park which was a Quaker establishment to which the famous West Country radical, Isaac Foot, sent his children. Burnam did not approve of Quakers or Feet. No boy of his would be going to Leighton Park.

Stack was the most gifted. He was taking the Winchester scholarship. No West Hill boy had ever even attempted such a thing. Winchester scholarships were left to the first eleven: Summerfields, Horris Hill, the Dragon. West Hill was not that sort of place, but Stack was an exception.

'How are the Latin verses, Stack?' he asked.

Stack's Latin verse was his weak subject. He would win, if he won, on his French and English.

'All right, thank you, sir.' Stack grinned and stared at his toes. He was a small, freckled child but strong. The school called him 'The Mighty Atom'.

'Only all right?'

'I think so, yes, sir.'

'What seems to be the trouble?'

They walked across the grass, gumboots leaving footprints in the dew.

'Well, sir, it just seems a bit, well, you know . . . pointless. I mean, I wouldn't mind writing English verse that people could understand but I don't see the point of writing poems in a language no one uses any more.'

'They use it at Winchester.'

No doubt about it, thought Burnam, Donald Stack needed to be put in his place. He grimaced ruefully. Donald Stack's place was too near the top for it to be an appropriate destination just now, and the trouble was that Stack knew it. He could not remember a more able boy; but ability in a thirteen-year-old was apt to breed bumptiousness and little Stack did have a high opinion of himself. The fact that it was

14

justified was no mitigation. Rather the reverse. Burnam attributed some of it to having lost his father during the war, but that was not the only reason. There was, in the CO's mind, a question mark against 'character' in Stack's file. If he were an adult Burnam would have said that he was 'not quite a gentleman'.

'Please, sir, my brother Freddie has a friend at Winchester and he says they use English just like everywhere else.' This was Fieldhouse. Fieldhouse thought he was funny and was unable to resist the opportunity of clever-clever remarks. They grated on Burnam's nerves, especially as the other boys invariably found them amusing. This time, as usual, there was a little chorus of girlish tittering.

Fieldhouse was the wettest of the school's three potential scholars, the only one who even began to conform to the stereotype notion of school swot. He was not very good at games though he tried desperately to make up for sporting deficiencies. It was a manifest truth in this as in most schools like it that you could get away with being a dunce provided you were a wizard centre forward or a demon leg-spin bowler. To be clever was allowable (though not particularly desirable) if you were a sporting hearty but a handicap if not. Better, in school life, to be hopeless at work *and* games. Burnam gave Fieldhouse credit for coming close to overcoming the stigma of 'weed' but privately awarded higher marks to Stack and Porter for sticking up for him. Without that, thugs like Ragwort I and Moberly would have made his life hell.

'You know perfectly well what I mean,' said Burnam stiffly. 'Latin verse is a compulsory subject in the Winchester scholarship because Winchester expects its scholars to be able to construe Latin verses. Winchester always has and Winchester always will. If Stack is to win a Winchester scholarship, his Latin verses will jolly well have to be up to scratch.'

He paused. They had arrived at the roller.

'Now, everybody get stuck into this rolling,' he said. 'Last time St Christopher's came their headmaster complained about bumps in the wicket. We don't want to give them any excuses this time, do we, eh? So heave-ho!'

He picked up the shaft of the roller and began to pull. The

15

boys surrounded it and bent like forwards in a rugby scrum. Muggins, the Irish setter, regarded them with disdain. Slowly, slowly, the heavy old iron creaked out across the turf, preparing the wicket for the afternoon match. Breath rose steamily in the morning air, and the boys in their elastic-topped navy shorts and light blue Aertex shirts grunted with the effort. Mr Burnam led from the front.

Dermot O'Rourke was homosexual. Not very homosexual, but homosexual. His homosexuality was not obvious, and certainly not in the fifties when homosexuals were supposed to be instantly recognizable by their limp wrists and their habit of calling other men 'dear' or 'dearie'. Dermot O'Rourke had never called anyone 'dear' or 'dearie' in his life. He had won the MC at Anzio with the Irish Guards and he had an iron handshake. When he practised his iron hand-shake he looked the recipient in the eyes with an unwavering steel-grey gaze. He had the reputation at West Hill of being a distinctly tough nut and if anyone had suggested that he was actually a bit of a fairy, they would have been laughed at.

Dermot O'Rourke was Somerset Burnam's number two. It was obvious to him and to some (though by no means all) others that there was only one reason why he was not the headmaster and Burnam *his* deputy, and that reason was money. O'Rourke had a modest private income, to be sure, but not the sort of money with which you could buy prep schools. This did not disturb him, for he was quite without ambition of the conventional kind. After the war his commanding officer had tried to persuade him to take a regular commission on the grounds that he would be a brigadier by the time he was forty. O'Rourke resigned at once.

He had taught at West Hill since being demobbed, apart from a six-month return trip to a part of Morocco he had discovered on leave a little earlier. He had intimated to Burnam when first interviewed for the job that he had gone native with a view to possibly settling permanently. Things, however, had not worked out and O'Rourke had moved on. Prep-school mastering had never occurred to him until he happened to notice the advertisement in the paper and had

16

answered it almost without thinking. Now, ten years on, he was content.

The work was far from arduous. Four months' holiday a year and practically all evenings off was a handy start; a modest amount of games coaching gave him just enough exercise to keep him in trim for occasional adult squash and tennis. He liked the boys (though he was scrupulously platonic in his affections) and the surroundings were pretty and agreeable. Others, he knew, regarded him as an awful waste, but when he looked at the careerists who were not, apparently, wasting themselves, he saw men who were almost all far less happy than he. In his quiet way he was satisfied with what he did. He took a mild but definite pride in inculcating questioning attitudes and open minds – though he acknowledged that part of this was a perverse pleasure in teasing the headmaster's orthodoxy and author-ity. There was nothing ignoble in being an assistant beak in a boys' preparatory school and, although his was an unusual view, he much preferred it to being a brigadier.

While Burnam and his senior pupils were rolling the wicket with conforming zeal, O'Rourke pushed the remains of his lightly boiled egg to one side, lit the second cigarette of the morning, and turned his attentions to the last third of the crossword. It was easier than usual, disappointingly so, since it provided the only foreseeable challenge of the day.

One across was 'Lord! Is Thomas sleepy, the ninny?' Three and five. 'Tom Noddy' he pencilled in, pursing his lips irritably. Two across was 'It is burnt in Fife.' 'Island' he wrote, grimacing again. Three: 'But don't they get permis-sion to go across the channel? 4, 5, 6.' 'Take French leave', he scrawled angrily. What *was The Times* coming to?

He had always been a *Times* man and, whatever its failings and foibles, *The Times* would always always claim his allegiance, just like the Liberal Party. And the Roman Catholic Church. He had reservations about the Pope and even more about the Liberals' new star, Jo Grimond, but the institution rose above the individual. If the compiler of the crossword had a substandard Saturday that was no reason to abandon the Thunderer, even if it invited insubordinate mutters.

In what he was beginning to find a disturbing world

O'Rourke considered *The Times* a good rock on which to base his day. That morning's had been no exception. In his paisley dressing gown with the first cigarette and the first cup of Earl Grey, he began with the front page. There was a charming dottiness about that grey front page of small-print advertisement. That morning he had been reassured by 'Mr Cuthbert's Weekly Garden Talk, number 1065' with its tetchily conservative opening ('Another word of undoubted American origin has crept into our daily language, "automation", although few of us really understand its true meaning.' Speak for yourself, thought O'Rourke. One day automation would look after his French classes for him.) Mr Cuthbert offered '12 dazzling Dahlias' for 15s. 'English Lady desires country post.' 'Lambswool twinset 63s.' Ah, England. 'Do you like kebabs?' inquired the proprietor of the fashionable White Tower restaurant. Familiarity with kebabs meant that 'you are a kebab initiate and clearly a gourmet *du premier ordre*'. O'Rourke smiled thinly but was strangely comforted.

He reserved the news for the loo. Even when experiencing rare bowel disorders he never sat there for more than five minutes but liked to take enough time to be tolerably briefed about the world situation. Once he had worked out what was worth more detailed analysis he could return to it later in the day.

He flipped quickly from beginning to end. Balliol were head of the river; Philius II was withdrawing from the Derby; at Taunton Somerset had lost by an innings to Hampshire; he would like to have seen Godfrey Evans going down to defeat against the championship leaders, Sussex; a six and seventeen fours in 93. The main home news was that a plan for a cultural centre and housing estate at the Barbican had just been announced. O'Rourke was not interested, much preferring the holidaymaker in Brixham who had been fined 10s for uprooting forty-two primroses from a roadside hedgerow. O'Rourke, who had a passion for wild flowers, considered he had been let off lightly. The Chancellor of the Exchequer, Mr Macmillan, warned about the danger of rising prices but said 'our traditional good humour and common sense would pull us through'. O'Rourke doubted it. He also doubted the Minister for Agriculture, Heathcot Amory, who had said, at

18

the Devon County Fair, that there would be 'just enough potatoes to get us through'. Not enough home-grown ones though. O'Rourke was unhappy with an England which was not even self-sufficient in potatoes. He was not happy with the botched talks on the future of Singapore where someone called Lee Kuan Yew looked like a young man in a hurry. He made a mental note to think about inviting himself to someone with a television set since England were playing Germany in Berlin that evening and *The Times* said that 'the match is to be televised on Eurovision and can thus be seen at British firesides'.

Finally he spent a second on the back-page photographs. The main one was of a man in a trilby hat fishing for trout in the river Itchen. This agreeable image restored his spirits enough for him to leave the lavatory, shave, dress, go downstairs, cook breakfast, resume his study of the newspaper in greater depth and finally proceed to the crossword. He frowned again at the three swiftly answered clues. They were distressingly banal. Not nearly up to the usual standard. Perhaps they were training up some new recruit. Or one of the old compilers was suffering from a hardening of intellectual arteries. If it got any worse a letter to the editor would have to be considered.

He tapped ash into the saucer and sighed. He had taken to breakfasting earlier than usual since St Aubyn had joined 'The Chummery.' in May. O'Rourke disliked conversation before breakfast and this prejudice was respected if not shared by 'Oily' Watkins who was his only regular companion at the meal. St Aubyn, however, had the irritating early-morning exuberance of youth, unlike Watkins, who was content to lurk grumpily and silently behind the *Telegraph.*

Most mornings nowadays O'Rourke managed to escape before St Aubyn came down to buttonhole him with his ceaseless questions about timetables and customs, observations on the weather, the county cricket championship, things he had heard on the wireless or seen in the Rialto Cinema, but today St Aubyn caught him.

'Ah!' he said, slamming the door behind him, 'I think perhaps today I shall have Grapenuts.'

The cereals were laid out on the dresser, which took up

19

most of one wall of the kitchen. It was or had been cream-coloured but was yellowing and cracked now and hung about with a job lot of mugs and cups and plates and bowls. None of them matched except for what might once have been a teaset in blue and white Cornish pottery. St Aubyn poured out Grapenuts from the stunted packet, covered them with milk from the jug on the table, then replaced the piece of muslin which covered it and which O'Rourke had left lying on the tabletop. It was weighted with garish beads and was useful for keeping out flies and the ash from O'Rourke's cigarettes.

'Grapenuts conquered Everest,' said St Aubyn, scattering sugar across the cereal's surface. 'In a manner of speaking. They took porridge too, but it was the Grapenuts that did it.'

O'Rourke pursed his lips and blew a ring of smoke at the crossword. The smoke fanned out and wafted across the table towards St Aubyn's Grapenuts like poison gas approaching the enemy trenches. St Aubyn was waiting to go up to Oxford where he had a place to read Modern Greats. Burnam knew his father. No need, therefore, for the personal columns of the *Daily Telegraph* or tortuous negotiations conducted through Messrs Gabbitas and Thring. Perfectly simple to fit him into what Burnam called 'the scheme of things' at West Hill for a summer term's teaching. Not that he had the first idea of how to teach. Normally O'Rourke was benign, even indulgent, with young men, especially if, like St Aubyn, they were comely, but he could not prevent himself being irritated by St Aubyn's exaggerated callowness, his effortless stupidity.

'Balls,' he said.

St Aubyn's first spoonful was en route for his mouth. It paused for a second. 'Sorry?' he said. 'What was that?'

'Balls,' said O'Rourke. 'Balls.'

'Oh.' St Aubyn seemed fazed. He covered his confusion by crunching the cereal around his mouth, making a sound which further infuriated O'Rourke.

'Perhaps,' said O'Rourke, 'Commander Crabb's unfortunate demise was due to the fact that he hadn't made a proper breakfast.'

'Come again?' St Aubyn frowned in that maddeningly bright and naive manner of his which suggested genuine perplexity combined with an equally genuine desire for enlightenment.

'Oh, nothing.' O'Rourke blew more smoke at the crossword. 'I was only suggesting that your equation of breakfast cereal and achievement had another side to it.'

Above them Oily Watkins could be heard moving about, his shoes loud on the lino. His bedroom was directly above the kitchen and the house was cheaply and poorly constructed so that noise carried. Although each man had his own room, privacy in the Chummery was relative. In the kitchen St Aubyn and O'Rourke sat silent except for the chewing of Grapenuts and the gentle exhalation of smoke. Upstairs Oily Watkins's iron bedstead shifted slightly, then he must have pulled the plug on his shaving water for there was a gurgling of water down lead followed by a liquid belch. O'Rourke continued to stare unfocused at the crossword. He was wondering whether in 1939, when he had arrived at the Guards depot in Caterham, he could possibly have been so perfectly, bloodily, aggravatingly wet behind the ears as St Aubyn. He thought not.

Presently they heard the loo flush and Oily Watkins's feet started to clump downstairs.

When he entered, an awkward, pot-bellied but otherwise rather gaunt fifty-year-old in assistant beak's uniform of leather-elbowed tweed jacket, grey flannel bags, and *Daily Telegraph* under arm stiff as a field marshal's baton, O'Rourke grinned at him.

'I'm worried about young St Aubyn,' said O'Rourke before Watkins could even pour out cornflakes. 'I don't think he's entirely in touch with the rest of his generation.'

Watkins affected not to hear but busied himself with breakfast.

'It says in today's paper . . .' O'Rourke made a play of turning pages and folding *The Times* very deliberately when he had found what he wanted, 'that our younger generation is a sight more solemn than we frivolous oldsters.'

Watkins crunched moodily on his flakes. St Aubyn pinkened.

'It's the editorial,' continued O'Rourke. 'It's about this chap Osborne's new play which it says, incidentally, is "good for people who like to leave the theatre in an argumentative

21

mood". Later on it says that the "prodigies celebrated by Mr Evelyn Waugh in 1930 or thereabouts" – that's us, Watkins – "organized parties in balloons and swimming baths".' He glanced up at Watkins and grinned. 'Not that I *ever* went to a party in a balloon. And it goes on to say "the youth of today visits prisons and reads Kierkegaard". Now, I ask you, Watkins, has our young friend here shown the slightest inclination of visiting a prison or reading Kierkegaard? I don't suppose he even knows who Kierkegaard is.'

'Oh leave him alone, O'Rourke,' said Watkins snappily.

O'Rourke shrugged and lit another cigarette. He could be a bit of a bully.

'Oily Watkins was a frogman,' said Donald Stack.

'Oily Watkins? Don't be silly. He can hardly swim.' Adrian Fieldhouse giggled. 'Haven't you seen him at the baths? One width doing breaststroke and that's his limit. And he did the most frightful belly flop diving in.'

'You don't have to swim to be a frogman, stupid,' said Stack. 'You've got flippers and things. You just wiggle your feet.'

They were standing in the hall waiting for breakfast. It was Stack's day as 'gong-basher'. As soon as breakfast was ready one of the maids would put her head round the green baize door that led into the pantry and nod at the day's gong-basher who would then go into an exaggerated J. Arthur Rank routine with the brass gong which stood on the hall table alongside the letter posting box and Mrs Burnam's flower arrangement.

'Even so . . .' Fieldhouse seemed doubtful, 'I don't see how Oily could have been a frogman even if he only had to wiggle his feet. Who told you?'

'Lorimer got it from matron,' said Stack. 'He says matron's brother was a frogman too. He got killed somewhere. In a fjord, I think.'

Fieldhouse remained sceptical. No one at the school had given much thought to frogmen until the other day when Commander Crabb had gone missing. It was the sort of story little boys adored: mysterious, threatening, with suggestions of personal gallantry and heroism deployed in the stirring battle against the horrible Russians. It was difficult for anyone, least of all prep-school boys, to work out what had happened.

In the House of Commons Mr Eden was so obviously evasive that it was self-defeating, his verbal contortions suggesting that his government had been up to something even more sinister than was alleged. jthe few available facts were admittedly embarrassing. Stalin's successors, an obviously doomed double act called 'B and K', were on a goodwill visit to Britain. Their transport, a Soviet cruiser of modern and sophisticated design, was anchored at Portsmouth. While she was there, it was alleged, Commander Crabb went for a swim in his wetsuit, never to return. In the House of Commons there were many who viewed the incident with distaste and embarrassment, but this was not the case at West Hill. In current affairs lessons all staff explained carefully that it was entirely proper for 'our side' to do whatever we liked where Russians were concerned. The Russians were the enemy, even if Marshal Bulganin and Mr Khrushchev *had* been invited. They were our guests but that didn't mean that they were our friends. It was perfectly all right for our chaps to go down and have a look at their ship in Portsmouth Harbour. Indeed, it would have been a dereliction of duty not to do so.

'But surely, sir,' said Fieldhouse when this was explained, 'that's spying?'

'No,' said the CO patiently. 'Spying is something quite different. Spying is deceitful and dishonest. The spy is someone who betrays the trust of others. Commander Crabb was a serving officer of the Royal Navy carrying out naval reconnaissance.'

Neither Fieldhouse nor the others were quite sure they followed the logic of this. What the CO and the boys all knew, however, though none actually voiced the thought, was that broadly speaking if *we* did it, it was all right, but if *they* did, it wasn't. That was what they taught at boarding school.

'I'm jolly peckish,' said Stack, standing on one leg and rubbing the toe of his open-toed Clark's sandal against the back of his calf. 'Is it a baked-beans day today?'

23

'It's Saturday, idiot,' said Fieldhouse.

'Ugh.' Stack held his nose and made lavatory-chain-pulling motions with his free hand. He was much given to gesture. 'I can't stand scrambled egg.'

'I don't mind real scrambled egg,' said Fieldhouse, 'like our cook makes at home. Real eggs and butter, not this putrid powder muck.'

The baize door opened and Elsie looked round it. Elsie was simple. She had a round, doughy face, a dark moustache and a vacant expression.

The maids were the lowest form of life at West Hill. They were generally, though quite erroneously, believed to be on day release from the local mental asylum ('looney bin' in school patois) and were known as 'Merry Maisies', to distinguish them from the two elderly odd-job men who were called 'Happy Harrys'. The Harrys were also supposed to come from the bin, though this too was untrue. They were no brighter than the Maisies but this did not make them certifiable or lock-up-able. Just stupid.

'You can bang the gong,' hissed Elsie, ' 'cos breakfast is on the table.' And she scuttled away, seeming embarrassed to have been seen at all.

Stack picked up the gong stick and banged: three well-spaced resonant thumps to start, followed by the gong's equivalent of a drum roll and a final brace of thumps.

By the time he had finished the whole house was alive with hurrying, pushing, shoving boys. Their summer sandals, rubber soled, made less noise than winter's heavy black walking shoes, but their scuffing shuffle still filled the corridors. Along with this there was a giggling, almost hysterical, communal whisper that sometimes exploded into shrill laughter. Some ran, some skipped, a very few walked. Occasionally one tripped or was shoved against a wall, only to ricochet back, laughing and expostulating until, on actually entering the dining hall, a sense of propriety attacked them and reduced the boys almost to silence. They fidgeted, smirked, elbowed each other in the ribs, glanced sidelong, rolled their eyes and contorted their faces. But they didn't talk.

The only two rooms big enough to accommodate all seventy-four boys and fourteen staff were the dining room and the assembly hall, which the CO had christened, rather

24

grandly, 'Big School'. (The library, much smaller, which in a normal house would have been called the library, was 'Little School'.) The dining room where the boys now gathered for scrambled egg (made as Fieldhouse quite accurately implied from large tins of dubiously labelled 'egg powder') had been the formal dining room in the old days when West Hill was privately occupied. It was panelled in oak, and as if this did not make it dark enough there were black honours boards hanging along three walls. The most pretentious of these announced awards won by West Hill boys to public schools; two slightly less grand ones gave the names of all those who had passed on to the Royal Naval colleges of Osborne and Dartmouth. On all these the lettering was gold. Another, larger, board, stained a mahogany brown, hung over the hot plate from which food was dispensed. On this the lettering was black and relatively small. Here were listed the heads of school since West Hill's foundation in 1874. At the top of all boards was the school crest – a bird, rather crudely represented and generally supposed to be an eagle. In its beak it held a sprig of foliage which was variously said to be an olive branch, an oak leaf and – by boys discovering the amusement of smutty jokes – a fig leaf. The bird, which ranged in colour from gold (suggesting eagle) to mouse-brown (suggesting sparrow), was perched on what appeared to be a stick of seaside rock in the school's pink and green. Underneath was the motto: *Nemo me impune lacessit*. West Hill's founder, the Reverend Fergusson, had been a Scot. 'No one provokes me with impunity,' he would thunder at his little boys, 'ancient motto of the Kings of Scotland *and* of the glorious Scottish regiments of the British Army. Remember it well for it is our motto too. Never provoke us with impunity for you do so at your peril.' Somerset Burnam invoked the tag less frequently but he would occasionally trot it out in one of his more formal orations.

Ritual was an essential element in life at West Hill. Ritual and routine, tradition and timetables. Never mind that the tradition was often ersatz; it was a necessary ingredient of the life Somerset Burnam gave to his boys and for which he was preparing them. Custom created precedent. Precedent was to be followed; change to be distrusted, especially for its

25

own sake. The breakfast gong was sounded every morning as near to eight as dammit. The boys entered the dining hall and went to their places at once. When they were settled and there was something approximating to hush, the monitors followed and took their places, scattered among the various tables of more junior boys. Then those few adults who regularly attended school breakfasts – matron and her two deputies, Mr and Mrs Burnam – entered in as stately a manner as possible. When this happened the silence, hitherto imperfect, became absolute. The CO stood at one end of High Table, cleared his throat with a portentous 'Ahem', and said grace. He had four graces, two English, two Latin. The first was 'For what we are about to receive may the Lord make us truly grateful'; the second was 'For these and all thy other gifts, we thank thee God'; and the third '*Benedicto, benedicatur*'. This morning, because he was in that sort of mood, he recited the most sonorous: '*Benedictus benedicat, Per Jesum Christum Dominum Nostrum.*'

Chairs scraped back, noise re-erupted. The two under-matrons, Miss Sparrow and Miss Battersby, began ladling porridge from cauldrons on the hot plate while the monitors queued in line to receive them. Stack as gong-basher had pride of place, which meant that he took the first two bowls and – more ceremony – presented the first to Mrs Burnam and the second to matron. Porter as head boy took the second two bowls, presented the first to the CO and the second to a newbug called Pimblott on Miss Battersby's table. Then the production line began in earnest.

As they passed one another the monitors exchanged hurried, corner-of-the-mouth intimacies.

'CO's in a bate this morning.'

'Mrs Burnam's got lipstick on her teeth again.'

'My uncle's going to get Keith Miller's autograph for me.'

'Figges I says the porridge is burned.'

'It's always burned.'

'Stiggworthy's got the most enormous lump in his you've ever seen. It's bigger than a gobstopper.'

Had Raymond Postgate conducted an inspection of the school for his five-year-old *Good Food Guide* the porridge would unquestionably have occasioned censure. It was invariably burned; lumps for the unwary like icebergs in the

26

North Atlantic. But boys and therefore staff were compelled to finish it. Times were not as difficult as they had been two or three years before. The school had survived the war and subsequent austerity by a combination of ingenuity and restraint. It helped that there was a home farm of sorts – enough to provide some milk and eggs. The walled vegetable garden was a boon too, but despite all this there was never *quite* enough food to go round. Boys did not actually starve but they always lost weight in term time. The annual fees were still only £70 a term and economy dictated privation. 'Dishes vary from day to day,' Mr Postgate might have warned, 'but not much.' 'Monday Muck' alias 'Beans and Bones' was a particular hazard, as were the oranges and cooking dates which frequently appeared for afternoon tea. The hated dates were usually smuggled out in trouser pockets and tossed into hedges or down the lavatories. Sometimes they were dropped into the flower vases on the dining tables, only to be discovered, days later, on account of the smell. 'Remember the starving millions!' the CO would admonish, as he ordered backsliders to finish up their mash (much like the porridge) or marge (butter at weekends only). Boys were unconvinced, but since the alternative was a beating, they usually did as they were told. Even when dishes had been interfered with they still managed somehow. One of Fieldhouse's recurring nightmares was of the orange marmalade steamed pudding he finally consumed under Burnam's unflinching stare. His neighbour, the Mighty Atom, had emptied half a pepper pot over it, but the penalty for sneaking was likely to involve more strokes of the riding crop than the punishment for not finishing food. 'Bugger the starving millions!' O'Rourke once muttered not quite under his breath, when the world's less privileged were once invoked as a reason to eat a particularly disgusting macaroni cheese. It had become a sotto voce school battle cry.

The school food, like the rugby, football and cricket, the Latin and Greek, the cold baths and the Boy Scouts, was all part of the process. It helped make men out of you. And, paradoxically, it appeared to have no lasting effect on the palate.

At High Table, Somerset Burnam smiled at his wife and daughter. Clarissa Burnam smiled back. Charlotte was

27

engrossed in her porridge and did not notice her father smiling. Charlotte was eight.

'Well, Menzies,' said Mr Burnam to the small boy on his right, 'I hope the catches stick this afternoon against St Christopher's.'

'Yes, sir.'

Menzies was the First XI wicketkeeper, only just eleven but precociously good. Burnam had hopes for him.

'We want to make up for last year's disaster.'

'Yes, sir.'

'And I should stand well back when Stack's bowling. He's beginning to work up quite a turn of speed.'

'Yes, sir.'

Inwardly Mr Burnam sighed. Small boys could be very heavy going. He turned to the post which lay on his side plate. It included some forbidding buff envelopes, a couple of khaki Forces airmail letter cards, presumably from military parents on foreign posting, and a few more local handwritten letters. He pushed the bills to one side and began to open the letters, starting with a Forces letter card which he saw came from William Porter's father in Malta.

Being a careful man Burnam slit the card neatly as directed along the requisite folds. If you didn't do that the letter became jumbled and out of sequence. Some correspondence between boys and parents was hopelessly garbled as a result, or from the impetuous tearing of paper with overanxious fingers. Not that it mattered. No one ever said anything of interest in an airmail letter card. There was scarcely enough space.

'Dear Burnam . . .' Prissy handwriting. Commander Porter was a prissy fellow, about to be passed over. William, luckily for him, inherited his intelligence and looks from his mother. Burnam had met her once at a May Ball in the thirties. She had been stunningly attractive and witty with it. Quite shocking when, a few years later, she had married a dim naval officer with few prospects. The marriage had endured but hardly prospered. Mrs Porter was said to have a roving eye and a dangerous appetite for midshipmen. The Commander's liking for pink gin was mentioned with increasing frequency too. Which was ironic in view of the letter.

28

Dear Burnam,

I hesitate to write what I'm afraid has to be a rather distressing letter but I'm afraid I'm really not left with any option. The fact of the matter is that yesterday morning in the garden shed I happened to come across three or four empty beer bottles and two empty cartons of John Player cigarettes together with a quantity of half-smoked stubs. After some inquiry I am driven to the conclusion that the culprit can only be William, spurred on no doubt by his friend Stack who, as you know, came to stay with us during the Easter holidays and who, between you and me, I found a little too much on the smooth side. I would not trouble you with this if it were not for the fact that on checking I find that a carton of 200 Players has gone missing. I hesitate to cast definite aspersions, particularly concerning my own son, but the conclusion does seem irresistible.

If you do discover that the cigarettes are in his possession I shall naturally fall in with whatever course of action you propose, although my own preference would be for a sound thrashing, after which the incident can be well and truly closed and one can begin with a clean sheet. I should absolutely understand if he were unable to continue as head of the school but I would be very sad if it were to interfere with his prospects of going on to Marlborough which is, as you know, the family school. I am truly sorry to be writing to you like this but will expect to hear from you in due course.

Yours sincerely,
Cecil Porter

Somerset Burnam refolded the letter card with the same precision that he had opened it, placed it on the table by his enormous willow-pattern coffee cup, and turned to the rest of the mail, hoping there were no more letter bombs. At the far end of the table his wife, Clarissa, noticed that there had been bad news but said nothing.

'William,' she said, 'would you be kind enough to fetch Mr Burnam's cup?'

Mrs Burnam, as headmaster's wife, provided the distaff side of 'in loco parentis'. She was the only adult who called boys by their Christian names.

'Yes, Mrs Burnam.' Porter's porridge was unfinished. He hoped forlornly that while he was on the coffee-cup errand it might be cleared away in error. There was, however, no such luck. He munched on his oats and wondered morosely how it was possible for them to be simultaneously raw *and* burned.

'Would you pass Mr Burnam's cup down to him?' asked Clarissa Burnam. This was the second part of the ritual. The full cup was passed down the table from hand to hand. Everyone was petrified of dropping it, but no one ever did. It would have been easy for Porter to have carried it back to the headmaster just as he had carried it up. Or it could have been placed at Mrs Burnam's end of the table in the first place. Or Mr Burnam could have had his own coffee pot. There were all sorts of more logical ways of making sure that the CO had a full cup of coffee for breakfast, but at West Hill logic yielded to tradition and ritual. It was always blue and white willow pattern; always coffee made with heavily sugared Camp essence; always passed from hand to hand. Ever thus.

Porter had noticed the airmail letter card and his father's handwriting. He had tried to read some of it while collecting the coffee cup but had failed. It was of no consequence. He knew his father wrote to the headmaster from time to time. Most fathers did and *his* father more than most. Porter was precocious and perceptive and though still impressed by his father's position and authority, by the red, white and blue ribbons on his chest and the scrambled-egg braid at his wrists, he was beginning to emerge from the childhood age of unquestioning respect and admiration into one of adolescent scepticism. By his late teens he would despise his father. Now, at thirteen, he was just beginning to take him with a pinch of salt.

'Penny for them?' said Mrs Burnam.

'What?' he blinked.

'Your thoughts, William. You're not eating your porridge. Your mind's miles away. Are you quite sure you're all right?'

'Yes, thank you, Mrs Burnam. I was just thinking.'

'Well, eat your porridge before it gets cold.'

'Yes, Mrs Burnam.' He wanted to say, 'It's cold already.'

She smiled at him. He was, she thought, a peculiar little boy. Not very strong. She was afraid the strains of being head boy and the apprehensions about taking the Marlborough scholarship were affecting him. She would have made Stack head of school. A much tougher customer. Somerset did not agree. 'I'm very much afraid,' he had said, 'that there's a flaw in that boy. A knot in the wood.'

The scrambled egg which followed was, as Fieldhouse had predicted, 'this putrid powder muck'. Full of nutritional value as demanded by the regulations of the Ministry of Food, but not appetizing: granular and watery. There was also sliced white bread, described by the makers as 'Best in the West' but so soggy that it was best used for compressing into small pellets to be flicked about the dining room when the CO and the matrons were not looking. At weekends there was butter in small round pats, a welcome change from weekday marge. To drink the boys were given home-produced milk, judiciously watered. Never tea or coffee on the grounds that caffeine and tannin were bad for them.

This feast took twenty minutes and was concluded by Somerset Burnam, who rose with a flourish, waited until everyone else was standing with heads bowed and hands clasped before them, and then delivered another grace. Today he decided on English. 'For what we have received, may the Lord make us truly grateful.' The school then said 'Amen' in a reasonable approximation to unison, waited until the adults filed out and then departed noisily to their dormitories for bedmaking.

2

'I do think something might be done to improve the cook-ing,' said Somerset. He gazed out of the drawing-room win-dow, across the lawn and over the ha-ha. It was Clarissa's room, chintzy and flower-filled. In the distance he could see Miss Murgatroyd pushing her bicycle up the hill through the park. It was not a very steep hill but it was beyond Miss Murgatroyd's pedalling capacity. She was very short of breath these days. Showing her age. Something would have to be done about her, but not just yet. She remained, for all her frailties, the best teacher on the staff.

'I'll speak to Elsie,' said Clarissa, contemplating her toenails and wondering if she was too old to go on painting them quite that shade of pink. On balance she thought not. They were pretty feet and she was proud of them.

'Hmmm. Will that have any effect?'

'None whatever.'

'So there's not much point.'

'Not really. I'm afraid edible porridge for eighty is beyond poor Elsie's capacity.'

'But you produce perfectly decent porridge in the school holidays.'

'*I'm* cooking for four in the holidays. And I usually use Quick Quaker which, as you know perfectly well, is far too expensive for school breakfast.'

'So what's to be done?'

'Hire a professional cook with experience of catering.'

'Which we can't afford.'

'Exactly.'

Burnam sighed. Miss Murgatroyd had made it to the flat now, had trundled across the cattlegrid and on two wheels was passing the cedar at a stately pace.

'So we have to live with the porridge,' he said.
'I'm afraid so.'

'Oh, well.' He turned and smiled at his wife, who returned the smile with interest and crossed her legs. She was still, in her early forties, a very attractive woman. Possibly more so than when young. Something to do with bones. And she had kept her figure.

'I had a disturbing letter from Commander Porter.'

'I don't awfully care for Commander Porter. Something about his mouth. He has too neat a bottom too. Pert.'

'Darling!'

'But it's true.'

'He says William has stolen some cigarettes. He also says that William and Donald Stack were smoking and drinking in the potting shed.'

'And you believe him?'

He shrugged. 'I don't know. But I shall have to find out.'

'And how are you going to find out?'

'I shall talk to William. Have it out with him. Man to man.'

'But he's not a man. He's a little boy. A very little boy, I sometimes think.'

'You know what I mean.'

Her turn to shrug.

Fieldhouse, Porter and Stack sat in the monitors' common-room waiting for the bell to go for morning assembly. Stack was reading the *Illustrated London News*.

'Hey, you chaps!' he said, 'listen to this: "The new Rank Organization Film *Reach for the Sky* is the story of a man's life. The story of Douglas Bader, who fought back against seemingly hopeless odds and won. In a wider sense it is the story of a nation. *Reach for the Sky* portrays with accuracy and delicate judgement the British reaction to fear, British sense of humour, British phlegm. It *had* to be made by a truly British film company."' He giggled.

'I should like to see that,' said Porter. 'Imagine doing all that with no legs.'

'What's phlegm?' asked Fieldhouse. 'I thought it was nose-blow.'

'No, stupid,' said Stack, 'it's keeping a stiff upper lip. Not blubbing when the CO beats you with the riding crop. All that rubbish.'

'I don't think it's rubbish,' said Porter.

'No,' said Fieldhouse. 'Why do you think it's rubbish?'

'It just is,' said Stack. 'Don't ask me why. I can't explain, but I know it's rubbish.'

The bell rang for prayers.

It was at morning prayers that the day's notices were given out to the school. Before that, Burnam briefed his colleagues in the staffroom. This was a painfully austere place, especially when contrasted with the Burnam's rather sumptuous private quarters in the main house. The staffroom was the ground floor of the old coach house, across a cobbled courtyard from the changing rooms. It was freezing in winter due to an absence of central heating and baking in summer thanks to the poor ventilation. There were few comforts: a gas ring for boiling a cheap tin kettle; two leatherette armchairs stuffed with horsehair. Decoration was perfunctory and eccentric: an owl in a glass dome; two posters advertising the Société Nationale des Chemins de Fer; portraits of the Queen and Winston Churchill. A long refectory table bisected the room and around it were a dozen ink-stained chairs made of tubular steel and canvas. The atmosphere was oppressively fusty. The school cat, Attlee, came in to pee from time to time and occasionally left a dead mouse behind the Cosi-Stove. It was also the only room in the school where smoking took place. The heavy smokers on staff were O'Rourke, and Oily Watkins who favoured a pipe and Three Nuns tobacco. Even if they were not actually alight the remembrance of fumes past hung in the air like spent cordite, mingling with the stale smell of people past and present.

Burnam coughed. It was a ham's cough, the throat-clearing of an old-fashioned actor–manager, full of self-conscious theatricality, not a real cough at all but a demand for the audience's attention. He had first adopted it because he could think of no spoken opening which was not either pompous or fatuous or both. Now that he had acquired the self-confidence to be either he could not be bothered to alter the cough. It had become standard procedure and was an essential part of the many not very good imitations of him practised behind his back by boys and staff.

'As you know, we have the St Christopher's match this afternoon,' he said, 'and as you also know, it's a long-established fixture. It's one which I'm keen to keep but which I'm afraid St Christopher's are inclined to drop. They have what, in my view, is an exaggerated idea of their own station in life. They see themselves as an "Eton prep" and they look on us as, well . . . better not mention names . . . as *not* an Eton prep. It is also true that over the last few years they have beaten us at all three major games rather more often than not. In fact, apart from last autumn's draw at rugby, they have won every encounter for the last three years. I think there's every chance that this will change this afternoon, but even if we don't manage a win it really is rather important that we put on a good show.'

'Must we win?' asked O'Rourke, not bothering to remove the cigarette from the corner of his mouth. 'Or is it enough to lose with dignity?'

'I should prefer a victory,' said Burnam, 'but one has to be realistic.'

'I don't see any need to be defeatist about it,' said David St Aubyn, fingering his Old Harrovian tie. 'We've only lost twice so far and from what I hear on the old grapevine St Kit's are having rather a dicey year.'

'Yes. Well,' said Burnam, 'as I said, it would be good if we could beat them for once but it's just as important to put on a really good show. And I don't simply mean on the cricket field. I want the school to consider itself on parade. Everything not only shipshape but absolutely spotless. Boys well turned out and clean. No litter. Absolutely no litter on any account whatever. Basil, I'm sorry to say there was quite a lot of mess in Little School when I did my rounds last night. I picked up several Sharp's toffee wrappers and there were books all over the place. There are plenty of waggers provided and you really must get boys to put the books back on the shelves. Frankly, if we're going to retain the St Christopher's fixture we've got to convince them that we run an absolutely first-rate show here. We simply can't afford any sloppiness in any department.'

Basil Roberts twitched but he said nothing. Nothing he could say. The twitch, an affliction which involved most of the right side of his face, was more or less permanent but accelerated in moments of stress. He had only been at West Hill for a fortnight. Smedley, the sixth-form history and English teacher, had gone down with a bad bout of hepatitis and Burnam had had to find a temporary replacement in a hurry. Under such circumstances one could not afford to be choosy and Basil Roberts had been the best of a bad lot on the books of Gabbitas and Thring. He was unquestionably able – a scholar of Queen's who had taken a first in modern history – but this itself was suspicious. If an Oxford history scholar was jobless in June there was something wrong with him.

Not for the first time the boys proved shrewder judges of character than their teachers. By lunch on Roberts's first day half the top two forms had developed a passable imitation of the twitch. That afternoon Roberts tested the sixth form on the kings and queens of England and their dates.

'Next. You boy. What's your name?'

'Fieldhouse, sir,' said Adrian, twitching frantically.

Mr Roberts pretended not to notice. 'Who came after Henry VII?'

'Henry VIII, sir.'

'Dates?'

'1509 to 1547, sir.'

'Good,' said Mr Roberts, reddening a little as Fieldhouse continued to twitch. His own tic began to speed up. A boy at the back started to giggle but concealed it in a cough.

'Next.'

'Stack, sir. Edward VI, sir. 1547 to 1553, sir. Donald twitched too.

'Next.'

Next was Fothergill. Fothergill might just scrape into one of the minor West Country public schools if lucky. He had trouble with concentration. At this moment he had just removed a gobbet of inky blotting paper from his mouth and was attempting to convert it from a ball to a worm by rolling it up and down his desktop. Gradually he became aware that the expectant silence was directed at him. He looked up to see Mr Roberts twitching at him.

'Who, sir? Me, sir?'

'Yes, you, boy. What's your name?'

'Fothergill, sir.'

'Well, Fothergill, who came next?'

A long pause. Then, 'Um,' said Fothergill.

'Come along, Fothergill . . . Queenie . . . Queenie . . . Queenie who?'

Finally Roberts gave up and threw the question open to the rest of the form. All hands went up; most of their owners were twitching ferociously.

'Well, Fieldhouse?' said Mr Roberts.

'Please, sir, Queenie Mary. 1553 to 1558.'

From then on Basil Roberts was universally known as Queenie except by those few smaller boys who called him 'Batty Roberts'. And the whole school imitated his twitch.

'Righty-ho, then,' said Somerset Burnam, jerking Queenie out of his Fothergill-like reverie, 'any questions?'

Matron, Mrs Hildesley, asked if boys not playing in the school teams should wear ties during the afternoon. Mr Burnam said he thought it would be all right if they wore their usual afternoon open-neck Aertex shirts, provided they were neat and tidy. Otherwise there were no questions.

Mr Burnam called Porter to his study immediately after prayers to discuss the matter of the missing Player's cigarettes. Man and boy were both apprehensive. Burnam did not want trouble. It was not that he was averse to beating, though he took no particular pleasure in the ritual. But he had only once caned a head of school. To do so – to be *compelled* to do so – was as much an admission of his own as the boy's failure. A successful head of school was as much a vindication of his own judgement in appointing him as a credit to the boy. So far, he reckoned, Porter had been adequate if not outstanding. No Churchill, but better than Eden. Other boys liked him and he had integrity. He was not, perhaps, a natural leader, but in later life, with luck, he could chair a committee with competence if not lead a cavalry charge. At the moment the boy seemed to be confident in his abilities and he had a real chance of an award in the exams later this term. Disturb that equilibrium with the disgrace of a caning and demotion and, Burnam told himself, anything could happen.

Porter's apprehensions were less complex. He and Stack *had* used the Maltese potting shed for illicit fags and beer and he *had* brought a carton of his father's NAAFI duty-free home from the holidays. He wouldn't have done it without Stack, though it would be unfair to say that it was therefore Stack's responsibility. The two had egged each other on. When he had seen his father's letter at breakfast and observed the CO's frown, Porter was inclined to fear that his father had shopped him. Now, standing on the chintz carpet before the headmaster's outsize mahogany desk, suspicion turned to certainty. The CO was wearing his 'This is going to hurt me a great deal more than it hurts you' expression above his red, yellow and black striped tie. Porter was not, for the moment, concerned with the hypocrisy of the CO's expression. He only knew that it was almost certainly bad news for him personally. He would bluff it through, of course, but the CO was an astute sniffer-out of deceit and, more importantly, of hidden contraband. The previous term he had conducted a swoop for forbidden comics – *Beano*, *Dandy*, *The Champion* or even the upmarket *Eagle*. 'Dan Dare' annuals and other 'trash' were also on the wanted list. The cache he discovered was enormous and some of it had been hidden with real ingenuity. Porter and other monitors suspected informers and sneaks, but whether the CO had recourse to a spy ring or relied on intuition and ratiocination, there was no avoiding the fact that the results were spectacular. Donald Stack maintained without conviction that it was due to his passion for Conan Doyle.

'I've had a letter from your father,' said the CO.

'Yes, sir,' said Porter. He rubbed his head. The hair on his crown was obstinately vertical. The school barbers – a lugubrious couple from Taunton who came once a month – couldn't have coiffed a hedge let alone a scalp and they always left him with a maddening and uncontrollable tuft which no amount of cold water could calm.

The CO was a master of the long silence. He now deployed one, gazing steadily at Commander Porter's only son. Porter himself, now used to the headmaster's silent stares, examined his fingers, especially the index finger of his right hand which was lightly stained with blue-black Quink.

Eventually Mr Burnam said, 'Is there anything you want to tell me?'

'No, sir,' said Porter, wondering as he did whether the words had come a little glibly and so qualifying them with, 'I don't think so, sir.'

'Donald Stack stayed with you in the holidays.'

'Yes, sir.'

'Your father seems to think that you and he were smoking in the potting shed.'

Porter coloured slightly and said nothing.

'There were empty beer bottles too.'

Porter still said nothing. He would like to have asked why his father was allowed to drink gin with water and Angostura Bitters and smoke twenty unfiltered Player's cigarettes a day, why indeed this seemed to be a symbol of nautical masculinity, if he was not even allowed a few uninhaled puffs and a quarter pint of Whitbread in the potting shed. In a sense this was an unfair question for the CO, who had never been seen to drink anything stronger than home-brewed cider and whose only smoking was a feast-day Manikin cigar after dinner perhaps six times a year. The CO, thought Porter, might even have been slightly shocked to hear about his father's gin and chain smoking. He would certainly have been shocked to hear about his mother's midshipmen but it would be a few years before young William found out about them.

'Naturally,' said the headmaster, 'what you get up to in the holidays is your own affair.' He rubbed his face with the palm of his hand as if thinking. This was mere subterfuge as he had done all his thinking before this little encounter began. He knew exactly what he was going to say. And how.

'However . . .' He paused to let the word lie between them like a playing card face down, then quickly played the rest of his hand, 'what you do in term time is not your own affair. There are school rules which everyone has to obey and which you as head of school have to obey even more than everyone else. Do you agree?'

'Yes, sir.'

'In his letter your father says he's missing a carton of two hundred Player's cigarettes. Do you have them?'

Porter judged it time to feign outrage. 'Me, sir! Why *me*, sir? It could have been anyone. The last cook was *always* watering the sherry. The Maltese are absolutely not to be trusted. My father's always saying so. And, frankly, I'm not sure I trust some of the men. They're a pretty rough lot.'

'I'm quite sure,' said the CO, 'that those thoughts will have crossed your father's mind and that he'll have made all the necessary inquiries. But the fact is that he has reason to think you and Stack were smoking his cigarettes and drinking his beer during the holidays and therefore he wants me to find out if you've taken the missing carton.' Inwardly Somerset Burnam sighed. The boy was not making it easy. This would have to happen on the day of the St Christopher's game. What a pest Commander Porter could be.

'No, sir.'

'No, what?'

'No, sir, I didn't take my father's cigarettes.'

This time Burnam's sigh was outward and, virtually, visible.

'Righty-ho,' he said, 'I'm going to be perfectly fair about this. More than fair. Your record has been a good one. I don't want to spoil things for you at this stage of your career here. If you have those cigarettes and bring them to me at once, I shall have to beat you, but that will be the end of it. We'll simply wash our hands of the affair and start again from scratch. If you continue to deny that you have them, I shall have to inspect your tuckbox and your hut and if I find them, then I'm afraid you're going to be in very hot water indeed. Do you understand?'

Porter nodded.

'Are you going to bring me the cigarettes?'

'No, sir. I don't have them, sir.' William hardly knew why he was being so perverse. It would have been simpler to go to his hut in the dingle, unearth the hundred or so cigarettes that remained and take his beating like a man. But, as Clarissa Burnam had observed earlier that morning, he was not yet a man. Having begun to lie, he could not see how to change tactics and tell the truth, a skill that he would only acquire in adult life. At thirteen, however, the loss of face was beyond him.

'You do understand that the one thing neither I nor the

school will put up with is lying?' said Burnam untruthfully.

'Yes, sir,' said Porter miserably.

'Very well.' The headmaster employed another of his devastating silences. 'In that case,' he said at last, 'I shall have to ask you to take me to your tuckbox; and if that produces nothing, we'll have to go the dingle. I hope you understand why I'm doing this, William.'

Porter did not particularly care about the motive. All that mattered was the effect. He felt a stinging sense of family betrayal. This was world's end and his own father was Iscariot. At least, that was how it seemed. The CO was doing what he was doing because he was the CO. The CO made the rules and the CO enforced the rules. *Why* he should do such a thing was not a matter of interest. He was simply a punctilious executor of his own orders.

'Yes, sir.'

'It's for your own good,' said Burnam, 'and the good of the school.'

The tuckboxes were in the cellars where once the house's owners had stored their wine. Steps led down from a kitchen corridor to a flagged subterranean alleyway containing two oil-fired boilers. Off this ran the changing rooms to one side and a tuckbox area on the other. This latter doubled up as a workshop. The current school obsession or craze was model aeroplanes, so the benches were a maze of glue, balsa, dope and blueprints. Miniature diesel engines were locked into vices and the walls were covered with posters of Spitfires and Hurricanes, Heinkels and Messerschmitts. One or two boys had Jetex solid-fuel acknowledgements of the post-propeller era. But Jetex was no more reliable than the new Comet airliner in real life – it had a nasty tendency to pack up in mid-flight.

Porter led the way to a bench in the left-hand corner, a privileged position because it was just below a barred window which allowed a corner of outdoor light from the world above. From underneath it he pulled out a grimy wooden box with black metal corners and the letters 'W. de V. P.' stencilled on the lid. It was secured with a small padlock and after some fumbling Porter unlocked it and opened his 'toey' for the CO's inspection. The contents were predictable: a tin of Dundee cake, half-eaten, now very stale; *Wisden's Cricketers'*

Almanack, cloth-bound, dog-eared; assorted pencils and crayons, glue and drawing pins; a Swiss Army knife; the components of a crystal radio set widely scattered; a pack of cards, similarly dispersed.

No cigarettes.

The CO rummaged ineffectively for a few moments.

'Good,' he said, 'good.' He straightened and looked at his watch. 'We've just time to get to the dingle and back before the end of this period. All right?'

Porter said it was all right. He had no alternative. Affable suggestions from the CO and other members of staff may have sounded like affable suggestions but they were still commands for all their apparent diffidence. The implication that there was an alternative was pure window dressing, a typically English piece of politesse. The question not only expected the answer yes, it demanded it. Officers and gentlemen always conveyed impossible demands in scrupulously sweet and reasonable tones. When asking one to die for one's country, one always said 'please'. West Hill boys were taught to do likewise.

The dingle was just over half a mile from the school buildings. You took the back drive past the old stables, turned sharp left along the path between the squash court and the greenhouses and herb beds, ducked through the low wicket gate in the rose-garden wall, across the rose garden, round the sundial, out the other end, past the Wellingtonia where *A Midsummer Night's Dream* was to be performed in three weeks' time, over the woodland garden, skirting the bamboo coppice until you arrived at the paling fence which separated the untamed dingle from the cultivated elegance of the grounds within the ha-ha and next to the house.

It was the one place at West Hill in which the official writ was hardly seen to run. Masters scarcely ever ventured into the dingle and if they did it was almost always at a time when the boys weren't there. At first glance there was nothing very appealing about it. Surrounded by a fringe of trees, mainly beech to the north and larch to the south, it was just a hole in the ground about a hundred yards long by thirty across. The hole was not clean or symmetrical but more like a miniature English Grand Canyon, a red earth landscape of warts and bunions with a five o'clock shadow of bramble, scrub and tree trunk. Elsewhere similar dingles were the favoured haunts of motorcyclists because the contours allowed for bumps and jumps which exhilarated without really frightening; here in the genteel laager of a boys' preparatory school the dingle provided the inhabitants with a different sort of illusion. In most of the place and for most of the time there was no escaping the apparatus of discipline and authority. Bells, whistles and shouted commands; lists, timetables and orders for the day, regularly recited. The call of the gong; the declension of verbs, regular and irregular, Latin and French. Pythagoras, Archimedes, Kennedy of *Latin Primer* fame and Howard Baker of the *Aide-Mémoire*; cricket nets in summer; hare and hounds in winter; no talking after lights-out; and always the realization that a member of staff might be lurking, like the Highway Patrol, round every corner. But the dingle was no-man's-land – a makebelieve no-man's-land, but none the less valuable for that. In the dingle boys reverted to the wild, or at least to an approximation of it. Life in the dingle was a little like a bowdlerized *Lord of the Flies*. Boys belong to 'gangs'; boys built 'huts' which were glorified bivouacs – holes scooped in the ground or burrowed in banks and overlaid with roofs of branches and leaves. Raw mud was used to construct crude walls and the same primitive adobe cemented sticks and leaves into screens almost, though never quite, strong enough to keep out rain and wind.

The hut was the social unit. Some huts were large warrens with ten or more members. Others were two-boy dwellings, desultorily constructed. No one knew, and certainly no one could explain, the rules of hut membership. It was simply something that happened. Boys were asked to join or they were not. A certain sort of boy built his own quite early in his West Hill career. Others were natural joiners and were quickly absorbed into one of the larger huts where they slowly graduated from menial-servant status to unofficial head of hut by the time they left. Some hardly ever went to the dingle and belonged to no hut. Of these there were very few.

School rules were relaxed in the dingle but in a curious unofficial fashion which, the CO believed, was a necessary preparation for life. Publicly he paid lip service to the notion that the Ten Commandments were of equal importance but in private even he was prepared to concede that it was worse to kill thy neighbour than to covet his wife, let alone his ass. Thus it was forbidden to possess comics in school whether they were annuals or weekly papers and even if they were as serious and respectable as the *Eagle*. In the dingle, however, it was accepted that you could get away with them. They were not to be flaunted. On those rare occasions when a master ventured into the dingle on a round of inspection the comics had to be hidden. The master might observe them being hidden, know perfectly well that they were being hidden, but there was a tacit understanding that he would turn a blind eye. Learning this lesson young would later enable West Hill's alumni to know precisely how far to go in fiddling expenses or income tax returns. (Or, come to that, precisely how far it was possible to go with thy neighbour's wife.)

Although it was forbidden everywhere else in the school, fire was allowed in the dingle. There was a myth that dingle fires could only be started by such honest Baden-Powell inspired methods as the rubbing together of sticks or the igniting of dried leaves with sun and magnifying glass. This was how Oily Watkins taught the Scout troop he purported to command, though it has to be said that as often as not Oily was unsuccessful in this and had to fall back on the services of Swan Vestas or Bryant and May. No boy in the dingle ever even attempted Scout methods. They all used matches. The big dingle occasions were Sunday afternoons. Then those boys who were not out on expeditions in the nearby hills or taking tea with doting parents would make a dingle fire and cook. Some of the food cooked would be sent from home by parents (Baxter's tinned chicken for the rich – Sona beans in tomato sauce for the poor). Some would be genuinely ingenious, a precocious attempt to live off the land. This last was never as successful as the commercially produced, parent-provided stuff, though nettle soup had its supporters and occasional raids on the vegetable garden yielded some dividends, especially chives.

Despite this, there was supposed to be fire without smoking. Smoking came into the same category as masturbation (especially mutual), and only just below cheating which

44

was, apart from murder, the school's single most serious offence. Murder had not yet occurred, cheating was rare, masturbation (especially mutual) confined almost exclusively to the senior boys and seldom discovered. Smoking, however, cropped up regularly, usually because some boy made himself ill by attempting to inhale smoke from a home-made cheroot of rolled leaves and pine needles. For this boys, once released from the sickroom, were beaten, though not with great severity. Possession of real cigarettes, containing real tobacco, was regarded less tolerantly. Which was partly why the CO and Porter were making such an unusual expedition during lessons this Saturday morning.

'I don't like having to search your hut,' said Burnam, 'but I'm afraid I have no alternative.' Inwardly he felt a flush of irritation at Commander Porter. If only the Commander had discovered the boys in the potting shed, none of this need have happened. Sometimes he felt parents asked too much for their money.

'No, sir.' Porter felt sick. It was not the physical fear of a beating but the apprehension of imminent discovery: the shame of it all.

They paused by the gate, an ugly iron-barred object on rusting hinges. The dingle was looking particularly peaceful. The sun filtered through leaves which still had the limy moist green of early summer; the rooks cawed but no man-made sound disturbed the moment. Porter wished he were alone.

From behind them there came the noise of a body crashing through undergrowth and suddenly Muggins, the school dog, emerged from the bamboos and bounded towards them grinning frantically. His obvious *joie de vivre* broke the sombreness of the occasion. He jumped up at Porter, trying to lick his face. Porter grinned. He liked dogs. Dogs liked him.

'Down, Muggins!' said Burnam sharply. Much as he enjoyed the animal, he was embarrassingly unruly. He would have to put him on a leash during St Christopher's visit. Or even lock him in his kennel. He opened the gate and they watched as the dog ran ahead, leaping the rim of the dingle, sliding and scampering down the incline, lost in the celebration of his exuberance and energy.

45

Then, without warning, the dog began to bark. Man and boy could tell at once that the tone of the bark meant something was wrong. It conveyed fear and threat in approximately equal measure, the sound of an animal confronted by enemy. The CO and Porter hurried forwards. At the edge of the dingle they both stopped and stared down at the floor below them.

Muggins was standing almost exactly in the middle of the bottom of the basin where the ground was at its most level. The hackles along his back had risen and he had his front feet splayed apart as if to say that despite the menace before him he was not going to retreat an inch. With his head slightly to one side he continued to emit a long rumbling growl punctuated by staccato barks. He was obviously very angry but also very scared.

About six feet from the dog stood three figures. At first glance the headmaster and his head prefect had thought they were human; at second they realized that they were too immobile, too fixed. They had something of the quality of scarecrows but scarecrows with a difference. As Burnam and Porter scrambled down the steep side of the dingle they began to understand the dog's reaction.

The three scarecrows were each two poles, nailed together in the shape of a crucifix. Across the horizontal of each one had been slung a pink and green striped West Hill blazer, at the neck of which was a West Hill tie. It was the heads which induced horror. Impaled on the upright stakes in grotesque parody of an ignoble historical tradition were three heads recently severed from living bodies. A thin trickle of blood ran from the mouths, eyes stared out blankly, flies buzzed. To complete the horrid joke, each head wore the hooped West Hill cap, jauntily angled. The heads were the heads of pigs, easily purchased for a few pence at any butcher's and more often used for making brawn or blood pudding. Had they been human the effect on Burnam, Porter and the dog could scarcely have been more upsetting.

'Good grief!' said the CO.

Porter made an inarticulate noise of disgust.

For a few moments they stood and stared at the uniformed pigs' heads while the dog continued to bark and growl. Then simultaneously they both turned to look around the dingle.

46

It was never the tidiest of places but today it was a shambles. Every hut had been systematically destroyed. Walls had been beaten in, roofs trampled and scattered. Luckily no one kept anything of great value in the dingle but various primitive kitchen utensils lay around: enamel saucepans and frying pans bent out of shape. One or two forks and spoons, cheap ones with a look of Woolworth's about them, had also been bent almost in half. China mugs and bowls had been smashed. Fragments of blue and white Cornish pottery lay everywhere. Porter guessed that anything which couldn't be destroyed had been taken away. He hoped that included the cigarettes, though faced with this disaster it seemed unlikely that the CO was going to remain unduly exercised by them.

'Well.' Burnam, who had seemed momentarily stunned, was never fazed for long. 'The first thing we'd better do is get these clothes together and see where they come from. Give me a hand, William.' The headmaster advanced on the nearest pig and removed cap, tie and blazer. When he had done so he peered inside the collar of the blazer, into the cap lining and the back of the tie. All boys at West Hill were required to have their names printed on Messrs Cash's nametapes and sewn into all items of clothing.

'As I suspected,' he said, 'the nametapes have been torn out.' He undressed another pig while William struggled with the third.

All the nametapes had been removed but the remains of the stitching could be seen clearly.

'Righty-ho, then,' said the CO. He put the three blazers under his arm and stuffed the ties in his pockets. Porter carried the caps. 'We'd better cut along home and see who's missing his blazer. As soon as we get back I want you to go round every class and say that there's a special assembly at,' he pulled out his gold hunter, 'at eleven. I'll tell Bert and the boys to clean up down here. And I suppose it's a police matter. I'll have to call Constable Taylor.'

Upsetting and dramatic though the experience had been, Porter had not forgotten the reason for their trip to the dingle. It seemed certain that whoever had carried out this raid had indeed made off with the cigarettes. His own hut was a write-off, so much so that he could not even make out where the cache of Player's had been hidden. They might

47

still be there, but it seemed highly improbable. They had only been under a thin layer of leaves. The vandals would almost certainly have found them. He was probably in the clear, but he knew that unless he had an articulated assurance from the CO, the accusation would nag at him for the rest of term. He had an uncommonly tidy mind which could not bear loose ends.

They had reached the iron gate when he decided he could stand it no longer. He finally broke in on the CO's thoughts out loud.

'I say, sir, what about the cigarettes, sir?'

'The cigarettes?'

'Yes, sir. The ones my father wrote to you about. The Maltese ones.'

'What about them?'

'Well . . . I mean . . .' Porter was nonplussed but the CO helped him out.

'I didn't find them, did I?'

'No, sir.'

The CO smiled a little thinly. 'So I shall write to your father and tell him so.'

'Yes, sir.'

There was an ambiguity in the headmaster's verdict and Porter knew it. He felt guilty, not proven. It was a weapon the CO often used: an implied withholding of judgement, a suggestion, unstated, that he knew more about you than you did yourself. Porter did not know whether Mr Burnam knew that he and Stack had stolen the cigarettes or not, but he sensed that the CO, as nearly always, was only too well aware of the truth. He would have been surprised to discover that, at this moment, the CO neither knew nor cared. But he was too astute a headmaster not to remember an important first principle: it did not matter if you *were* omniscient, provided the boys *thought* you were.

Nevertheless, Porter accepted that the question of the contraband Player's was now closed. That, since he was guilty, was a relief. The matter of the pigs in the dingle was very much open. And that, since he was a wholly innocent party, was distinctly thrilling.

3

Special assemblies were a rarity at West Hill. Normal business could be conducted quite adequately at morning prayers. So indeed could much abnormal business. A special assembly meant haste, urgency, high drama and was as much a dramatic device as a genuinely useful forum. The last one had been three years earlier when two boys had run away in the spring term and, inexplicably, set fire to a railway carriage a few miles east of Shepton Mallet. There had been a special assembly in 1945 when the CO had passed on Churchill's announcement of the German surrender, and another on Coronation Day in 1953, not because of the Coronation but in order to tell the school that a British expedition had conquered Mount Everest.

As Porter went from classroom to classroom with his announcement of a special assembly at eleven – or 1100 hours as the CO insisted on calling it – he left behind an audible buzz of apprehension. The staff were as agog as the boys. It was barely two hours since prayers. Nothing untoward had been suggested then nor at the staff briefing.

'A what?' said O'Rourke, halfway through giving a Maupassant short story to Form One as a dictation. 'Have the Russians dropped an atom bomb on Taunton? Have the Ashes been stolen? *De quoi s'agit-il, mon petit?*'

Porter's lips were sealed. He was enjoying the occasion as much as, he rather suspected, the CO.

'Dear me,' said matron starchily, when he found her dispensing quinine to a hypochondriacal fourth former named Fingest, 'is it really necessary for the matrons to be there, Porter? I'm sure it's nothing to do with us?'

William explained that Mr Burnam wanted everyone to be present except for those too unwell to attend. That,

49

presumably, let off Fingest. Matron sighed, and poured water into the medicine glass. When it mixed with the quinine it turned milky like Pernod. The taste, however, was one of the horrors of West Hill.

Eleven hundred hours found the CO standing at the lectern in Big School, black gown billowing, gold and orange MCC tie glowing. At prayers the custom was for the staff, followed by the headmaster, to enter Big School after the boys were in place; but on this occasion Burnam had decided to reverse the procedure by getting there five minutes early. As boys approached the entrance they were chattering and giggling but as they entered the room Burnam reduced them to silence with one of his ferocious stares, delivered pensively while he chewed on one end of his spectacles.

The lectern was in the centre of Big School, just in front of the organ. In the days of private occupation Big School had been the ballroom, though quite why a private ballroom should need an organ no one seemed to know. A ballroom organ smacked of Blackpool and working-class knees-ups. The general assumption was that the ballroom had doubled up as a chapel and that the organ was installed for rousing voluntaries and hymns. Certainly that was its latter-day purpose. Mr Friendly, the music master, was quite competent at Purcell and *Hymns Ancient and Modern*, but he would never have dreamed of attempting anything as vulgar as dance music.

On either side of the lectern were rows of desks. These were simply sloping fronts of wood with evenly disposed inkwells and a groove for resting your pen. They were attached to backless benches. Boys filed into these pews according to order of seniority, while the staff, instead of sitting on some sort of central platform as they would have done in most schools, were scattered around the walls on wooden chairs with backs, arms and rather motheaten cushions. This meant that they were behind the boys and could, as it were, see without being seen. It made misbehaviour more easily detected and also allowed the staff to shut their eyes, pick their noses or indulge any other disrespectful habits without being stared at by little boys.

The CO conducted the school as if it were an orchestra. Despite his dampening stare there was an early element of

50

pre-performance restlessness. A handful of late arrivals scurried in, crimson-faced, shoving over other boys' knees as they struggled to their places. The latest arrival, characteristically, was O'Rourke. He could be heard whistling 'Lillibullero' as he ambled down the corridor and only stopped as he entered, hands deep in pockets, apparently oblivious to the significance of the occasion. One or two boys tittered but Burnam silenced them as effectively as any maestro disciplining errant spirits in the brass or woodwind. A flick of the eyes in their direction and order was restored. No need for anything as crude as a spoken rebuke.

'You may close the door now, Fieldhouse,' he said, looking across to Adrian who was the week's official 'door monitor', a sort of sentry-cum-commissionaire. Adrian shut the door and slid into his corner seat at the back of the room. He wished he had had a chance to talk to William but he had only managed a snatched interrogatory whisper when O'Rourke's back was turned. Porter had just smiled smugly.

The glasses went on and were pushed a little down the large fleshy nose; the gown was hitched; papers on the lectern frowned at; an all-encompassing, frankly hostile perusal of the room as if checking (an impossibility) that all were present; another frown at the papers; the famous cough; tension now raised to highest desirable level; eyes fixed firmly on the third pew to the left (eyes always fixed firmly on someone or other so that by the time he had finished all boys were convinced he had been talking to them personally and individually). And off.

'Bad news,' he said. Long pause and gaze transferred to other side of room, fourth row. 'Sometime during the night it seems that vandals broke into the school grounds, stole various articles of clothing and destroyed all the huts in the dingle.'

The flat statement of such dramatic events was astutely judged and received with a gratifyingly stunned silence. Porter, the only listener not stunned by the revelations, was impressed. Quite succinctly Burnam now described their discovery. He did not embellish. There was no need. He had a good story and he told it simply. When he had finished he took a handkerchief from his trouser pocket and rubbed the lenses of his spectacles.

51

'I have in my study,' he said, 'three blazers, three ties and three school caps. None of them is marked. After leaving here I want all of you to go to the changing room and check to see if you're missing any of these clothes. If so, come to my study at once and report it.'

Some clothes were kept in dormitories, but blazers and caps being for outdoor and semi-ceremonial use were usually in the changing room. Ties, of which all boys were required to have three, were often to be found in dormitory and changing room. The changing room had doors which led straight outside as well as stairs leading up to the interior of the house. There were also windows. They were often left open. Security was lax. There was no reason for it to be otherwise. Crime was hardly a major cause for concern in rural Somerset in the mid 1950s. The theft of West Hill school uniforms presented no problems for even the most amateur burglar. No reason why it should. The idea of anyone wanting to steal them was, until now, inherently improbable.

'Obviously,' he continued, 'steps will have to be taken to discover who is responsible for what has happened. I have already been in touch with the police' (he gave the word 'police' the slightest extra emphasis and was rewarded with a scattered but quite audible intake of breath from perhaps a third of his audience) 'and, of course, they will be making investigations. If anyone thinks he can help in any way, if anyone saw anyone hanging around the grounds last night, or saw anything at all suspicious, then come to my study as soon as possible.

'Now,' he leaned forward with his elbows on the lectern and smiled, for the first time since beginning to speak. Most of the school leaned forward an inch or two to share the confidence. 'I don't want to be alarmist, but there is always the possibility that whoever did this may strike again. So I want you to be particularly watchful. You all know the people who live here, whether they're boys or members of staff. Most of you also know about the people who visit us regularly, whether it's the postman or Dr Blenkinsop or the padre. I don't want boys rushing in to tell me there's some intruder in the grounds and then find that someone has reported the bread delivery man.' (Laughter.) 'But if you *do*

52

see strange people whom you don't recognize, then tell me or one of the staff or one of the monitors. I'm confident that the police will catch the culprits pretty jolly quickly but there's no point in taking risks. So I'm asking you all to keep on your toes and keep a good lookout.

'And one final thing. As you know, it's the St Christopher's match this afternoon and it's important that we put up a first-rate show. I'd prefer it if nothing at all was said about this when you meet their chaps. Until the matter's solved, remember, it's in the hands of the police. The fewer outsiders that know about it the better. Otherwise it'll make their job that much harder. And, for the time being,' he added, 'I'd prefer you not to mention it in your letters home.' Fat chance, he thought to himself ruefully. Little boys were inveterate gossips. Someone was bound to spill the beans during team tea and by the time St Christopher's got home the news would be all round the southwestern prep-school circuit.

'That's all for now,' he concluded, making a show of shutting his glasses with a snap. 'Just check on your clothes and then report to your classrooms after break.' He gathered up the papers from the lectern and marched out magisterially, gown billowing like bats' wings. As he passed the pensive figure of his second-in-command, slumped in his corner, he stopped briefly to say he'd like a word. O'Rourke said yes, of course, at once.

They were an intriguing contrast, Burnam and O'Rourke. Burnam, much the bigger of the two, a shade over six foot and broad with it, was a Labrador alongside O'Rourke's whippet. O'Rourke was just under five ten but looked smaller. Burnam was dressed as country gentleman with his brown brogues, his cavalry twills, long-waisted hacking jacket, discreet check shirt and sleeveless brown pullover. Above all, the rhubarb and custard striped tie. O'Rourke did have a military air but, despite the neat David Niven moustache, in no way did he give a conventional or parade-ground impression. You would be more likely to have classed him as one of Orde Wingate's Chindits or David Stirling's Long-Range Desert Group. He had a raffishness which Burnam at once envied and deplored. The light tan cords were just a touch too tight, the ankle-length brothel

53

creepers a little too vulgar, and he wore a belt which might almost have been lizard. His sportscoat and shirt were not, superficially, unlike Burnam's but they had a Bohemian left-bank quality which was difficult to pin down. His tie, which might have been the respectable blue and magenta of the Brigade of Guards, was a canary number knitted from string. At some times they complemented each other, these two types. At others not. It would be misleading to say they did not get on. Not entirely true to say that they did. The relationship was wary and fraught with crossed purpose, but for ten years it had survived.

O'Rourke knocked on the study door, waited politely for Burnam's 'Come!' but sat down without waiting to be asked. He always did. It irritated Burnam which was why O'Rourke did it.

'Wretched business,' said Burnam.

'Mind if I smoke?' asked O'Rourke, taking out a packet of Navy Cut.

Burnam did mind but did not object. Instead he pushed a heavy glass ashtray across the desk and watched impatiently as O'Rourke tapped the cigarette several times on the back of his left hand before lighting it with a battered lighter.

'So,' said O'Rourke, blowing a perfect ring, 'you're going to leave no stone unturned?'

'How do you mean?'

'I mean, you're determined to get to the bottom of this. Identify the guilty parties, bring them to trial, have them flogged or put away or whatever the bench decides.'

'From your tone,' said the CO, 'I gather you think that's not the proper course.'

O'Rourke thought for a moment. 'It's one way of doing it. It's not the way I'd do it. Not if you want my advice.'

'It's because I want your advice that I asked you in here.'

'Well,' said O'Rourke, 'I'd let it rest if I were you.'

'What? Condone it?'

'I didn't say that. Just treat it with the contempt it deserves.' O'Rourke watched the ash accumulating on the end of his cigarette and tapped it into the glass dish just in time to prevent it falling to the carpet. 'You could be using a sledgehammer to crack eggs. If you know what I mean. Might make things a lot worse.'

Burnam frowned. 'I'm sorry,' he said, 'I'm not with you.' O'Rourke was wearing that supercilious, 'what did *you* do in the war?' expression: the one which implied that he, O'Rourke, had knocked around a bit and knew what was what. Burnam had learned, more or less, to live with it, relatively secure in the knowledge that he was in charge at West Hill and could fire O'Rourke whenever he felt so inclined. But he had learned over the years that when O'Rourke did put it on, it usually meant he did have a trump. Better to yield and let him play it.

'You told the school it was a police matter. I don't think we should bring the police into it. If it is a crime then it's not that sort of crime.'

'I've already been on to the police.'

'You mean Constable Taylor?'

'Yes.'

O'Rourke smiled. 'Oh,' he said, 'we surely don't think of Constable Taylor as "police"?'

'He's not exactly the Flying Squad,' conceded Burnam. He smiled back. 'But I've always thought him quite competent within his limits. And if he can't cope, I'm sure he'll have the sense to send for help.'

' "Help",' said O'Rourke, 'would mean a lot of callow, heavy-footed strangers from the CID in Taunton. That's exactly what we don't want. Taylor doesn't matter. He's local and he doesn't go by the book. I agree with you. He *is* competent within his limits and he also knows his place. He'll do as he's told.'

'Up to a point. He can hardly ignore a crime.'

'That's what I mean.' O'Rourke ground out the cigarette and lit another. 'It's not a crime. Not that sort of crime.'

'What do you mean? "Not a crime"? Trespass. Breaking and entering. Theft. Damage to property. Of course it is.'

'You know what I mean.' O'Rourke was unable to keep the edge of exasperation out of his voice. Burnam could be so bloody obstinate. He almost caught himself muttering 'pig-headed' under his breath, but caught himself in time. Sotto voce, or even silently, that was hardly the phrase. The trouble with Burnam was that he saw things so starkly. Too much cricket and too many westerns. You were either in or out – no half measures. You were a good guy or a bad guy.

Good guys wore white hats, bad ones wore black. No one in Burnam's world wore grey. Gary Cooper good; Boris Karloff bad. O'Rourke's character assessments were based on the premise that everyone wore grey.

'Look.' Burnam was just as exasperated, partly because of O'Rourke's insufferable one-upmanship, partly because, yet again, he seemed to be trimming and equivocating. O'Rourke, it seemed to him, was always facing both ways, seeing all sides of the argument, unable to accept that there was a time when you had to stand up and be counted. It was, apart from anything else, a bad example for the boys. 'Am I right in thinking you know something I don't?'

'It depends,' said O'Rourke, smiling again, 'what you know.'

'For heaven's sake, stop playing games, Dermot. You don't seem to understand. This is serious.'

'It's because it's serious that I don't think you should take it too seriously.'

'Oh, for crying out loud! I'm really not in the mood for riddles. Explain.'

O'Rourke explained. It was a hunch more than a certainty but it was a pretty good hunch all the same. As Burnam knew, he spent a certain amount of time down at the Plume of Feathers. Burnam nodded. Frankly, he disapproved, though he had no control over the staff's out-of-school activities. He himself would never be seen dead in the Plume of Feathers, not even in the saloon bar, and his information was that O'Rourke hung out in the public. Well, he had to accept that O'Rourke was unconventional, that was all.

'I know,' O'Rourke was being patronizing again, 'that the Plume of Feathers isn't exactly the officers' mess, but I happen to like it. The draught bitter's first class and I enjoy the atmosphere. Besides which, you learn things.'

Burnam didn't doubt it. His intelligence came from local dinner tables, the occasional meet of the local foxhounds. It was as good as O'Rourke's but it was different.

'I sometimes play dominoes with Richard Odstock.'

'The village schoolmaster?'

'The same.'

'So?'

'Well, he's a nice chap but a bit of a bolshie. Argumentative.

56

Fond of quoting Orwell. Especially on the public schools.'

'Oh? You're not suggesting he had anything to do with it?'

'Of course not. As I said, he's a decent sort even if his politics are Bevanite. He doesn't like private education. Doesn't like any sort of privilege. Now, I don't know what you think, but it strikes me that the dingle incident is a child's prank. Not an adult's.'

'Prank is hardly the word I'd have chosen.'

'Oh, all right. Bad choice. I agree there's a viciousness involved. Criminal, if you insist. But I don't think it's adult.'

'So you're suggesting that you have a quiet word over the dominoes with your charming Mr Odstock and we all forget it?'

'I'm saying that if you make a meal out of it and bring in the strong arm of the law, then you're going to set the village against you. That would be foolish.'

Burnam ran a hand across his scalp. O'Rourke had a point. 'I'm not sure I have an alternative.'

O'Rourke stood up. 'You talk to the constable. I'll talk to Odstock. Then let's discuss it again. But if it *was* children from the village school, I think it would be much better to ask Odstock to sort it out informally.'

'All right.' The CO was weary in defeat.

'Good. I knew you'd agree,' said O'Rourke.

His hand was on the door when there was a knock from the other side. Burnam called 'Come,' and the door opened to reveal a grinning Basil Roberts, though it did not look as if this was because he had found anything amusing.

'Ah, headmaster,' said Roberts, grin widening still farther until it seemed to be causing him actual physical pain, 'ah, Major.' No one else called O'Rourke 'Major'. No one knew where Roberts had got the idea. 'I'm not disturbing you?'

'I was just leaving,' said O'Rourke irritably.

'Oh, do stay half a mo,' said Roberts. He closed the door behind him and then, with his hands still clutching the knob behind him, he shut his eyes and began to recite:

> 'The Boar's Head in hand bear I,
> Bedecked with bays and rosemary,
> And I pray you, my masters be merry,
> *Quot estis in convivio*.

The Boar's Head, as I understand,
Is the rarest dish in all this land,
Which thus bedecked with a gay garland
Let us *servire cantico*.

Our steward hath provided this,
In honour of the King of Bliss,
Which on this day to be served is,
In Reginensi atrio.'

Mr Roberts opened his eyes. 'So you see,' he said, 'the Boar's Head is a *tremendously* ancient image. It goes back quite *tremendously* far into our heritage. Quite tremendously. We've sung that at my college since the late fourteenth century.'

Neither the CO nor O'Rourke was sure how to take this. Eventually the CO said rattily, 'They weren't boars' heads. They were pigs' heads. Rather small pigs, if you must know.'

'No, no,' said Mr Roberts excitedly, 'it's the idea, the image, don't you see. *Tremendously* potent and quite unchanged through the centuries. Rural England is the most extraordinary phenomenon. Always who knows what lurking in the hedgerows and under the thatch of the most modest cottage but so seldom manifested in such . . . such a *visible* manner.'

Burnam and O'Rourke were looking at each other blankly and incredulously, an incomprehension which Roberts, even though he was obviously operating on another plane altogether, obviously caught. 'Witchcraft,' he said, 'witchcraft.'

'Oh really, Mr Roberts!' The CO was at his most reasonable and level-headed. 'I hardly think that in this day and age . . .'

'Oh, there's no doubt about it.' Roberts shook his head. 'I know it's fashionable to pooh-pooh the notion that the black arts still flourish, but I assure you they do. My postgraduate thesis was on the occult in sixteenth-century Surrey, so I know what I'm talking about.'

'This is 1956,' said the CO equably.

Roberts took a step towards the desk. 'I could tell you stories about Haselmere and Godalming which would turn

58

your blood to milk,' he said. 'Not history. Contemporary stories. Stories of our times. There's a myth that we live in a Christian country and so perhaps we do, but it's a pagan country too. It always has been. And that's what those heads in the dingle are all about. Don't worry about the police. The only man who can help you is the priest.'

'I came across a lot of it in Italy,' said O'Rourke surprisingly, 'particularly in the south.' He took Roberts genially but firmly by the elbow. 'Look,' he said, 'the headmaster's got an awful lot on his plate just at the moment. Why don't you and I nip off and talk it through over a cup of coffee? Then if we decide on a course of action, we can make a simple recommendation without having to waste his time talking about it.'

Burnam was greatly relieved that as his number two guided the history teacher out of the room he still found time to look quickly over his shoulder and wink.

It might have surprised the staff, even O'Rourke, to know that some of the boys' analyses of the situation were better informed and nearer the mark than those of Burnam, O'Rourke and Roberts.

'A hundred to one it's those oiks from the village,' said Donald Stack, lobbing a piece of gravel idly towards the front door. He, Fieldhouse and Porter were sitting on the wall which separated the drive from the tennis courts and croquet lawn. They often came out here in morning break, especially if the weather was fine. It was a sun trap.

'I'm surprised they had the guts,' said Fieldhouse. 'Supposing they got caught?'

'They've got plenty of guts,' said Stack, 'they're just vile yobbos. I can't stand the way they talk. Like that ghastly gamekeeper in the Archers. Ooh aar, ooh aar, ooh aar. Do anybody wanna come aowtsoid so oi can push his face in for him? Why can't they talk English? It's not difficult. *We* all do it.'

'Quite a clever idea, though,' said Porter. 'They did look extraordinary standing there in the dingle. Really upset Muggins. He was in an incredible state.'

'Do you think they'll catch them now?' said Fieldhouse.

'What, with PC 49 from the village?' said Stack. 'Ooh aar, ooh aar, oooh aar. I was proceeding in a northeasterly direction when I observed that a crime had been committed and I have reason to believe . . .' Stack coupled his verbal imitation with a physical one of a PC Plod-like, bandy-legged, flat-footed walk. His friends laughed dutifully. 'Besides,' he said, 'he's one of them, isn't he? Even if he does know, he'll turn a blind eye.'

'Oh, come on,' said Fieldhouse, 'it doesn't work like that. The law's the law, and the police have to uphold the law. And they do too. My father's a lawyer, remember. We know the Chief Constable, actually. He just wouldn't let that sort of thing happen.'

'Fieldhouse believes in Father Christmas,' jeered Stack.

'Fieldhouse believes in fairies,' said Porter.

Fieldhouse turned puce. 'Come on, you chaps,' he said, 'what's so bloody funny? I just said the law's the law and the police enforce it. What's wrong with that?'

'Listen,' said Stack, 'when you were a newbug you thought monitors were Lord God Almighty. Is that right?'

'I suppose so.' Fieldhouse said it grudgingly.

'And now you are a monitor yourself, do you still think they're Lord God Almighty?'

'Course he does,' said Porter, 'that's why he thinks he's going to get a scholarship to Sherborne.'

'What's wrong with that? You both think you're going to get scholarships.'

'What's wrong with that, Fieldhouse, is that we're right and you're wrong,' Stack laughed.

Fieldhouse jumped down from the wall. 'You're so pleased with yourself, Stack,' he shouted. 'Just because your father got the VC. I'd like to see you get the VC. Stupid little runt.'

'Batey bo,' said Stack, thumbing his nose at Fieldhouse's departing back and then, turning to Porter, 'What's the matter with him, then?'

'I wish you wouldn't tease him like that,' said Porter, loyalty divided.

'Well, he shouldn't be so pompous.'

'You were being vile about his father.'

'I was not. I just suggested that PC Taylor wasn't exactly Sexton Blake. Anyway, you agreed.'

'I know. But his father's a lawyer.'

'So what? You don't get all excited when people are rude about the Navy.'

'That's just it. Nobody ever is rude about the Navy.' Porter felt he had scored an important point.

'Well,' said Stack lamely, 'you know what I mean.'

'I wish you wouldn't do it.' Porter consolidated his attack. 'I *like* Fieldhouse.'

'*I* like Fieldhouse too,' said Stack. 'That's part of the reason I do it. I'm trying to educate him.'

'Oh, gosh, you do talk a lot of bilge.'

'Yes,' said Stack, grinning, 'don't I?'

For a while they continued to sit on the wall kicking their heels in the sunlight. Then Stack said, 'If it was the yobbos, and if they get away with it, what should we do?'

'How do you mean?'

'Well,' said Stack, 'should we let them get away with it?'

'It's not up to us.'

'Not to start with, but if the CO and the police don't sort them out, then we'll have to do it, don't you think?'

Porter looked at Stack quizzically and rather uneasily. 'Do what exactly?'

'Dunno yet,' said Stack, 'but if they can pinch a whole lot of school uniforms and stick them up on pigs' heads in the dingle, then so can we.'

'They don't wear uniform at the village school,' said Porter prosaically. 'And there's no dingle.'

'Don't be silly.' There was a dangerous glint in the Mighty Atom's eyes. 'You know what I mean. We have to find some really clever kind of revenge. Something that'll make them wish they'd never even thought of pigs' heads.'

They were interrupted by the bell for the end of break and these embryonic plans were left unresolved. Porter hoped they would stay that way. Not for nothing, he reflected as they scuffed across the gravel, was his friend the son of Stack VC.

O'Rourke had a free period immediately before lunch. This gave him time, were he so inclined, to take a quick shufty down to the Plume of Feathers, sink a pint of Starkey, Knight and Ford's best bitter, exchange a little chat about cricket and weather with whoever happened to be in there and then walk briskly back. Most Saturdays he *was* so inclined and he had refined the practice to a precise ritual. If he started out from school the minute the period ended at 12.15 he could get himself into the pub at 12.30, which gave him a quarter of an hour's drinking time. If he left the Plume when their clock showed 12.45 he would be entering the front hall of West Hill just as the luncheon gong was sounding. If, which he very occasionally did, he fancied another half, he could always drive there and back in Wilfred, his bottle green MG sports car. But as a rule he preferred to walk, particularly if it was fine, and today was fine.

He knew that the CO was aware of this practice and he knew that the CO disapproved. Burnam never took liquor until the sun was over the yardarm, and even then it was only a small glass of medium-dry South African sherry. For once, however, Burnam would presumably waive his censure because the probability, the extreme probability, was that Richard Odstock would be on his usual stool at the far end of the bar chatting up whoever was behind the bar and toying with a pint and the *Manchester Guardian* crossword.

O'Rourke enjoyed the beer but he also enjoyed the walk. The house although not beautiful had a certain early-Victorian impressiveness which fell short of grandeur but still conveyed substance. As he strode away from it, swinging his blackthorn, O'Rourke liked to half pretend that he was the owner, Squire O'Rourke, taking a turn about the policies and inspecting the tenantry. He walked briskly with that distinctive swagger and flick of the wrist characteristic of the Irish Guards, and as he walked he daydreamed, absorbing rather than consciously appreciating the countryside. He was aware of the great cedar with the climbing ropes and of the three copper beeches on the lawn to his right. He skipped nimbly across the cattlegrid which divided the gardens from the park, but he did not have to look down to make sure his feet did not catch in the gaps. He managed it instinctively, from habit. All through the park his nostrils inhaled the aroma of grass and cowdung and sun on soil, but if you had asked him to say what he was smelling he would at first have denied he was smelling anything at all. The effect on his senses of the rolling parkland, the palisade-surrounded elms and oaks, the scattered Friesians was real enough but subliminal. It induced peace and wellbeing, an at-one-ness with the world. Although he attended mass every Sunday, O'Rourke was an instinctive rather than a thinking Christian. He felt more spiritual inspiration on a walk through the park to the pub than he ever did in the cramped corrugated-iron Catholic church with its mean pews and its crabby priest. If there was a God, he was out here in the countryside under the sky, not locked up in a damp shed. O'Rourke would rather smell cowdung than incense. Matter of taste, he supposed. He would have denied it was an indication of character, though the suggestion would, secretly, have appealed to him.

At the door of the Plume of Feathers the trance-like state subsided and he became once more the sardonic, marginal failure of a prep-school master as which he was universally accepted.

He pushed open the door of the public and blinked a couple of times to acclimatize to the gloom. There were very few windows in the bar and they were seldom if ever opened so that the fetid smoke of last night, last week and possibly even last year was a permanent lingering part of the atmosphere. It was a particularly smelly pub. It was not just the smoke, ancient and modern, but also the beer and the fact that few of the regulars were much given to soap and water. Hardly any had indoor baths.

Odstock was there all right, frowning at the crossword. 'Morning, sir,' he said, looking up briefly. The 'sir' was half sarcastic, half instinctive. Odstock was too young to have served in the war but he had done National Service as a sergeant in the Education Corps. Madge, the publican's busty daughter, rouged and peroxided, said, 'Morning, Mr O'Rourke,' and began drawing off a pint without being asked. O'Rourke said, 'Morning,' in a general sort of way, though Madge and Odstock were the only two inhabitants, placed his walking stick in the ancient motheared elephant's foot to the left of the dartboard and slid onto the stool alongside the village schoolmaster.

'It's a crime,' said Odstock, pencilling in an answer to 23 across, 'that England don't choose Gimblett.'

63

'If England chose Gimblett,' retorted O'Rourke, 'Somerset would never even make double figures.'

Odstock grunted. There was some truth in this. The Somerset cricket team was a disaster. Harold Gimblett, their star opening batsman, was the only player who ever made runs.

'It'll be better in the holidays,' O'Rourke blew the froth off his beer and smiled at Madge, 'once the schoolmasters are available.'

'Bloody amateurs,' said Odstock.

'Ah, but gentlemen,' O'Rourke grinned teasingly.

'If I had my way,' said Odstock, 'there wouldn't be any amateurs or gentlemen. It would be players only. I mean, what sort of world do people think this is? "Gimblett, H.; M. M. Walford." '

Odstock was referring to the prevailing practice, in newspapers and on scorecards, of allowing amateurs (i.e. gentlemen) the privilege of having their initials before their names while professional players (i.e. yobbos) had them after.

'Well, at least they all use the same changing room and come out of the same gate.'

It was not so long since they hadn't.

'Makes you sick,' said Odstock. 'You'd think the war never happened.'

O'Rourke let this curious remark pass. Instead of replying, he took a mouthful of lukewarm bitter, swilled it round thoughtfully and said, 'Any news from Lord's?'

'Australians are batting,' said Odstock. 'No one out yet.' He had been listening to the BBC Home Service.

'I'm glad I found you here. I wanted a word.'

'Well, carry on.'

Odstock continued to suck his pencil and, apparently, worry the crossword, but O'Rourke sensed an apprehension in him. Something about the tips of the ears. Perhaps a general tension.

'I think you know why.'

'Do I?'

Much too studiedly casual, thought O'Rourke. Still, he didn't have time to faff around. He told him about the pigs in the dingle.

'Very interesting,' said Odstock when he'd finished.

64

'Is that all you have to say?'

'What do you expect me to say?'

'Listen,' O'Rourke was anxious to appear as reasonable as possible, 'there's no point in pretending. We both know whodunnit.'

'Who?'

'It's your precious Gavin and Chrissie.'

'How do you know?'

'Intuition,' said O'Rourke honestly.

'You can't prove it. Even if it was them.'

'We could. In time.'

'Who's we?'

'Me. Burnam. The police. No great problem. Footprints, fingerprints all over the place.'

'Police?'

For the first time O'Rourke felt he was getting through. Odstock was worried by the idea of police.

'Look.' O'Rourke glanced up at the clock. He had five minutes left before departure time. 'I'm not suggesting you had anything to do with it. I'm not even suggesting you knew anything about it. But I do know that you've done your level best to turn those children into a couple of what most of my colleagues would refer to as "dangerous bolshies". And I also infer, from what you've told me in the past, that you have some influence with them. Now, I'm suggesting you use it to stop them getting into real trouble.'

Odstock said nothing. He continued to stare at the cross-word.

'Are you listening?' asked O'Rourke.

'I'm listening.'

'Well, I think that this time, maybe, I can persuade Bur-nam to hold his horses. But only if I can get an undertaking that nothing like this is going to happen again. I've no objection to people holding political views but I do object to cheap hooliganism.'

'I wouldn't call it that.'

'What would you call it then?'

'A gesture. A symbol. Quite a clever one in its way.'

O'Rourke looked at Odstock sharply and wondered if he was mistaken, if the village schoolmaster had been actively involved.

65

'If,' he said, 'I can't hold Burnam back, there'll be a prosecution. They'll be found guilty and in all probability they'll be taken into care, put into some sort of institution, removed from their parents, their roots, everything. You don't want that.'

'For a first-time offence? Thirteen-year-olds?'

'You've seen the local bench in operation. Justice of the Peace is a total misnomer. If those children come up before any sort of local authority round here they'll get more than the book thrown at them. And from what you've told me, if any do-gooding welfare officer gets a peek inside their hovel and manages to hold an intelligible conversation with the parents, they'll be whisked off into a home for deprived delinquents before you can say knife. Best place for them probably.'

'They're very clever children,' said Odstock.

'OK,' said O'Rourke, 'then tell them to start acting clever. Otherwise they're in dead trouble.' He drained his pint and stood up. 'Well,' he said, 'will you talk to them?'

'I'll talk to them. But it's not fair.'

'Who said anything about fair? Of course it's not fair. Life isn't fair. Never has been, never will be.'

'One law for the rich and another for the poor.'

O'Rourke grinned. 'Laws grind the poor,' he said, 'and rich men rule the law, etcetera, etcetera.'

'That's going to change,' said Odstock, 'and Gavin and Chrissie's generation are the ones who'll change it.'

'Oh, yes?' O'Rourke was still grinning. 'Well, they'll have Stack and Porter and Fieldhouse's generation to contend with. I don't see them getting a great deal of change out of them. But we shall see.'

O'Rourke walked home whistling.

4

Gavin and Chrissie Smith were genetic freaks – the very clever children of very stupid parents, probably educationally subnormal parents (the concept did not exist in their own childhood and adolescence). George Smith was a farm labourer, the latest in an unending line of farm labourers, not one of whom had ever strayed more than five miles from the centre of the village of Nether King's Compton. His wife, Gertrude, *née* Cooper, boasted similar lineage. For centuries the male Coopers of Nether King's Compton had been labourers. The female Coopers had, like Gertie, married the labourers and washed and cooked for them and borne them children who in their turn had become the Georges and Gertrudes of their generation. Rural life was like that. Not just in Somerset. Not just in England. But every century or so some fluke combination of apparently dim spouses would bring forth not just progeny but prodigy. Not all these flourished, but if someone – schoolmaster, rector, even squire – noticed this deviation from the norm and nourished it, then from the mute and inglorious there did indeed emerge a Milton. Gavin and Chrissie might not be modern Miltons, but they were bright and, thanks to Odstock, their brightness was noticed, and educated.

They were pleased with themselves that afternoon. All the way back to Compton on the Puffing Billy branch line which transported them to and from the grammar school five miles away, they had been hugging themselves and each other with joy at a job well done. They had no real hatred of individuals, but they had a very real hatred of symbols, a hatred which had been carefully cultivated by Odstock during their years at the village school. Now that they had passed the eleven-plus and moved on to the more sophisticated

67

atmosphere of the grammar school, Odstock's influence
was formally diminished but actually enhanced. He was
in the process of passing from pedagogue to friend. No
longer someone to obey without question, not yet merely
someone to listen to with interest, but a man at whose feet
you still sat and whom you respected. Last night's efforts,
they felt, were an offering he would enjoy.

They were pleased, though slightly surprised, when
Odstock appeared standing by the ticket barrier as they
passed through. He looked unhappy. And it was not just
because Neil Harvey was collaring the MCC bowling.

'Hello, you two,' he said.

They had been looking forward to this moment, but now,
for reasons they could not properly understand, they felt flat
and anticlimactic. They did, however, say hello.

'It's hot,' said Odstock truthfully. 'Would you like a
drink?'

Gavin and Chrissie said they wouldn't mind if they did.
Their father wouldn't be home and their mother might or
might not, depending on whether she was needed up at the
big house – the *other* big house – where she worked part time,
bedmaking, cleaning and generally skivvying about. Gavin
removed his maroon blazer and slung it over his shoulder.
He slouched. So did Chrissie.

'Good day at school?' asked Odstock.

' 's all right,' muttered Chrissie, pushing auburn hair out
of her eyes. She would be a pretty girl before long but was
gawkily plain at the beginning of adolescence and, like
Gavin, inclined to acne. She had grown six inches in the last
year.

They walked slowly down the station approach towards
the village; past Harris, the coal merchant; past Irving's,
whose bull-nosed Morris was the only taxi between here and
Taunton; then into the main street. The general store and
post office, seemingly obsessional about wellington boots
which hung in ranks from string along the ceiling, also sold
soft drinks. Odstock bought Gavin a Vimto and Chrissie a
Tizer ('The Appetizer') and paid in coppers. They took
them outside into the street and walked across to the war
memorial. This grim obelisk was embossed with the names
of those men (forty-one in the first war, twelve in the second)

and women (two nurses and an ambulance driver) who had given their all for king and country.

There were seats around the memorial, which was at the foot of wide steps leading up to the churchyard. Most days the seats were occupied by old men with heavy oak walking-sticks and nothing better to do than watch the world go by. Or that small part of it which passed up and down the main street of Nether King's Compton in the middle of the day. Today there were none. Probably watching the village play cricket. Or perhaps even West Hill versus St Christopher's. The school ground ran alongside a lane leading down the hills and occasionally one or two villagers would lean over the fence and watch. There was no law against it and no one seemed to mind.

'I had a talk with Mr O'Rourke from West Hill this morning,' said Odstock.

'Yeah?' Gavin wiped his mouth with the back of his hand.

'He told me they had a break-in last night. Vandals. Some things were stolen.'

'Yeah?' Gavin managed to keep anything more than passing interest out of his voice.

'Some things were stolen, Gavin.' Odstock sounded censorious voice raised a notch.

'Can't have been,' said Chrissie. 'Property's theft. 's wot you always tell us. Marx, innit?'

'No,' said Odstock prissily, 'it wasn't Marx. As a matter of fact, it was Proudhon.'

'Oh,' said Gavin, laughing unpleasantly, 'French bloke, was he?'

'Come on, you two. This is serious.' Odstock sighed. 'Was it you?'

'Didn't steal nuffin',' said Gavin sullenly. 'Threw it in the lake.'

'So you admit it. It was you.'

Gavin shrugged. The church clock struck the half hour. The three of them sat silently contemplating the gap between theory and practice. It was quite true that Odstock had preached the doctrine that property was theft, just as he had insisted that all men were equal, that justice should be accessible and that Jack was as good as his neighbour. It had been implicit in his teaching while they had still been at his

69

school. He had explained why Cromwell's cause was preferable to the King's, that the revolutions in France and Russia and even America were necessary. He had spurred them on so that they would pass the eleven-plus and go to the grammar school because that way they could pass on to university and begin to compete on equal terms with the nobs, the Little Lord Fauntleroys up at West Hill. People, he had explained, both in and out of school hours and after they had left his little school for the grammar in Taunton, people should not be able to buy superior medicine and superior education. In the bad old days men had bought commissions in the Army, been granted church livings by the aristocrats who owned them. Not any more, but there was still intolerable injustice in Britain, he explained, a great social injustice which he wanted to eradicate.

Gavin and Chrissie were to be the weapons in his private fight to change the system, and Gavin and Chrissie, though they might not yet be able to formulate the idea articulately, were aware of this. So, like dogs wanting to please a beloved master, they had gone out and killed for him. Now when they came back and dropped their prey at his feet, he was ungrateful. Gavin and Chrissie reacted like any spurned pets. They were cowed and resentful. They didn't understand and, making it worse for them all, nor did their master.

'You shouldn't have done it,' said Odstock eventually.

'Why not?' asked Chrissie. Odstock often thought Chrissie would be the more successful of the twins. It was not just that she was cleverer. She was more combative.

'Because,' Odstock began and then stopped. He had been going to say it was wrong but that was not quite true. Besides which, if he approved of revolution he ought to approve of Gavin and Chrissie; he could hardly justify Madame Guillotine and frown on their beating up West Hill's dingle and mocking its inmates in effigy.

'Listen,' he began a second time, 'you have to be realistic. What you did was against the law. Now the law may be wrong, but the law is the law, and if the West Hill people want to make trouble they can use the law to protect themselves and make life miserable for you. They could get you taken away from home, expelled from the grammar school. Heaven knows what.'

70

'They don't know we dunnit,' said Chrissie.

'Yes they do.'

'How?' asked Gavin.

'That doesn't matter. Even if they didn't know, it wouldn't take long to find out. I gather there are footprints all over the place. Fingerprints as well, I imagine. If they set their minds to it, they'd have you in no time.'

Gavin looked at him suspiciously but said nothing.

'They goin' to do that?' asked Chrissie.

'Not if I can help it.' Odstock scratched his head. 'Look,' he said, 'I know it's difficult to understand, but you have to pick your time and place. You'll be able to get even in time because you're bright kids, but the best way to do it is to work hard, pass your exams and fight them with your intelligence and your qualifications. Later. When you're grown up. At the moment you don't have the strength to take them on. They'll win, and they'll destroy you.'

'We did though. Didn't we?' Gavin smiled slowly. 'Loik to have seen their faces.' He talked with some of the Somerset burr that Stack and his friends so mocked. It made him seem slow-witted, but the quick ferret eyes and mobile features should have disabused anyone who bothered to look as well as listen. Also a term at grammar school in town was doing much to urbanize the accent and iron out its distinctiveness. He would soon be difficult to place.

'Can you stop them making trouble?' asked Chrissie. She flicked at the permanently errant hair. An irritating tic.

'Only if you help.'

'Yeah?' They both looked at him sceptically. Some trust had been eroded by this. Might never be regained.

'You have to promise it won't happen again. You must agree that you're not going to conduct a sort of EOKA campaign against West Hill. No guerrilla warfare. No more pigs' heads.'

'EOKA,' said Gavin, grinning, 'I like that. Slit their fucking throats.' He put down the empty Vimto bottle and kicked it towards the gutter.

'I wish you wouldn't use that word, Gavin,' said Odstock mildly, 'and don't let the hatred take over. You can hate the system but it doesn't mean you have to hate the individual.'

'You sound like the bleedin' vicar,' said Gavin. He put on

71

an exaggerated posh parody of Alvar Liddell or John Snagge only less virile. 'Love thy neighbour and do unto others as thou would they wouldst do unto thee!' He relapsed into Somerset. 'Those stuck-ups at West Hill'd slit *my* throat if I let 'em.'

'What if we don't promise?' asked Chrissie, squinting in the sunlight. Odstock was struck suddenly by her freckles. He supposed they must come out in the warm weather. He had never thought of her being *quite* so freckle-faced.

'Then they'll use the law to punish you. And they can do it. You'll be made to look like mindless juvenile delinquents. Frankly, they can very nearly destroy you.'

'No choice then?'

'No.'

'Well, that's it then, innit?' She stood up and swung her satchel over her shoulder. 'C'mon, Gav,' she said, 'no point sitting about. Might as well go on 'ome.'

'You promise then?'

'Yeah,' she said over her shoulder, 'we promise. Thanks for the drink. See you around.'

'And you, Gavin,' he called as they slouched off, 'do you promise?'

' 'spose so.' The boy did not even bother to turn.

He watched them move up the street towards the new pebbledashed council houses which clustered in a planners' ghetto on the outskirts of the village near the other pub, the Garibaldi, also new, characterless, drab but draughtproof and even, within limitations, comfortable. Whereas the Plume smelled of booze and fags and people, the Garibaldi smelled of disinfectant and not quite melting plastic. Symbol of the new Britain. He wondered if the Smiths' promises were worth anything. Not much probably. But enough to keep the vengeful West Hillians at bay, at least until the next time.

On the West Hill 'Upper' the cricket match against St Christopher's was progressing reasonably satisfactorily. The ground itself was a picture. Bert and the Happy Harrys had worked their ever green fingers to the bone. Bert himself had carried out the final cut with the heavy duty Atco

72

lawnmower so that the entire field was striped in meticulously executed swathes of alternating light and dark green. Not a daisy, let alone a buttercup, to be seen anywhere. The boundary line had been freshly whitewashed by the Harrys that morning, as had the crease marks on the wicket, itself close-shaved to the texture of a St Andrews putting green by Bert himself. From the flagpole alongside the thatched pavilion the pink and green of West Hill fluttered above the rather vulgar (thought Burnam) black and gold of St Christopher's. Around the ground at thirty-yard intervals were smaller West Hill pennants on smaller poles. There was just enough breeze to make them ripple.

Only a few miles to the north the Quantock Hills formed a backdrop of red and green checked fields, topped by woods and iced with dots and lines of bare moorland at the summits and along the spine. The crumbling red-brick wall of the old vegetable garden ran along one side of the ground, pear trees trained carefully to wires screwed into the bricks. Opposite, partly shielding the lane which ran from Cothelstone to the village, was a line of elms. On the north a grassy bank led up to an orchard and the small lawn around the pavilion. The pavilion was a white-boarded, one-storey building erected in the 1890s when a cricketing squire had entertained his friends to cricketing house parties and even cricketing weeks. On the verandah just next to the scoreboard ('The Tally' in West Hill argot) sat the scoreres, one from each school, carefully entering in the record of the afternoon, ball by gentle ball. They worked in pencil so that mistakes could be easily and unmessily corrected. A large rubber 'bunjie', or 'mystic eraser' as O'Rourke called it, was an essential part of the scorers' equipment.

This year's scorer was April, the Burnams' twelve-year-old daughter, destined shortly, examination results willing, for the girls' school at Sherborne. She would be glad to escape from the peculiar freakish position of being the school's only girl. There was her younger sister Charlotte as well but she was only eight and was in her first year. At that age the difference in sex scarcely seemed to matter. Besides, Charlotte was a tearaway and a tomboy and she, emphatically, was not.

'Was that a bye?' she asked the St Christopher scorer, a

bookish-looking child, pallid, with an owlish pair of tortoiseshell giglamps.

'He didn't signal it,' said the boy, 'so I'm putting it down as a run. Though, if you ask me, he didn't hit it.'

'OK,' said April, 'I'll put it down as a run too.'

West Hill were batting. The score was advancing with a languor befitting such a sunny summer day and the wickets were falling with similar lethargy. The school were 62 for 5. Donald Stack was doing what April's father called 'holding the innings together'. Adrian Fieldhouse was at the other end prodding around ineffectually. Not much cop at cricket, thought April. April didn't think he was a lot of cop at anything. In fact, she regarded him as the school drip. Too bad that it should be him and not William Porter who was going on to Sherborne Boys'. She had a crush on Porter.

Stack hit another run. She supposed she liked Stack. She would have liked him more if he hadn't been such a little runt. Though she had to admit that for such a tiny person he was awfully good at games. He wasn't called the Mighty Atom for nothing. Precocious too. The other day in history he had passed her a note. When she opened it, hiding it behind a pile of books on her desk, she found that it said:

> 'It's only human nature after all
> For a boy to take a girl behind a wall
> And pull down their protections
> And plug in their connections
> It's only human nature after all.'

Rude beast. She had been unable to stop herself going a violent pink. It was fantastically risky too. What if she'd been spotted. Suppose the teacher had asked her to read it out to the class. Luckily it was only Queenie Roberts so she'd have refused. But what if Mr Roberts had asked her to give it to him? She supposed she'd have stuffed it in her mouth and swallowed it like Odette and all those spies eating their secret instructions.

'He's out,' said the boy with the tortoiseshell spectacles. 'Jolly rotten shot.'

'Who? Oh, Fieldhouse,' she said, watching Adrian's crest-fallen figure sloping towards them. 'How was he out? I'm afraid I wasn't looking.'

74

'Bowled,' said the St Christopher's boy. 'Middle stump. He was playing a cowshot. It looked to me as if he had his eyes shut.'

'Probably,' conceded April. She pencilled a stiff double line in the shape of an angular closed bracket sign and wrote 'bowled Snow 0' in the columns provided, after Fieldhouse's name.

'Bad luck, Fieldhouse,' she called to him as he walked past in the pavilion, removing his gloves. He glanced up and smiled ruefully.

'Thanks,' he said. 'I'm afraid I wasn't concentrating. It was a lousy shot. Your father looked livid.'

'Oh, well,' she said, 'I shouldn't worry about it. There's more to life than cricket.'

The innings continued its frankly boring course. Shortly before four she saw her mother's cream Commer van come round the corner of the drive and then turn left along the elm trees. There was just enough grass between the boundary and the trees for the van to pass. April smiled. Teatime. Tea was the only bit she liked about cricket matches. She watched as the van jolted over the grass. Elsie sat in the passenger seat and from the open back she could see two pairs of boys' legs. They, she knew, belonged to the 'urn guarders', two junior boys whose punishment for some relatively minor misdemeanor was to spend the afternoon helping her mother cut sandwiches and then set them out on trestle tables. On the drive from the kitchens to the pavilion they sat in the rear of the Commer and clutched the tea urn to prevent it falling out. It was not, in April's book, a punishment at all. She would love to spend the afternoon with her mother making tea. Instead she had to endure the purgatory of scoring for the First XI. Ironically this was not perceived as a punishment but as a great honour. Too silly.

Today's timing was more than usually adroit. Just as the last plate of sandwiches was put out, so the last wicket fell. West Hill had made 93 with Donald Stack the not-out batsman on 47. Just over half the runs but three short of the coveted half century. Fifties were not often achieved by West Hill boys. When they were, Burnam presented the successful boy with a prize of a new Denis Compton Slazenger cricket bat.

'Thanks *very* much, Lindsay,' said Stack to poor Peregrine Lindsay, the eleventh man and his final partner. 'All you had to do was block the last couple of balls.'

'I'm sorry, Stack,' said Lindsay, 'I just didn't see it.' This was a perfectly plausible explanation. Lindsay was very short-sighted.

Burnam patted Stack on the back. He was wearing a long white coat and a panama hat with the red, gold and black ribbon of I Zingari. Like the headmaster of St Christopher's, Ormsby-Percival, he had been umpiring. The convention was that you always had one home-team umpire and one visitor. Privately no one believed you would ever achieve impartiality but that way you could at least hope for an equalization of bias.

'Very well played, Donald, I really thought I was going to have to fork up for a bat.'

'Thank you, sir,' said Stack rather grumpily. 'I thought so too, sir.'

Ormsby-Percival, bare-headed, though also in a white surgical-looking coat, joined them from square leg. 'Well played, boy,' he said in a voice that both Burnam and Stack found unpleasantly patronizing. 'We've only had one fifty scored against us all season. That cover drive of yours is a promising shot. You work on that and you'll be a proper little Hutton.'

'Yes, sir,' said Stack. 'Thank you, sir, I will.'

'Well, Burnam,' Ormsby-Percival's bonhomie sounded forced, as always. 'Think you've got enough runs on the board?'

'I'd have liked a few more,' said the CO, 'but we'll make a game of it.' Privately he was delighted. Two years ago the eleven had been all out for single figures in the St Christopher's match. He had no idea how they had retained the fixture.

'I'm sure you will,' said Ormsby-Percival half-heartedly. 'I'm sure you will.'

They ascended the pavilion slope and Burnam led his guest to the trestle tables. The convention was that the headmasters helped themselves first, then the visiting team, then the home team. Scorers, though entitled to eat and drink, came last, thus adding insult to injury for April Bur-

76

nam. 'I thought ladies were supposed to come first,' she complained to her mother.

'Only when it doesn't matter, darling,' said Clarissa Burnam with feeling. 'And don't mention it to your father, he'll just be cross.'

'I know. He'd say, "You're not a lady, you're just the scorer." '

They had both laughed indulgently enough but still ruefully.

'We had an exceptional game against St Dunstan's last week,' said Ormsby-Percival. 'Nip and tuck till the very last ball. We just squeaked home. Awfully nice school, St Dunstan's.'

'Awfully nice,' agreed the CO.

'But not,' Ormsby-Percival paused to deal with too large a mouthful of *mille-feuille* (though that was a rather Ormsby-Percival term for what the manufacturers called a custard slice and the boys referred to as a soap cake), 'but not,' he dabbed at the corners of his mouth with red and white spotted handkerchief, 'not absolutely in the top flight. An awfully nice sort of boy but not . . . well, you know what I mean. Rather a lot of parents in trade.' He pronounced 'trade' as if it were a disreputable disease brought on by disgusting habits. The social equivalent of syphilis or cirrhosis of the liver.

'*Non-U* seems to be the latest way of describing it.'

'Yes, I've been reading about that too. Seems to me to be a rather vulgar notion. The Mitford woman has breeding but that Evelyn Waugh fellow's no gentleman.' Burnam felt suitably abashed. He disliked Ormsby-Percival and did not actually, when he thought about it later, regard himself as in any way inferior to him, socially or intellectually. But that didn't prevent him from feeling that his place, in which Ormsby-Percival put him as often as possible, was uncomfortably far below the salt. Ridiculous.

Ormsby-Percival was blathering on about the new Douglas Bader film. 'Fearfully good,' he said, tucking into a Marmite sandwich, 'that Kenneth More chappie. Always thought of him as a bit of a pansy until now. Funny enough in his way, but not really one of the boys, if you know what I mean, but I must say in this he's got old Bader to a T. An absolute T. He really has. It's extraordinary what these film wallahs can do nowadays, don't you think?'

Burnam said, 'Yes.'

A small boy came across and asked if they would like more tea. The headmaster gave him their empty cups. 'Two lumps,' said Ormsby-Percival, 'and if there are any more Marmite sandwiches going, I wouldn't say no. Thanks awfully.' He turned back to Burnam. 'Well,' he said, 'exams any moment. How's your stable? Any high fliers?'

The CO said he couldn't grumble and that actually they did have one or two rather bright boys.

'Good, good,' said Ormsby-Percival. 'Maybe we shall be competing for places in college, eh?'

The CO realized that Ormsby-Percival was talking about Eton. As far as Ormsby-Percival was concerned there *was* no other school unless you included Stowe, which was where places like St Christopher's sent those who were unable to pass the Eton entrance.

Burnam decided the best thing to do was to make a noncommittal noise somewhere between a cough and a grunt and a light laugh. This he did, following up quickly with 'If you'll forgive me, I think I ought to go and have a word with my chaps.' He was pleased to see that although there was a myth that these team teas were occasions for fraternization between the opposing sides, nothing of the kind was going on. Occasionally there were teams in which boys knew each other from the holidays, but this didn't seem to be the case here. The two teams were in two separate groups apart from an occasional 'After you, Claud, No, after *you*, Cecil' act when one or other of them wanted a sandwich or a cup of tea. Normally he might have been peeved but this time it meant that there was no chance of anybody inadvertently spilling the beans about the pigs' heads. He suspected his boys found the St Christopher's lot as stuck up and phoney as he did. At any event, they kept their distance.

'Cave,' said Stack, halfway through his second soap cake, 'CO's coming.'

'He's impossible at St Christopher's matches. I can't think why,' said Porter.

'Oh, it's Eton,' said Stack. 'He's batty about Eton. He tried to make my stepfather send me there. My stepfather

78

told him an Old Etonian shot a dog of his once and he wasn't having a boy of his turning into a dog shooter. The CO didn't think that was funny.'

The headmaster arrived within easy earshot.

'Righty-ho,' he said, 'gather round and let's have a bit of a chinwag. Stack, you'll open the bowling with Allen. Then Jameson comes on as first change and Dunstable-Smith second. Fieldhouse for emergencies. I think we can win this one, don't you, Stack?'

Donald was not only the best player on the side. He was also the captain.

'Yes, sir,' he said dutifully. Privately he had his doubts. Ninety-three wasn't enough. St Kit's always batted well.

It proved, at first, to be very much what he had feared. Of the two opening batsmen, one was a dour grafting player in the manner of Hutton in later years and duller moments. The other was a Gimblett, a swashbuckler. Gimblett himself had scored his maiden century nearby at Frome in three minutes over the hour. This boy, Prideaux, showed signs of doing the same. He cut and he drove and he hooked. No matter what Stack and the others could throw at him. They bowled short and they bowled yorkers. In desperation Stack even tried Fieldhouse with his lazy donkey drops. Disaster. Prideaux took 14 from the over. Ormsby-Percival smirked. April Burnam pencilled the runs into her book and was not only bored but also depressed. It was becoming humiliating.

Prideaux was, however, vulnerable. This plundering progress was too easy and it made him overconfident. He became visibly irritated when his grafting partner got the bowling and played out a tentative maiden over blocking every long hop and full toss as if he were facing Trueman and Statham on a grassy wicket in near darkness. Such was his enthusiasm for batting himself that he started to back up quite recklessly. By the time the bowler delivered the ball he was miles out of his ground.

At the end of a maiden over from Peter Allen, a thoughtful red-haired child who was good at chess, Porter and Stack conferred.

'This is awful,' said Porter. 'The CO will never forgive us. Have you looked at him recently? He's in the most ghastly bate.'

They both glanced over to square leg where the CO had taken up his position on his shooting stick. His panama was pulled down over his nose. His body gave off fury like steam.

'I've got an idea,' said Stack, rubbing the ball up and down on his trousers and leaving a smear of red dye and green grass stain which he and matron would later discuss quite heatedly.

'What?'

'I'm going to run the swine out.'

'How?'

'You've seen how far he's backing up. I'll just knock the bails off instead of bowling.'

'You have to warn him first.'

'Don't be silly. If I warn him he'll stop doing it and I won't be able to get him out.'

Porter looked appalled. 'You can't do that. It's not . . . I mean you can't.'

'If you've got a better way then tell me.'

'But it's not cricket.'

'Don't be wet. There's nothing in the rules against it.'

The CO's voice came irritably over the grass. 'We haven't got all day, you two. Come on, for Pete's sake.'

Donald winked at his friend, the head of school, and marched to the end of his run-up, rubbing the ball fiercely on his bottom. Death to all goody-goodies, thought Stack. He wanted to win – wanted it badly. Prideaux was facing him and hit the first ball of Stack's over firmly to Porter at cover point. They ran one.

This, of course, brought Prideaux to the non-striker's end where he was vulnerable to Stack's plan. Once again Donald paced back to the beginning of his run. It was far too long. He would have delivered the ball just as fast if he had only taken a few paces, but he was a fan of Fiery Fred and he believed, with some justification, that it frightened less intrepid opponents. He turned, gave the ball another rub on his flannels and began. Walk, trot, canter. He could see Prideaux beginning to move. With five strides to go he saw that Prideaux was well out of his ground. He increased speed and then, just as he seemed to be on the point of delivery, smashed his right hand and the ball down onto the wicket and shouted exultantly, 'How was that!'

For a second everyone froze, speechless.

The first person to break silence was Prideaux.

'You can't do that,' he said, thin-lipped and priggish. The expression of a boy born to the magistrates' bench.

'I've just done it,' said Stack, grinning. 'You're out.'

Behind him the CO emerged from shock.

'You're supposed to give a warning, Stack,' he said.

'But, sir, it's not in the rules, sir.'

The CO echoed Porter. 'It's not cricket, Stack. That's all there is to it. It's not done. We'll count that as a warning.' He began to straighten the stumps.

'Cheat!' Prideaux said in a stage whisper only Stack was supposed to hear.

Now Ormsby-Percival approached from square leg. He was wearing the pained expression of an English gentleman whose proprieties have been outraged, whose sense of all that is most English and gentlemanly has been deeply offended, who has seen the spirit of Dr Arnold and all who follow him travestied. But who nevertheless recognizes the force of law.

'I'm afraid,' he said to the CO, 'the boy's within his rights. Technically speaking, Prideaux is out. You'll have to go, Prideaux.' The two headmasters were waging a ritual war, striving to outdo each other in their Britishness.

'No, no,' said the CO, fiddling with his shooting stick, 'I can't allow it. Technicalities don't come into it. It's only a game and it should be played in the spirit of the game. Stack will apologize to your chaps and we'll treat it as a warning.'

Ormsby-Percival took Burnam by the elbow and led him a little way from the stump out of earshot of the boys.

'Very unfortunate,' he said.

'Very,' conceded Burnam. He could kill Stack. After all he had said that morning, after all he had tried to teach him these last five years, to do this. It was as if Ormsby-Percival had caught him picking his nose or dropping his aitches. Too humiliating. He supposed he would beat the boy and strip him of his captaincy of the eleven. Behind their backs Stack and Porter were also conversing. Porter was saying, but not too truculently, that he had told him so. Stack wasn't saying anything much.

Ormsby-Percival chewed his lip. 'Is he English?' he

inquired. 'He has a faintly foreign look about him.' This was plainly untrue. Donald Stack's face was monkeyish but not alien. It was the face of a cheeky chimpanzee but a perfectly British chimpanzee.

'His father was Stack VC.' Burnam was stung. *He* was allowed to be unpleasant to and about Stack. Not visiting headmasters of rival schools.

Ormsby-Percival made a tutting sound and stared up at the sky as if invoking divine guidance.

'Nevertheless,' he said, 'according to the law, my boy's out.'

'That's the *letter* of the law.' Burnam felt on sure ground here. 'But hardly the spirit. And it's the spirit that matters, surely?'

Ormsby-Percival grunted. 'Since you're the home headmaster, I have to defer to you,' he said. 'We'll pretend it was an overzealous warning, and leave it at that.'

'All right.' The CO was relieved. He felt he had found face.

'Stack VC, eh?' muttered Ormsby-Percival as they returned to the wicket. This did not appear to be addressed to anyone. Nor was it clear what it meant. However, the headmaster of St Christopher's had clearly been given food for thought.

Burnam replaced the bails.

'Righty-ho,' he said, 'no more bezonian antics from you please, Stack. Let's get on with the game.'

'Is he still in, sir?'

'Yes, he is.'

Prideaux grinned. 'Thank you, sir,' he said ingratiatingly.

The CO was not to be ingratiated. 'But that counts as a first warning. You'd better be jolly careful about your backing up from now on.'

Stack's reaction to all this was predictable. Or would have been if his teachers and colleagues had been clearer about his emerging character.

He retreated to his bowling mark, frowning thoughtfully and still rubbing the ball on his white trousers, the green and red stain growing increasingly lurid. His next ball was so abjectly anaemic that even the Huttonian plodder could not resist poking it into the covers for a single. That brought Prideaux down to the batting crease. This time a perceptive observer would have noticed the little hitch Stack gave to his pink and green belt, the increase in swagger and the sheer malice in his expression and posture as he turned to come in again. He ran fast and when he bowled he swung his whole body into the action. He was little but he was strong and this was yards faster than anything he had bowled all day. It was also yards shorter. Prideaux, who had been waving his bat nonchalantly and peering about the field as if to say that he could hit the next ball anywhere he wanted, went, to his credit, for the most dangerous shot of all: the hook. He might normally have got away with it but this ball was much more venomous than anything he had faced before. It came straight up off the pitch and hit him full in the face.

Reactions to this second extraordinary incident were speedier than last time. Stack, young Menzies the wicket-keeper and both headmasters were off and running the second Prideaux hit the ground, which he did almost instantly. There was a second when he dropped the bat and staggered back, blood already streaming from his nose. Then he just seemed to crumple. Several boys agreed later that they thought he was dead, but by the time a crowd gathered round he was beginning to twitch.

Under a pretence of cool, calm collectedness, Ormsby-Percival and Burnam showed every sign of panic and confusion.

'Give him air.'
'Let him breathe.'
'Get his pads off.'
'Loosen his belt.'
'Don't touch him.'
'Untie his laces.'
'Stop the bleeding.'
'Can anyone do a tourniquet?'
And so on.

From the pavilion, however, there presently emerged the comforting figure of matron escorting the two urn guarders who had been transformed into stretcher bearers. They marched briskly, carrying between them a canvas litter on wooden poles which looked as if it had been left over from the Somme and which for years had hung on the pavilion wall waiting for just such an emergency. Mrs Hildesley's starched white cap and businesslike manner were reassuring. Marginally less so was the large box with a red cross which she was carrying in her right hand. This, like the stretcher, had been in the pavilion for as long as anyone could remember. It seemed unlikely that it would contain anything terribly helpful. If it did, it would almost certainly have gone off.

Meanwhile Clarissa Burnam, doing a commendable imitation of Stirling Moss, the school's number one national hero after Winston Churchill, had leaped into the Commer, and gunned it into action with much gusto and exhaust smoke, arriving at the wicket at much the same time as Mrs Hildesley's stretcher party and leaving startled little white-clad figures in her wake.

With the arrival of these reinforcements the gentlemen drew back. Matron knelt down in what looked like an expert and professional manner, while Mrs Burnam produced a pair of tartan travelling rugs, dusted with dog hair, from the interior of the van.

'His pulse is fine,' said Mrs Hildesley, releasing Prideaux's wrist, 'and his breathing's not too bad.'

Prideaux moaned and opened his eyes briefly. They seemed curiously unfocused and reshut rapidly. He moved his arm ineffectually.

'Lie still, dear,' said Mrs Hildesley, eyes bright through her steel-rimmed spectacles. For such a very small woman she had surprising self-confidence. Almost too much. That and her angular, almost brittle, appearance made boys nervous of her, which was sad, and in a sense unfair. She would like them to have thought her maternal.

'Broken nose and concussion,' she said, straightening. 'But he'll live. We'd better get him into hospital as quickly as possible. Mrs Burnam, if you can drive the Commer, I'll come with you and hold his hand.'

So that was settled. Prideaux was loaded, none too efficiently, onto the stretcher, which mercifully did not come apart at the seams or crack, and thence into the back of the van. Clarissa and matron got in and drove off, a little less like Stirling Moss but still with a fine sense of drama, double-declutching and smoke. They left behind an anticlimax.

Stack was brooding. He had not actually meant to hurt

84

him. Well, not hurt him quite so badly. He'd like to have removed his cap, or winded him. He hadn't meant to knock him out. The experience had chastened and frightened him, though not out of his wits.

'I say, sir,' he said to the headmaster, 'I am awfully sorry. The ball just seemed to slip.'

'These things do happen,' said Ormsby-Percival tersely. He turned to the CO. 'Though I must say it didn't look accidental. Any more than Larwood looked accidental in Australia in thirty-three.'

The CO did not know what to say and therefore took refuge in repeating the first half of Ormsby-Percival's remark.

'Quite,' he said, 'these things do happen. You can't eliminate risk altogether.'

Ormsby-Percival glanced sharply at the CO, but if he had been about to say something hostile, he bit it back. Instead, in a matter-of-fact BBC newscaster's 'We are losing the war but keeping perfectly calm about it' tone of voice, he said, 'Well we'd better get on with the game.'

At the scorers' table April Burnam and the boy with the giglamps pencilled in against Prideaux' name: 'Retired hurt, 42.'

In the normal course of events St Christopher's would have cruised to victory in less than an hour. Their only casualty so far was Prideaux and they had fewer than 30 runs to make. However, this was not the normal course of events. St Christopher's were manifestly the better side. They always were. They were known throughout the southwest as a 'damn fine cricketing school'. There was invariably an Old St Christopher in the Eton XI, and often one in the Varsity match. Two Old St Christophers had played for England.

Today, however, West Hill, who had a wide reputation for being 'not much cop at cricket', brought off an upset. To be fair, St Christopher's contributed greatly to their own defeat for their usual phlegm and assurance seemed to have suffered more than their opponents', who in any case, never had much in the first place. There were two foolish run-outs and one boy hit his wicket. But West Hill also played above themselves. They caught catches they might not normally have held; they stopped what on other days would have been certain fours. Stack and Jameson, a burly oaf whose father was something in biscuits, shared the bowling with more than their customary control and with much more than their usual aggression. The plodder who had opened the innings with Prideaux continued to block stoically but in the end he ran out of partners. While still 7 runs short, the St Christopher's number eleven, a faintly improbable African fast bowler with an unpronounceable but reputably ancient title, tried to hit Stack back over his head, got a thin but unmistakable edge and was well caught by Menzies behind the wicket.

The West Hill boys were, naturally enough, elated. Burnam was depressed. He recognized that this was illogical. It was the first time since he had taken over the school that they had ever beaten St Christopher's, and he knew that the news would circulate around the incestuous prep-school circuit, causing surprise, admiration, envy and all that he most wanted for his school. But he also sensed that Ormsby-Percival would manage to suggest – though he would be too careful to put it into words – that West Hill had only won by cheating. What made this worse was that, although he could not quite bring himself to admit it, he had a nagging feeling that Ormsby-Percival was right.

The farewell ceremonies were tense and muted. As usual the West Hill captain, Stack, shook hands with the St Christopher's captain, or in this case with the vice-captain, since the captain, Prideaux, was otherwise engaged. The last man into the bus, a modern, slightly vulgar coach unlike the prewar charabanc habitually hired by West Hill, was Ormsby-Percival. He was now in a Hawks Club blazer with a matching cravat or square around his neck. He was also smoking a pipe. This he removed as he shook hands, standing on the bottom step at the bus's open door, thus giving himself a head-and-shoulder advantage over his hosts.

'Well,' he said stiffly, 'congratulations.'

'Thank you,' said the CO a trifle wanly. 'I'm awfully sorry about your boy, Prideaux. If there's anything Clarissa or I can do . . .'

'No, thank you, you've done quite enough already,' said Ormsby-Percival ambiguously. 'I'll have to telegraph his parents, of course. His father's our man in Bogotá. Luckily he has an aunt nearby. I just hope there's no permanent damage.'

He smiled thinly. The CO winced.

'Well,' said Ormsby-Percival, beginning to close the door, 'can't be helped. No use crying over spilt milk.' And then, just before the door was quite shut and only half aloud, 'Stack VC, eh?'

There was almost worse to come.

Because St Christopher's was almost forty miles to the west it was quicker for the bus to reach the main road by the back drive, rather than go out across the park and through the main gates. The back drive ran through various out-buildings and then plunged down a steep incline between high banks just to the right of the dingle. After five hundred yards the drive emerged from what was virtually a tunnel and joined the Minehead road by the back lodge. This modest building was the Chummery.

The atmosphere aboard the St Christopher's bus was strained as it moved slowly down hill in second gear. Ormsby-Percival sat alone in the front seat, thoughtfully smoking his pipe; the boys were unusually quiet. The banks were almost up to the top of the bus and the trees linked branches overhead so it was quite dark. The sun was pinkening at the gills and only a little soft light filtered through leaves.

The bus was about thirty yards short of the Chummery when Ormsby-Percival leaped up, lurched towards the steering wheel and shouted out, 'Brake! Stop!' The driver obliged with a crash stop and Ormsby-Percival managed to rotate the steering wheel a half turn, so that the right wing of the bus bruised the muddy wall – though not, as it turned out, doing any damage.

The passengers were jolted and shocked but no one was hurt. Ormsby-Percival himself had suffered nothing more than the temporary loss of his pipe and a bowlful of Three Nuns which lay smouldering on the floor. In seconds he was down the steps and onto the drive where, no more than six feet from the front bumper, lay the second prostrate form of the day.

The driver followed him out with ashen face, peaked cap pushed back off his forehead.

'Gawd!' he said. 'I never saw 'im. Is he dead?'

Ormsby-Percival was getting used to this sort of thing.

'He wasn't a few seconds ago,' he said. 'I saw him clambering down the bank, then he slipped and fell into the drive.' He knelt beside the body in a passable imitation of matron beside Prideaux. The body, which wore grey flannel trousers and a tweed sportscoat, was obviously alive since it was snoring with evenly punctuated wheezing gasps. Ormsby-Percival recoiled, screwing up his nose. There was green glass on the drive. He could see from the label that it was the remains of a Gordon's gin bottle.

In the Chummery, O'Rourke and Oily Watkins were playing chess while listening to the closing overs of the Lord's Test on the wireless. They had heard the sound of the coach's sudden stop, gone to the window, peered out, seen that it was the St Christopher's school bus and gone back to their game. After O'Rourke had made his move – which put Oily Watkins in check – he returned to the window.

'It's still there,' he said. 'I think I'd better take a quick shufty and see what crisis has befallen them. Some little bleeder being car sick, no doubt.'

Oily, frowning at his predicament, merely grunted.

'Hello,' said O'Rourke to Ormsby-Percival, whom he loathed. 'Can I help?'

'Oh,' said Ormsby-Percival, 'it's O'Rourke, isn't it?' He indicated the body which seemed to be regaining consciousness and was bleeding from a cut lip. 'We almost ran over the village drunk.'

O'Rourke looked down and raised an eyebrow.

'Oh,' he said, 'him.'

'You know him?' Ormsby-Percival looked sceptical, censorious and, finally, incredulous.

'Not socially,' said O'Rourke, 'but he's a fairly familiar figure around these parts, especially at weekends. I'm glad you didn't run over him. That would have been awkward.'

'Quite.' Ormsby-Percival sighed. 'I suppose we'd better phone the police. Or an ambulance. Or both. May I use yours?'

The corpse tried to sit up, and succeeded for a moment or two. Then it fell back onto the gravel, hitting its head with an unpleasant crack.

'You've got a long drive,' O'Rourke said. 'You just leave him to me.' Saying which, he quite suddenly and unexpectedly pulled the drunken man to a sitting position and smacked both cheeks with the palm of his hand.

'Not the first drunk I've had to deal with,' he said. 'Come along, matey. You and I are going to get a bucket of cold water and a mug of black coffee.' He smiled at Ormsby-Percival. 'Don't worry, old bean. I can cope.' He put his hands under the drunk's armpits and lifted him easily to his feet. The knees buckled slightly so O'Rourke shook him.

'Sad case,' he said to the St Christopher's headmaster. 'Shellshock. Or something like it. Japanese POW, or so they say.' He pulled the man's shoulder over his and began to half drag him towards the Chummery.

'Toodle-pip,' he called. 'Drive carefully and don't give it a second thought.'

After a few steps, the drunk belched twice and tried to walk. Falteringly, he and O'Rourke negotiated the trip to the Chummery just as the St Christopher's bus passed them on its way home. The front door was still open and Oily Watkins did not look up as they entered.

'I think it's mate,' he said gloomily, picking at his scalp.

'Look who's here!' said O'Rourke gaily.

Oily Watkins shook his head in sorrow at the lost game and then looked up in a casual manner which was not sustained. His eyes widened.

'Good grief!' he said. 'What are you doing with Basil Roberts?'

5

If the Church of England was the Tory Party at prayer and the *Daily Telegraph* the Tory Party at breakfast, then the Rover 75 was the Tory Party at the wheel. If the Tory Party could be made flesh and be embodied in just one single couple which epitomized everything the party was about, then that couple would have been Mr and Mrs Geoffrey Fieldhouse.

Shortly after noon on the Sunday following the St Christopher's game, Mr and Mrs Fieldhouse were bowling along the road towards West Hill in their grey Rover. The upholstery was leather and smelled of it, the dashboard was wooden and the yellow and chrome Automobile Association badge elicited a smart salute from the AA patrolman on motorbike and sidecar who passed them in Norton Fitzwarren. Mr and Mrs Fieldhouse both wore tweed suits, though she had a string of pearls around her neck and he sported an old (Blundell's) school tie. They had both eaten a breakfast of boiled eggs, toast and marmalade and they had both been to matins at the village church. Mr Fieldhouse had read the first lesson. Apart from the thin drizzle which smeared the windscreen and gave the green countryside a monochrome dullness, all was right with their world.

'I do hope he hasn't been working too hard,' said Mrs Fieldhouse. 'I sometimes wonder if it was wise to let him sit the scholarship. I'm not sure he's that sort of boy.'

'Burnam thought it was worth trying,' said Mr Fieldhouse, 'and he's the boss.'

Mrs Fieldhouse smiled. She was an insipid-looking woman. She seemed older than her forty-one years and not awfully well. Her husband, on the other hand, was almost aggressively robust and had that very black hair which some men keep into their fifties or beyond.

'Yes, dear,' said Mrs Fieldhouse. She looked out at a herd of Friesians swishing their tails bleakly in the rain.

'Did you read John Gordon in today's *Express*?' asked Mr Fieldhouse. The *Telegraph* had yet to launch its Sunday edition and so the Fieldhouses took the *Sunday Times* and the *Express*. Mr Fieldhouse only read the sports pages in the *Sunday Times* but was an avid *Express* fan, especially of John Gordon, whose column was an articulation of what the average Conservative voter was thinking that week. Mrs Fieldhouse preferred Veronica Papworth. John Gordon was too fierce for her taste.

'I thought he talked a lot of sense about the canal,' continued Mr Fieldhouse. 'It's an absolute fallacy for this chap Nasser to say it belongs to him. It was built by us and the French as an international waterway, and an international waterway is what it is. I don't really understand what the Gippoes are getting so excited about.'

The windscreen wipers clicked steadily back and forth. Mrs Fieldhouse continued to gaze out of the window, her thoughts concentrated on her little boy and on lunch, which was under the temporary supervision of Mrs Perryman, the distaff side of the Fieldhouses' 'couple' of servants.

'Besides which, it's ridiculous to think that the Egyptians are capable of keeping the canal running properly. Their experience of navigation is limited to putting out in bumboats and trying to sell leather poufs and each other's sisters in Port Said harbour.'

'Geoffrey!' Mrs Fieldhouse was jolted from contemplation of Sunday lunch by this sudden, unexpected crudity.

'I'm afraid it's perfectly true, darling.' Mr Fieldhouse sighed. 'Your average Gippo's simply not competent to organize his own affairs, let alone the world's most important waterway. It's just not on.'

'They built the pyramids.' Mrs Fieldhouse spoke with surprising vehemence.

'That was a very long time ago,' said Mr Fieldhouse, gripping the wheel fiercely so that the veins stood out on the backs of his hands underneath the string of his driving gloves.

91

He had not realized, sixteen years ago, that he had married a *silly* woman.

On the other side of Nether King's Compton they joined a convoy of similar middle-class cars. One boy's family, the Weatherby-Browns, had a Bentley. Mr Weatherby-Brown was a company director in Bristol and his car, though privately envied, was publicly considered vulgar. Jameson's father, the one who was big in biscuits, owned a Jaguar which was thought vulgar in private as well as in public. Some of the local farmers owned ancient Austins and Morrises which had seen better days and tended to be spattered with mud, or worse, but most West Hill parents were of the Rover-owning class. Here and there a Vauxhall or Triumph or one of the new Riley Pathfinders, but never, ever, anything as vulgar as a Ford Consul or Zodiac. Today, on this 'going-out Sunday', the West Hill mothers and fathers, all of whom had spent their day so far in much the same way as Mr and Mrs Fieldhouse, drove in a sedate crocodile across the park and over the cattlegrid in order to take their little dears out to lunch and tea.

There were three main classes of parent. The biggest was the local one which lived within easy driving distance of school and could take their offspring home with them. Another sizable number lived in London and the home counties (there were two or three Scots too) and were forced to put up in the County or Castle Hotel in Taunton. The smallest was the armed forces/diplomatic and international company set who lived abroad. The children in this group saw their parents during Christmas and summer holidays. Their 'going-out weekends' were spent at the school or with more distant relations who lived in England, or if their friends and contemporaries felt so inclined, with other people's parents.

As the cortege of cars arrived in the yard by the back door, small faces pressed against window panes to see if their family had arrived. Larger boys affected a studied nonchalance and relied on smaller ones to tell them excitedly.

'I say, Fieldhouse, please, your parents are here.'

The Fieldhouses were giving Stack and Porter a lift. Donald's stepfather farmed outside Bishop's Lydeard, close enough to the Fieldhouses to make the sharing of transport to and from West Hill a sensible arrangement, though transport was practically all they did share. Stack's stepfather, Travis-Gunn, had nothing in common with the Fieldhouses or people like them. He was very much the sort of man you would have expected the widow of Stack VC to marry. Wild.

'Thanks, Anderson,' said Fieldhouse. He looked straight through the ingratiating little newbug and snapped shut the anthology of Maupassant short stories he had been grinding through. Stack and Porter were engrossed in a game of card cricket.

'Hang on a mo',' said Stack, 'I'm in the middle of Lindwall's last over before lunch.'

It was several minutes before the three of them were in the back of the Fieldhouse Rover.

'We've been here ages,' said Mr Fieldhouse irritably. 'What kept you?'

'I'm awfully sorry, sir,' said Stack. 'It was my fault. I was in the middle of some Latin verse for Mr Watkins, sir.'

'Oh. I see.' Mr Fieldhouse appeared mollified by this. 'How was the match yesterday?'

'We won,' said Fieldhouse. 'Donald took six wickets and almost made a fifty.'

'That's very good, Donald,' said Mrs Fieldhouse as her husband crashed the gears past the cedar. 'You don't often beat St Christopher's. Mr Burnam must have been pleased. He loves beating St Christopher's.'

'Actually, he wasn't as pleased as he might have been,' said Stack. 'One of their chaps got hit on the head ahd had to retire hurt.'

'It was a bumper,' said Adrian, 'Donald bowled a bumper.'

'Actually, sir,' said Stack, 'the ball sort of slipped. I didn't do it on purpose.'

'Good,' said Mr Fieldhouse, as the Rover passed through the park gates and out into the real world. 'Bumpers are extremely unsporting. "It matters not who won or lost but how you played the game." W. E. Henley. He's what I call a real poet. Not like that creature T. S. Eliot. He can't even rhyme.'

'No rhymes in a lot of Shakespeare,' protested Stack.

Mrs Fieldhouse turned and smiled condescendingly.

'Shakespeare wrote plays, Donald. That's quite different.'

Stack and Porter were glad to escape the leathery claustrophobia of the Fieldhouse automobile. Life at Bowling Green Farm was more raffish and relaxed than the starchy atmosphere at the Fieldhouses' Old Rectory. Travis-Gunn allowed the boys cider. Dorothy Travis-Gunn, Donald's mother, smoked cigarettes through a holder and had been known to wear trousers. This sort of thing did not go on at the Old Rectory, even though it had to be admitted that the food was better.

'Hello, darling.' Donald's mother put down the *News of the World* and kissed her son on both cheeks, leaving behind a smudge of scarlet lipstick. 'Hello, William. Nice to see you. Lunch will be ready in half an hour. Scatty's up in Long Meadow doing something with cows. Why don't you two run up and help him. Work up an appetite.'

'Scatty' was Travis-Gunn's nickname, acquired as a child. It had stuck. Odd though it was, it was an improvement on Henry.

'Might,' said Donald. 'What's for lunch?'

'Joint,' said Dorothy. 'Beef.'

'Yorkshire pudding?'

'Well.' Mrs Travis-Gunn frowned at the Aga cooker. 'I'm not sure I awfully like Yorkshire pudding, and . . .'

'Oh, Mummy, please,' said Donald, 'Yorkshire pudding's William's absolute all-time favourite food and they never get it in Malta. Please. Just for William. He won't be able to eat his beef without it.'

'Oh, darling.' She smiled. 'You are absolutely incorrigible. How's work?'

' 's all right.'

'Only all right?'

'No, it's fine, actually. Only we've got a rotten replacement for Mr Smedley. He knows *nothing*.'

'Oh,' Porter was no fan of Queenie Roberts but he felt he should be accused on accurate grounds, 'he knows the stuff,' he said. 'He's just clueless at explaining it.'

'He drinks too,' said Donald.

'Well, darling, we all drink,' said Mrs Travis-Gunn.

'No, but he *really* drinks. I think he has a bottle in his cupboard.'

'Oh, come on,' said Porter.

'No,' said Stack, 'honestly. I caught him the other day. I came in early after break and he was coming out of the cupboard wiping his lips and looking, you know, guilty.'

Dorothy Travis-Gunn attempted to hit her son's bottom with the *News of the World*.

'Darling,' she said, 'you absolutely must not say things like that about the staff. If they found out you were spreading that sort of rumour there'd be ghastly trouble. And quite right too. Now do get out of the kitchen, both of you, and tell Scatty it's time for a glass of sherry. Otherwise you'll never get Yorkshire pudding.'

The boys scuttled out into the yard, grinning and giggling. The rain had stopped now and a lemon sun was trying ineffectually to penetrate the summer mist. Donald picked a couple of chives from a tub just outside the kitchen door and gave one to his friend. They chewed them as they walked towards Long Meadow. Their gumboots sploshed in the mud; rooks cawed; sheep baaed; somewhere quite a long way away a tractor throbbed.

Porter shifted his chive to the corner of his mouth so that he could talk round it. 'Do you really think Queenie Roberts drinks?'

'Probably,' said Stack. 'Why? What do you think?'

'It hadn't occurred to me, actually,' said Porter, 'but now you mention it, it would explain one or two things.'

'Like the mints.'

'How do you mean?'

'Those Polos he keeps stuffing in his gob. They're to get rid of the smell of booze. Oldest trick in the book.'

Porter hadn't known about this though he remembered, with misgivings, that his father, the Commander, was rather given to a morning mint.

There was a five-bar gate into Long Meadow and they both vaulted it in the head-over-heels 'gate vault' taught in gym by O'Rourke. The grass was long and yellow with buttercups. In the middle of the field Scatty Travis-Gunn was standing some way away from his cows, holding a stick in both hands and staring at it very hard.

'Oh, God!' said Stack. 'He's water divining. He's always in a foul mood when he's been water divining. He never finds

95

water. He thinks he has Celtic blood. Sshh! Don't make too much noise or he'll be hysterical.'

The boys crept, suppressing giggles, across the grass which swished damply with every footstep. Travis-Gunn had his back to them but while they were still more than thirty yards from him he called out, 'I don't know if you two are trying to stalk me but you sound like a herd of stampeding buffalo. Baden-Powell would have you shot. Don't they teach you anything in Scouts?'

The answer to this was an emphatic no. Oily Watkins took the Scouts, if anything, even less seriously than the boys themselves. However, when they did try stalking in the woodland gardens or dingle the boys usually managed to surprise poor Oily. This was not because of any skill on their part. Oily was invariably engrossed in a book, usually of a trashy kind that Burnam would not have allowed the boys to read. On the last stalk he had been discovered fast asleep with the new Bond, *Diamonds are Forever*, open across his face. If they *had* been stampeding buffalo the West Hill Scouts would still have succeeded in surprising him.

Scatty Travis-Gunn remained bent over his divining stick.

'I'm sure there's water down there,' he said, straightening at last, 'but there's not a twitch in this.' He spun the stick away from him in exasperation and pushed his tweed cap back on his head. He had straw-coloured hair which should have been cut weeks back and stuck out from under the cap like a scarecrow's; a rather high complexion; and goose-blue eyes. He, like the boys, had gumboots on. Also a cream riding mac from Burberry.

'Donald. William.' He shook both boys' hands. 'All well?'

The boys said yes.

'Mummy said it's time for a glass of sherry,' said Stack.

'Well,' Travis-Gunn smiled, 'if Mummy says it's time for sherry, then it's time for sherry.' He put an arm round Stack's shoulders. 'Did Mummy tell you Mrs Wodehouse had had her litter?'

Mrs Wodehouse was the prize sow, named in an oddly circuitous way after P. G. Wodehouse, creator of the Empress of Blandings.

'Oh, good,' said Donald, 'how many?'

'Twelve,' said his stepfather, 'and mother and children are all doing well.'

'Can we have a look?' asked William.

'It'll keep Donald's mother from the sherry,' said Travis-Gunn, 'but I dare say she'll survive it. Yes, of course.'

'She's making Yorkshire pudding actually,' said Donald.

'Good grief! That should be an experience.' Travis-Gunn grimaced. 'I should think we'd be well advised to keep her away from the sherry until after she's done whatever it is you do to make Yorkshire pudding. Even so, I'm not optimistic.'

They sauntered across Long Meadow and through the five-bar gate, down the track to the house and outbuildings. In her sty Mrs Wodehouse was lying on her side, hugely pink and whiskery, while her tiny offspring rooted and sucked at her flabby teats.

Porter winced involuntarily. These were the first pigs he had seen since the dingle. These were living and, in their porcine way, not unattractive. But he could not help being reminded of the three bloody heads in their striped caps and ties and blazers.

Travis-Gunn noticed.

'Not care for pigs, William?' he asked.

'No, sir, it's not that. I . . . I . . . well . . . no, I'm very fond of pigs.'

Travis-Gunn leaned over the stall and scooped up one of the piglets in large grubby hands. The animal wriggled and squeaked but failed to escape. 'Here,' he said, handing it to William, 'hold him tight. He's like an electric eel. Well, more like an electric slug.'

William held very tight.

'See, he's still quite blind.' Travis-Gunn took him back quickly before William could drop him. 'Stop wriggling, you little cuss,' he said sharply to the pig, 'or we'll make you into breakfast before your time.' He replaced him by his mother's ample flanks and watched as the piglet found a spare teat and started to suck again, its nervous frenzy quietly and slowly disappearing. 'You wouldn't think he'd look just like his mother in a few months' time, would you?' he said. He ruffled his stepson's hair. 'Take more than a few months to make you look like your mother. Come on, let's get some lunch before she's burned it all to a frazzle.'

Stack held Porter's elbow as they walked to the house, restraining him so that they were, if they whispered, just about out of earshot.

'An eye for an eye,' hissed Stack, 'and a pig for a pig.'

'What?' asked Porter. 'I'm not with you.'

'Tell you later,' said his friend.

The kitchen's thin blue haze of smoke warned them that Travis-Gunn's pessimism about the lunch was justified.

'I don't know what it is about Yorkshire puddings,' complained his wife, 'it doesn't matter what I do to them, they're never right.'

'Never mind.' Travis-Gunn was carving. He was not drinking sherry but Whitbread Pale Ale, from a pewter tankard with his initials carved in italics on one side. Oddly enough it had been a present from Donald's father. 'I didn't marry you for your cooking. Marvellous piece of beef though. Carves like butter. Or marge. You boys still getting marge all the time?'

'Butter at weekends,' said William, eyeing the rather blackened roast potatoes with apprehension.

'Underdone or overdone?' asked Dorothy.

'Neither,' lied Travis-Gunn, 'it's just how I like it.'

'Liar,' she said. 'You boys help yourselves to cider. I'm going to have a beer too.'

She helped herself, watched the boys draw off a glass each from the wooden keg on the sideboard, and told them to take gravy and vegetables. 'Don't feel you have to eat the Yorkshire pudding,' she said.

Everyone took Yorkshire pudding which somehow contrived to be burned on the outside and pasty raw on the inside.

'I think it's very interesting Yorkshire pudding, actually, Mrs Travis-Gunn,' said Porter.

Everyone laughed. William blushed and joined in.

'It's sweet of you to say so, William,' said Dorothy. 'Donald, I hope you're as polite when you're in other people's houses. I must say if it does nothing else, West Hill does teach boys good manners.'

'I should damn well hope it does teach something else,' said Travis-Gunn. 'Burnam's putting the fees up yet again next term.'

'Donald should be at Winchester so it hardly matters.'

'You know what I mean. And Angela's fees aren't exactly chickenfeed.' Angela was Stack's elder sister, a boarder at Cheltenham Ladies' College. There were no Travis-Gunn children.

Conversation swiftly shifted from the dodgy ground of Travis-Gunn's stepchildren's school fees to safer more general matters. The Travis-Gunns asked politely about William's parents. They discussed Malta, cricket, both national and parochial, and the different schools that various West Hill boys were moving on to at the end of term. After the first course the boys cleared away the plates and Dorothy produced strawberries and cream. The cream was their own, as were the strawberries. William breathed silent relief. You couldn't burn strawbugs.

'Were you at Winchester with Mr Gaitskell?' asked William.

Scatty said the Labour Party leader was older than him and had left for Oxford a year or so before Scatty got to Winchester.

'Why do you ask?' Scatty wanted to know.

'I don't know. Mr Burnam says that people like Gaitskell are "class traitors". I just wondered if you knew him.'

'I suppose I shouldn't say it,' said Travis-Gunn, saying it, 'but your headmaster does talk an awful lot of tripe. Anyone would think it was a crime to be a member of the Labour Party.'

'It is round here,' said his wife a shade viciously.

'You're not a member of the Labour Party are you, sir?' asked William, wondering if the question was safe.

'No, I'm not, as it happens.' Travis-Gunn swallowed a strawberry and looked thoughtful. 'But some of what they say makes a lot of sense. And some of what the Conservatives say makes no sense at all. And as for Hugh Gaitskell himself, I think he's honest and intelligent and a very fine leader of the Opposition. In fact, if it were a simple choice between personalities, I'd sooner have Gaitskell than Eden.'

Porter was almost shocked. It was as if someone had said they would be happy to see the Australians win at Lord's. Or as if the Fleet Chaplain had put in a good word for the Pope. Mr Gaitskell was captain of the other side.

'Do they teach you politics at West Hill?' asked Travis-Gunn after a couple more strawberries.

'The CO sometimes gives us current affairs instead of Bible reading,' said Donald.

'That follows.' Travis-Gunn grinned.

'Some of the other beaks sometimes do a bit of chat about what's in the newspapers,' said Porter. 'Oily Watkins gave Form Five a talk about Commander Crabb the other day.'

'And what did Mr Watkins have to say about Commander Crabb?' asked Travis-Gunn, still grinning.

'Someone said he used to be a frogman himself.' Porter giggled. 'Only if you saw him in Taunton baths you'd realize how silly that was. Oh, I say, Donald, do do your imitation of Oily.'

Donald needed little persuasion. He put his head on one side, half closed his eyes, and said in a flat, unctuous voice, 'Commander Crabb was a British officer and ahem er gentleman engaged in ahem er active service against ahem er our as it were enemies, the Russians. The Russians, ahem ah er, are not like you and me.'

'That's enough, Donald,' said his mother surprisingly sharply. 'Scatty, I don't think you should encourage them to mock their teachers. They should have more respect.'

'I'm not a great one for respect,' said Scatty, 'and I'm afraid a lot of their teachers do seem to ask for it.' He turned back to the boys. 'So, in effect, the only politics you get is from Mr Burnam.'

'Yes.'

'And I suppose everyone else on the staff is to the right of Genghis Khan as well.'

'Oh, not as bad as that,' said Donald. 'I think Mr O'Rourke may vote Liberal.'

'Hmmm,' his stepfather mused. 'Coffee?' he asked of his wife, and when she nodded, went to the sink, filled the heavy black kettle and put it on the Aga's front burner. 'Talking of politics,' he said, 'which I think is what we are, I see that Eifion Hughes is coming to the constituency the week after next.'

'Really?' Mrs Travis-Gunn seemed surprised, as well she might. Quantock was one of the ten most Conservative constituencies in the country. The Liberal got to within fifteen thousand votes at the end of really unpopular Tory governments, and the Labour candidate lost his deposit even in years of Labour landslide. Eifion Hughes was, next to his compatriot Aneurin Bevan, the most lyrically eloquent orator of a notoriously silver-tongued race. He was also unequivocally radical, espousing a fierce form of Valley Baptist refusal to compromise which had kept him, unlike Bevan, firmly on the back benches. From there he conducted guerrilla warfare on the 'crypto-Socialists', public-school men like Gaitskell, who dominated his party. He made headlines wherever he went, which was mainly South Wales and a handful of depressed industrial towns where he preached enthusiastically to the converted. The idea of Eifion Hughes in Quantock, even for the briefest of whistle stops, was remarkable.

'Oh, the new Labour chap's some sort of Welshman too. I expect they were in the same pit together. The old-boy network isn't just for the gentry, you know.' Travis-Gunn took a packet of Abdullas from his jacket pocket, removed one of them and tapped it several times on the kitchen table. 'It's a form of showing the flag,' he said. 'The new chap's still in his twenties. Obviously bright. He'll get a safe seat in Glamorgan next time round. Meanwhile our Eifion's demonstrating that he's not entirely on his own.'

'Gosh,' said Donald, eyes gleaming, 'do you think there'll be trouble?'

'Trouble?' said his stepfather. 'I should doubt it.'

'Didn't they kick Mr Bevan down the steps of some club when he went in there?' asked Porter.

'Silly ass said Conservatives were all vermin and then expected to be treated civilly in White's of all places,' said Travis-Gunn. 'Served him right. This is quite different. It's a free country. Hughes is exercising his right to free speech in a public place. A number of public places. Including, by the way, Nether King's Norton village hall. But I don't imagine Somerset Burnam and the staff of West Hill will be outside with placards, much less rotten eggs. They'll simply pretend he's not there and nothing's happening. They're good at that. An awful lot of middle-class thinking is based on the idea that if you ignore it, it'll go away. Doesn't always work. That's what Chamberlain thought about Hitler: "Nasty little foreign oik. Let's pretend he doesn't exist, then he'll just shut up and disappear." Only he didn't.'

'That's an awfully long speech for a man of few words,' said his wife, smiling indulgently.

'Was it?' said Travis-Gunn. 'Sorry. I'm going to take my coffee and read the paper in the library. Then, if anyone's game, I'm on for a round of croquet before tea.'

After he had gone Donald asked his mother if Diggory was around. Diggory had served as Travis-Gunn's batman during the war and now worked on the farm in an ill-defined position well below that of farm manager but significantly above that of general farm labourer. If Travis-Gunn was considered 'wild', Diggory was generally held to be a menace. It was Mrs Travis-Gunn's opinion, often expressed, that if it weren't for her and her husband, Diggory would be behind bars. He was, on the other hand, loyal as a dog and fundamentally well disposed.

'I saw him this morning,' said Dorothy, 'he came with roses from his garden. He's probably at home sleeping off lunch. No, wait a minute. There's a cricket match. He'll be at the green. Why don't you nip down there for half an hour or so if you want to see him, then come back here and set up the croquet?'

Donald said that sounded like a good idea and the boys begged a couple of Mars Bars from the canary-coloured Dundee cake tin on top of the Boulton and Paul fridge, then scampered out into the yard.

The mist had lifted when they got outside. They sniffed the drying moisture and watched the steam rising from the grass.

'What's up?' asked William.

'Even more than before lunch,' said Donald. 'It was half an idea before lunch. Now it's a whole one.'

'What is it?' Porter was agog but also alarmed. Stack had often seemed incipiently dangerous in the past but nothing had really ever come of it. They had been beaten often for ragging in the dormitories, talking after lights-out. They had stolen (though they never said 'stolen') apples and pears from the West Hill orchards, occasionally cheated (they called that 'borrowing' each other's papers). And, there had been the business of the booze and fags in Commander

102

Porter's Maltese potting shed. That had, conceded Porter, very nearly turned nasty. But at no time had he ever thought Stack was leading him on to places where he really did not want to go.

Yesterday, however, was different. What Stack had done ran counter to everything Burnam and West Hill stood for. The CO had said he would talk to Donald tonight after prayers. God knew what would happen then. Stack being Stack would probably get away with it, but that wasn't the point. Hitherto he had broken the rules in a way that was acceptable. Now he had not only broken the rules but offended against the code. It was the spirit of the game which mattered, not the letter of the law. Stack had not played in the right spirit. Worse still, he seemed to have enjoyed it. There was a new devil in his manner, a reckless chancing of the arm which had always seemed a possibility but had never before surfaced. Porter caught the excitement of this but was frightened by it too.

'Can't you guess?' asked Stack. 'You're scholarship material, you ought to be able to put two and two together.'

'Not *Winchester* scholarship material,' said Porter sarcastically, 'only boring old Marlborough.'

'Oh, ha, ha!' Stack laughed. 'You can be an awful weed sometimes, Porter. Come on. I'll race you down to the green. Bet you sixpence.'

And so they ran down the gravelled avenue of elms and along the lane with its thick hedges scented with honeysuckle and pink with dog rose, their breath coming in thicker and thicker pants, gumboots beating an irregular rubber rhythm on the tarmac, until they emerged three quarters of a mile later at the village green, Porter leading by about ten yards.

'I win,' he said. 'That'll be sixpence.'

'What do you mean?' Stack put his head between his knees and gasped. 'It's too far to run in gumboots. I'm not paying you anything. You've got longer legs than me, so it's not fair.'

'All right then, I'll have an ice lolly. A Mivvi, please.'

Stack grimaced. But Porter knew that, unlike everyone else, he always had money, so he did not make an issue of it. There were always ice creams on sale at the back window of the pavilion.

'All right,' he said.

The game had not been going long and the opening pair of the home team was still at the wicket. That meant that Diggory would be sitting around somewhere, padded up and ready to bat. He always went in at number three. They found him sitting on a bench in front of the Six Balls pub, universally known as the Three Men. One hand was round the dregs of a pint of bitter, the other round a peroxide blonde with a low-cut cotton dress.

'Wotcher cocks,' he said as the boys came into view. 'Come and sit down and have a chat with old Diggory. Budge up, Scarlett.' The girl, whose mother had been reading *Gone with the Wind* immediately before her birth, duly budged, though grudgingly. 'Scarlett, these are my mates Don and Bill,' said Diggory.

Scarlett smiled rather sourly and said she was pleased to meet them, she was sure.

'I say, Diggory,' said Donald before there was a chance of any further inconsequentials, 'can you help us? We've got a plan for revenge.'

'*You've* got a plan,' said Porter, 'I don't know anything about it.' He bit into the pink outer casing of his ice lolly until he came to the ice cream inside. Strawberry without, vanilla within. On reflection, the Mivvi, coming so soon after the Mars Bar and the strawbugs, might not have been such a good idea.

'Come again?' said Diggory. 'I'm not with you.'

'Well,' said Donald, breathing in, 'we've been having trouble with some oiks in Nether King's Norton and . . .'

He managed to tell the story moderately succinctly without leaving out any of the best bits.

'Cor,' said Diggory, 'took a bit of nerve, dinnit?'

'They're not wet,' said William. 'Actually I think they've got a lot of guts.'

'Which is all the more reason for us to do something really gutsy in return,' said Stack.

Diggory grunted questioningly, one eye on the wicket, where the opening pair looked safe as houses.

'We were looking at Mrs Wodehouse's litter before lunch,' said Donald. 'They'll be quite big by the week after next, won't they?'

104

Diggory nodded, perplexed. The more aggressive of the two batsmen played a crisp cover drive. The ball sped across the boundary line to where the vicar was sitting in a deck chair. The vicar stood and threw it back awkwardly, underarm.

'Good throw, padre!' called Diggory.

The vicar turned and waved in embarrassed acknowledgement.

'Good bloke, the padre,' said Diggory, then turned back to Donald. 'Not big enough to go to market so you can 'ave their 'eads stuck up on poles.'

'That wasn't what I meant,' said Stack. 'But they'll be running around?'

'Oh, ah,' said Diggory, which meant yes, ' 'ell of a job catching one of the little bleeders if they get loose.'

'Smashing,' said Stack, 'just what I thought.'

'I wish you'd tell us what on earth was going on.' Porter was plaintive.

'Oh, do shut up and listen,' said Stack. 'I'm getting to the point as fast as I can. So if you were to rub one of them all over with Vaseline you'd never be able to catch it.'

'Who'd be daft enough to do that?' asked Diggory.

'Someone who wanted to get his own back,' said Stack. 'Diggory, will you do me a big favour?'

Diggory said, 'Ah,' an abbreviated form of yes.

'One evening the week after next I want you to put one of the piglets in the back of the van and bring it over to . . . oh . . . there's a tiny road called Pig Trough Lane about two hundred yards from the back gate at West Hill. And bring a jar of Vaseline and some blue paint and brushes. *Dark* blue.'

Diggory looked down at Stack and frowned. 'Wass this all about, then?' he wanted to know.

From the centre of the green came the wooden tinkle of broken stumps and falling bails. White-flannelled visitors clapped. So did the vicar and one or two other recumbent figures about the ground. One of the batsmen glanced briefly at his wicket, turned, put his bat under one arm and started to unwind his brown, sausage-like batting gloves as he walked towards the pavilion. Diggory put his beer down and let go of Scarlett.

'Me next,' he said, stuffing a stray piece of shirt tail into his too tight cream trousers.

'Will you do it?' asked Donald urgently.

Diggory pushed his dark blue cap back on his head and grinned. 'Sounds a laugh,' he said. 'One piglet. One jar Vaseline. One pot paint. You ring me at home and tell me when.' He bent down so that his face was very close to Donald's. 'Only one thing. I don't want trouble with Scatty. You promise it's safe enough not to bother him.'

'Oh relax, Diggory,' Stack laughed airily, 'you know I wouldn't want to upset Scatty any more than you would.'

'Right then.' Diggory unbent and marched to the wicket, flexing his shoulders and twirling his bat as if it were an Indian club.

'I still don't get it.' Porter was now thoroughly perplexed and even more alarmed.

'Don't you?' said Stack with a knowing look. 'You know, Porter, I begin to have serious doubts about your scholarship. Even at Marlborough.'

'Oh do put a sock in it.' He crunched the last of his Mivvi and threw the stick on the grass. 'Hadn't we better go and set up the croquet?'

They stood and began to walk slowly round the ground in the direction of Bowling Green Farm, staying long enough to see Diggory flail at one ball, miss completely; snick a streaky four over the slips and hit the third ball for a resounding straight six into the churchyard.

'You really are a bit slow on the uptake,' said Donald as they started to walk up the lane.

'I give up,' said William. 'You want to get poor old Diggory to bring a piglet and some blue paint and Vaseline to school. It's like a really silly crossword clue.'

'What happens the week after next?' asked Donald.

'Oh, endless things,' said William. 'There's a monthly half. It's the last week before the scholarships. There's a match against someone. St Dunstan's or Perrot Hill.'

'Don't you remember what Scatty said at lunch?'

'Oh, you mean about Eifion Hughes. Yes.'

'Well, stupid, that's our big revenge.' Stack looked positively feverish. 'We're going to get a greased pig in Conservative colours into Eifion Hughes's meeting in the village hall.'

106

6

'How did you deal with Donald Stack?' asked Clarissa Burnam. She was sitting at her dressing table brushing her hair. It was ten o'clock and her husband had just brought in the cocoa. He had made them cocoa every night since they had married and took a pernickety pleasure in stomping the lumps out of the Bourneville chocolate powder with a teaspoon. All through the war and during the grim Labour years of ration books he had used boiling water with a dash of milk and half the usual sugar allowance. Now, under a Conservative government and the imminent arrival of 'Never-had-it-so-goodery', he had reverted to 100 per cent milk. He boiled the milk after making his final rounds of inspection; locking up, turning off, tiptoeing into the occasional dormitory. Then into the cavernous kitchen where he made the cocoa in silence, the school (with the exception of matron and her deputies) sleeping above him. A time for contemplation and stocktaking. Finally lights-out in the kitchen too and the journey up to their private sleeping quarters through the green baize door. He turned the lights out as he went, leaving darkness behind him and no sound but the creaks and groans of pipes and boards. It was a noisy house in that way. A malfunctioning stomach of a mansion.

'Stack?' he said. 'Oh, Stack.'

'Well?' Clarissa put down the silver-backed brush and dabbed at the crowsfeet at the corners of her eyes. Getting old, she thought, think of them as life lines, evidence of experience and amusement past and present. She turned to look at her husband who was standing at the window in shirtsleeves. He was wearing the gold-yellow braces April had given him for Christmas.

'Oh, Stack and I sorted things out.' He took a sip of cocoa, still searingly hot, and replaced cup and saucer on the chest of drawers. 'We agreed to put it down to overenthusiasm.' He stuck a thumb in his braces and looked sage. Clarissa smiled indulgently. She was used to his self-importance.

'I'm glad.' She got up and went to the window where she too stood looking out across the park. It was a clear night and the half moon was bright enough to silhouette the timber. 'I thought you were going to take away the captaincy and do all sorts of unmentionable things to him. Didn't you even beat him?'

'Didn't even beat him,' said Burnam, kissing his wife chastely on the cheek. He turned to go to his dressing room. 'I tried putting myself in his position. O'Rourke's advice, I have to confess, and sound, as usual.' The bitterness was inescapable. In so many ways O'Rourke was a lamentable burned-out case, but you had to grant him a certain shrewdness. He supposed that too often, in his case, an adherence to principle made that sort of intuitive understanding difficult. When you came down to it, men were either trimmers or they were not.

'I suppose . . .' He raised his voice so that it would carry to his wife. She was now in bed with last year's Agatha Christie, *Hickory, Dickory, Dock*. Clarissa was fond of Mrs Christie's ridiculous Belgian detective. 'I suppose,' he said, 'my enemies would say it was because of the Winchester scholarship.'

'I'm sorry, darling. Come again.'

'I said that some people would say I'd been soft on Stack because I wanted him to get a Winchester scholarship. For the good of the school.'

Clarissa said nothing, attention hopelessly divided between her husband and the printed page. Presently he came back into the room in his dressing gown and slippers.

'What do you think, darling?' he asked.

'About what, darling?'

'About Donald Stack.'

'I think you did absolutely the right thing, darling.'

'Really?'

She forced herself to concentrate and raised her eyes from her book. She cared very little about scholarships but she realized they mattered to Somerset. 'Yes, darling. He was

108

only trying to please you. I'm sure he knows what beating St Christopher's means to you. He just got carried away. And the Winchester scholarship's even more important to him than it is to you. It would be very wrong to get him in such a state that he didn't do himself justice.' She shut the book. 'I'm going to clean my teeth,' she said.

When she returned she found her husband kneeling by the bedside, eyes shut, palms together. She too, as always, knelt down and closed her eyes, though unlike Somerset she said no prayers, just tried to let her mind go as blank as possible in the hope that something reassuring would somehow float into the vacuum. She wasn't at all sure about God. Hadn't been for ages.

The Fieldhouses said prayers at the Old Rectory. Theirs was a ritual rendering of the Lord's Prayer, out loud, then a small reflective silence, before they climbed into their separate beds. Lights went out straightaway and there was no talking or reading. Mr Fieldhouse went to sleep, as always, immediately, snoring lightly within seconds of pulling up the sheets. Mrs Fieldhouse lay awake worrying, as always, about her only son. She wished, secretly, that he did not have to go to boarding school. Yet, as she knew quite well, there was no alternative. Boarding school was where one went, that was all there was to it.

Officially the lights went out immediately after prayers in all the dormitories at West Hill: in Nelson and Marlborough; Kitchener and Haig; Montgomery and Alexander. That meant nine o'clock even for the most senior boys. It was silly to risk talking. Someone nearly always heard and when you were talking you forgot to listen for the footsteps of matron or CO, footsteps which invariably made the floorboards creak. Neither of them was actually much better at stalking than the Boy Scouts, but it was not a risk to be taken lightly. Justice was summary. The CO made the offender grip the rail at the foot of his bed and bend over to present full bottom. He used his slippers, which were scarlet and springy and leather, like every shoe in the school made by Clark's, and he never gave fewer than four strokes. Pyjamas were not thick, even the standard issue Viyella ones, with their dull muted stripes and flannelly material.

Since you were allowed to read *before* lights-out there was always a book on every bedside chair along with the neatly folded uniform, and most boys simply picked up their Buchan or Biggles after matron had closed the door and began to read again. When it got too dark the avid book-worm and the chronic insomniac produced torches and moved their books under the bedclothes. Some played dab cricket using a self-constructed dart board and shutting the eyes before dabbing to see what the verdict was. Others played Howzat, in which metal rollers marked '6', '4', 'LBW', and so on were thrown like dice. Card cricket was generally considered too complicated for after lights-out.

By ten, when the Burnams and the Fieldhouses were saying their prayers, most little boys really were asleep. The oldest, however, still tended to be awake, especially the monitors, each of whom was in charge of a dormitory of younger boys. Porter had Alfred, named after the cake burner; Stack was the boss of Wolfe, the large seven-boy dormitory next door. Fieldhouse was up in Auchinleck, which, as the name suggested, was the newest of the dor-mitories, an attic conversion which had been made only two years before to cope with the overcrowding. Field Marshal Auchinleck had been asked to its opening but no reply was ever received.

Adrian Fieldhouse, as his mother feared, had been unable to sleep. He had learned to worry early in life. There had never been anything very carefree about him, even as an infant. Now, at twelve, he had obviously inherited his mother's tendency to fuss, an inheritance which was com-pounded by the unreasonably (he thought) high expecta-tions his father had of him. Tonight his worries ranged from the specific to the general. He was worried about when, if ever, his voice was going to break. Both Stack and Porter were exhibiting the first tentative signs of voice breakage and Porter had an obtrusive enough swansdown on his upper lip to make the CO wonder if he might be the first West Hill boy ever to shave. Fieldhouse showed no such signs. His voice remained resolutely alto and he did not even have the beginnings of acne. That was one problem. Then there was the French prose that O'Rourke was due to give back next morning. He was sure it was riddled with careless mistakes. He was always forgetting apostrophes and accents. O'Rourke took off double marks for both. Too often he had got work back from O'Rourke with 'Gamma – *Far* too many careless mistakes'. You could tell how peeved O'Rourke was by the degeneration of the scrawl. All that red ink. Like spider's blood. He was afraid that would happen again tomorrow. He still couldn't remember if there was a circumflex on '*gateau*'. He was also worried about the Sherbourne scholarship exam. Petrified in fact. He was worried about not liking his father enough. Worried about liking his mother too much. Worried about whether he was popular. Worried about not being better at games. Worried about the way the hair at the back of his crown stuck up and could not be coaxed back with water and harsh brushing. Worry, worry, worry. In middle age it would be the mortgage; giving up smoking; not fancying his wife any more. One day it would give him ulcers. Tonight it just meant he could not sleep.

Shortly after ten he decided to help himself to a drink of water. There were no hot and cold taps in Auchinleck but a marble-topped washstand held a pitcher and an enamel 'spit bowl' together with a plastic mug for each boy. Each mug contained a toothbrush identified by a Cash's name tape, usually red on white.

The other boys were asleep so he got out of bed carefully. The springs were primitive and creaked alarmingly, but no one stirred. He tiptoed to the washstand, absurdly over-conscious of the sound of his naked toes on the wood; also of the noise of the water as it poured from the pitcher into his toothmug. He tried not to gulp.

It was wonderfully still and solitary as he stood sipping silently at his water. Although he had not yet articulated the idea, he was not what a certain sort of (American) magazine would later call a 'people person'. He stared out across the grounds and felt alone but not lonely. As if he were the only person on earth, and enjoying it. As his eyes grew accustomed to the darkness he could make out the shapes of the trees in the park, see the darker line of the ha-ha. The stars

111

were bright, which helped. Mr Friendly had told them something about the constellations using an ingenious plastic
device called a 'Phillips' Planisphere'. It was a sort of move-
able map of the heavens with all the names written on it. In
spite of it he could still only distinguish the Plough. He
screwed up his eyes and turned his head so that he was
properly aligned . . . that meant that north was over there.
He checked his finding against what he already knew, which
was that he was looking almost due south. In daylight you
could just glimpse the Lake District through a fringe of trees.
Could you see it reflecting moon and stars? He wasn't sure.
He stared harder. There *was* something, but it did not look
natural. A light. It was moving. It swayed slightly and
seemed to be travelling at a slow walking pace. He felt a
frisson of excitement. Could it be burglars? Or the village
troublemakers on another pig-planting expedition? Or
something still more exotic? He thought of the Russians'
visit, Bulganin and Khrushchev, Commander Crabb missing, presumed dead in Portsmouth Harbour. He thought of
James Bond and of Richard Hannay in John Buchan's
books. *Greenmantle*, *Mr Standfast*, *The Thirty-Nine Steps*. Just
thinking of the names made him shiver.

The light continued to move. Flying saucers? Men from
Mars? He had never lacked imagination and now he willed it
into flight. After a minute or so of overheated contemplation
he decided that it was too exotic a mystery to be kept to
himself.

Wolfe, named for the victor of Quebec, was down one
flight of stairs and halfway along the passage which culmi-
nated in Alfred. Fieldhouse moved stealthily towards it,
adrenaline tempering fear but not eliminating caution. As he
opened the door he heard the sudden rustling of bedclothes
which meant that one or more boys were still reading or
playing cricket. Inside it seemed that everyone was in a deep
sleep. Too deep to be real. As he tiptoed over to Donald
Stack's bed, Stack sat up very awake indeed.

'Fieldhouse!' he whispered. 'What on *earth* are you doing?'

'Shh,' said Fieldhouse. 'I want you to come and look out of
the window. I can see a light. Moving.'

Stack regarded Fieldhouse with a slightly mocking
curiosity.

'You're not sleep-walking, are you?' he asked, waving a hand in front of Fieldhouse's eyes.

Fieldhouse told him not to be stupid. 'Come and look,' he said, 'please.'

Stack continued to stare at him but then, without warning, threw back his bedclothes with a decisive air.

'OK,' he said, 'but if the CO finds us, I've had it. He said the St Christopher's thing was the last straw but one. I've got to write to Prideaux and apologize.'

'Who's Prideaux?'

'The little twerp I hit on the head.'

'Oh.'

'Where's this light, then?'

They stood staring out of the window.

'There! Look!'

Stack followed the line of Fieldhouse's pointed arm. 'Yes,' he said, 'so there is.' His voice included a note of surprise and even, thought Fieldhouse, of admiration. The light still seemed to be moving. At least it was definitely bobbing about, though it was difficult to tell whether it was also proceeding in a consistent direction.

'Hey,' said Stack after watching it intently and silently for a few minutes, 'it's gone out.'

'I expect it's only gone behind something. Just hang on a mo' and we'll see.'

They waited.

'It's gone,' said Stack.

'But it can't just have disappeared.'

'I imagine someone's turned it off.' Stack sounded impatient. 'Or that it's gone out.'

'Maybe it fell in the lake?'

'We'd have heard a splash.'

There was a pause while they continued to stare. Eventually Stack said, 'It's no use. It's not coming on again. It was a torch. Obviously. And someone's turned it off.'

'But why,' Fieldhouse wanted to know, quite reasonably, 'would anyone take a torch down to the Lake District, and then turn it off?'

'Search me,' said Stack.

'I suppose they must have got to wherever it was they were going. I mean, they needed the torch to find it, but now

113

they've got there they don't need it any longer. If you see what I mean.'

'Maybe we should go and have a look,' said Stack.

'What?' Fieldhouse was horrified. 'We can't,' he said, and then, practically, 'We'd never find anything anyway. Not unless they turn the torch on. It would be a waste of time.'

Stack shrugged. 'I suppose so. Pity. Might have been rather fun.'

Fieldhouse shivered. 'I think I'm going back to bed,' he said. 'We can talk about it in the morning.'

'Oh,' said Stack, 'all right.'

At Bowling Green Farm, Scatty and Dorothy Travis-Gunn never said bedtime prayers and tonight, as they did more often than not, they had made enthusiastic and efficient love, with the light on. Afterwards Dorothy would have liked a cigarette but could not be bothered to go and get one. Besides, it would have meant cleaning her teeth afterwards. Altogether too much trouble. Instead she said, 'How did you think he was?'

'Who?' asked Scatty, who was lying on his stomach slipping away into a self-satisfied sleep.

'Donald, of course. Who do you think?'

'He seemed all right to me.'

'I do worry about him, you know.'

'Only natural. It's what mothers are for.'

'No, but seriously. He's starting to be a bit of a tearaway. That cricket-match business. Hitting the wretched boy on the head. You don't think he did it on purpose?'

'Oh, do go to sleep.' Travis-Gunn was always up at five. He needed sleep.

'I shouldn't like him to turn into quite as much of a tearaway as his father.'

'He's his father's son. You can't get away from that.'

'No. I suppose not.'

'And I'm sure his father would be very proud of him. *Especially* if he hit the boy on purpose. Now, for Pete's sake, put a sock in it and let me get some shut-eye.'

* * *

It was much much later that O'Rourke went to sleep. After an early supper of macaroni cheese and rissoles prepared by Oily Watkins, he had spent a tedious hour or so correcting French proses. They had been irritatingly full of avoidable error and careless mistake. He had wielded his black Waterman, the one with the red ink that he kept specially for marking, with increasing ferocity, until he broke off for a large Scotch and the nine o'clock news. The news was not encouraging. It looked as if the Egyptian and British governments were painting themselves into corners. The cricket wasn't much better either – Australians winning, Somerset losing. Shortly before ten O'Rourke retired to bed in order to reread *War and Peace*. He must have dozed off because he woke with a start to find that the book was lying face down on the floor beside his head. 'Oh, hell,' he said, wondering why he had nodded off and what had woken him, and realizing that he wanted to pee. That, presumably, was what had woken him. The bladder was not functioning with its old efficiency. There had been a time when he could last all day provided he didn't drink anything more than a single cup of tea. Rather like a camel. Just as well he hadn't been smoking. He often had a gasper or two while reading in bed. It was like drinking in the bath. Pleasantly wicked feeling.

He got out of bed and walked irritably across the landing to the lavatory, wishing as he did that he had bothered to put on slippers. The lino was cold. Urination brought release though there was lino in the loo too and it was just as cold as the lino on the landing. He wondered whether to have a good-night cigarette now that he was awake again, but decided against. His watch said it was five minutes after midnight. He never smoked before seven in the morning.

On the landing en route for bed, he paused as he heard the front door open and close, and waited, despite his freezing feet, to see who it was, then smiled indulgently as young St Aubyn came slowly up the stairs, hair tousled, jacket slung over one shoulder. He too was smiling.

O'Rourke watched him wistfully for a second, then coughed.

St Aubyn looked up, startled. 'Oh,' he said, 'hello. I didn't think anyone would still be up.'

'I'm not,' said O'Rourke, 'just went for a pee.' The refilling of the cistern confirmed the truth of this.

'Oh,' said St Aubyn, 'I see. Well. Good night, then.'

'Lipstick on your collar.'

'Oh.' St Aubyn blushed and rubbed furtively at his shirt.

O'Rourke grunted. 'Figure of speech,' he said.

St Aubyn blushed deeper. 'Oh,' he said, but before he could think of anything more coherent, O'Rourke had disappeared into his bedroom, wondering once more if he, in youth, could ever have been quite so callow, so impossibly wet behind the ears.

Like the authors of musicals, textbook authors always seemed to come in pairs: North and Hillard, Hillard and Botting. Whatever happened to North? Why did Hillard make off with Botting? Discuss.

Sellar and Yeatman were not, of course, textbook writers; they were funny writers who wrote for *Punch*. Nevertheless, it was an article of faith propounded by Smedley, the history beak who had gone down with hepatitis, that *Ten Sixty-Six and All That* was the best history book ever written. At least for small boys. Categorizing the great events of the past into 'Good Things' and 'Bad Things' was a 'Good Thing'. To say that King John was a 'Bad King' and Queen Elizabeth a 'Good Queen' made them more memorable. Besides, it accorded with the school philosophy, namely, that in 'Real Life' there is no such thing as a 'Grey Area'. Things are Good and Things are Bad; there is Black and there is White.

This was one of the devices Smedley employed for making history interesting. The other was to use the school for analogies. Thus: 'The feudal system is just like school. Mr Burnam is at the top because he's the king. At the bottom are the serfs, villeins and cottars. Who are they, Fieldhouse?' 'Newbugs, sir.' 'Go to the top of the class, Fieldhouse.' Or: 'Let's assume that West Hill are the English and St Christopher's are the Spanish Armada.'

The feudal analogy was a particularly happy one. Stack and Porter often argued about whether monitors were knights or barons and where exactly the bishops could be made to fit in.

Like feudal society, West Hill was intensely hierarchical. Each layer was superior to the one below. It was not 'form'

116

for a junior to initiate conversation with a senior, even if the difference between them was a single term or a single form. Boys were all too aware of those senior to them but they scarcely noticed those below them; and a boy found his friends from within his own age group. To do otherwise would have been regarded as a serious offence, suggesting sexual impropriety.

Because there were only a dozen or so new boys each term, one's social horizons were thus rather limited, but it was odd that from the very beginning boys voluntarily subdivided still further. The basic social units in the school were either pairs of 'best friends' or 'gangs' of three. Stack, Fieldhouse and Porter had been a gang from the very first week of their very first term. As such they had stayed in each other's homes, cribbed from each other's homework, borrowed each other's socks and handkerchiefs and shared each other's bathwater. They also excluded everybody else. In fact, most of the time they were oblivious to the fact that anybody else in the school existed. The others were just bodies ('bods' for short). It was essential to have another eight bods to make up a cricket team but that didn't mean you had to know anything whatever about them or even exchange anything but the barest civilities with them. As far as the three of them were concerned, their own private gang was all that mattered. 'Three for one and one for three,' they used to chant during their first year, though now that they were more grown up the assumption had become tacit.

Next morning Porter, Stack and Fieldhouse held a conference during break. They always held conferences in break, always had. Stack and Porter sat on a radiator in the First Form classroom, each sucking rather watery milk through a straw. 'Elevenses' was another of the West Hill rituals. Daily milk was as important for growing boys as daily bread. Good for the bones. Fieldhouse ate a rich tea biscuit and paced. Porter, not having seen the light, was sceptical. Also practical.

'All right,' he said, 'so you didn't imagine it. It was a real light. If it is Russian spies or flying saucers, I'm certainly not going to go out and get myself shot or frizzled up by a gamma-ray gun. And if it's burglars or oiks from the village, then the CO specifically asked us to tell him about it.'

117

'I think you're being incredibly wet, Porter,' said Stack, 'just because you're head of school.'

'Oh, come on,' said Porter, 'we've had enough trouble already with the fags and the St Christopher's match.'

'He never found the fags, and he's forgiven us for the match.' Stack opened his mouth and belched noisily and deliberately.

'Don't be foul,' said Fieldhouse. 'I think Porter's right. First of all, it might actually be dangerous. And second, the CO asked us to report anything suspicious. It might be different if he hadn't asked, but he did. I don't see how we can not tell him after that. After all, we are monitors, Stack. You can't get out of that.'

'I'm not trying to get out of it.' Stack was tetchy now, sensing that it was two against one and he was on the wrong end of the argument. 'Because we're monitors we're supposed to use our initiative. We're practising to be leaders, not to go running to the CO or some other beak every time something difficult crops up. If we did that we'd be just like the oiks from the village.'

'You mean we're officers and gentlemen and they're just yobbos?' asked Porter with unusual sharpness.

'Yes, actually,' said Stack, 'that's exactly what I mean.' He slid off the radiator. 'OK. Go ahead and tell the CO. But I think you're being fantastically drippy.' He stalked off.

'What's the matter with him?' asked Fieldhouse.

'Oh, just in a bate,' said Porter. 'I think he's worried about the exam.'

'We're all worried about the exams,' said Fieldhouse with feeling.

'*Genou, hibou, joujou, pou,*' he recited, 'that's as far as I can get.'

'My problem's the gerund,' said Porter. 'I don't see the point of it.'

Despite the continuing trench warfare at the Chummery, David St Aubyn was enjoying his term at West Hill. In fact, he got along perfectly well with Oily Watkins and even Queenie Roberts. The relationship was formal and distant but not unfriendly. It was much like sharing a study, which

118

he had been doing for the previous five years at Stowe in any case. He was used to living in close proximity to other males even though they were usually males of his own generation. The worst thing about living with one's elders, he decided, was the smell. All three of the others had pronounced bachelor smells, a compound of stalenesses to which they seemed cheerfully oblivious. Old cigarette clung to everything, even the loo. He wished they would not smoke in the loo. Every day he pulled the wick in the bottle of Airwick to its fullest extent, only to find that someone else pushed it down again on their next visit. Probably O'Rourke. He was at a loss as to why O'Rourke apparently disliked him so much, but although he did not particularly enjoy their spiky bickering and occasional spats he refused to let them interfere with his enjoyment.

His pleasure in life that summer was partly a simple function of age. To be eighteen and newly released from the routines and petty restrictions of public school was a happiness in itself. His short-term future was assured. He had a place at a good Oxford college (Magdalen), which took care of three years beginning in September, and after that he was due for two years' deferred National Service in a good regiment (cavalry). After which it would be the Foreign Office or merchant banking, depending on what sort of degree he got. In the meantime he was killing time in a thoroughly agreeable part of the world in a thoroughly agreeable manner. He enjoyed coaching the Under XI cricket team; he enjoyed teaching every conceivable subject at a level so elementary that it was not in the least intellectually taxing; above all he was enjoying Miss Battersby.

Helen Battersby was the third and most junior matron. First there was Mrs Hildesley, almost as permanent a fixture in the scheme of West Hill things as the CO himself. Then there was Miss Sparrow, the under-matron, an incipiently spinsterish figure who would, if the precedents were anything to go by, last about three years before moving on to another similar school, hoping to achieve her goal of ensnaring a male counterpart into matrimony. This was almost certainly an unrealizable ambition since unmarried prep-school masters were usually unmarried because they liked it that way. Those, like David St Aubyn, who were maritally desirable, were, as he was, far too young for Miss Sparrow's mature and not immediately apparent charms.

Miss Battersby was something altogether else. She was eighteen months younger than St Aubyn and had recently left a nice but dim convent school with an O level in English language. She had flunked needlework. 'Not a lot upstairs' was O'Rourke's verdict on Miss Battersby and no one disagreed. Nor did anyone care. Least of all St Aubyn. Miss Battersby's body amply compensated for any deficiency of intellect. It was just what St Aubyn wanted. His sexual experience was limited to unsatisfactory and fleeting mutual masturbation during school termtime and some tentative fumbling in the back row of the Gaumont in Godalming. Most of his knowledge of girls was based on the photographs in *Health and Efficiency* and unspeakable Surrey dances. He was passably expert at chastely clutching nervous partners in waltzes and quicksteps and even more chaste Gay Gordons and Sir Roger de Coverleys. Anaemic cider punch was the prevailing tipple, so there wasn't even the chance of alcohol unshackling inhibition and letting loose the libido. At eighteen, therefore, David St Aubyn was not only a virgin but also virginal, sexually useless, emotionally illiterate. He had never unhooked a bra, or been in a French kiss.

Until Miss Battersby. Miss Battersby not only had a body like Diana Dors but she was keen to put it to good use. She was not necessarily keen to go all the way just yet, but she was keen to go as far as was safe and had indeed managed to do so twice, on both occasions with older men. Her parents, dismayed by her burgeoning sexuality as much as her O level results, consigned her to the safekeeping of Mr and Mrs Burnam until they could think what to do with her. For weeks she had suffered sexual deprivation. The boys were too young and, in any case, too risky. The male staff too old, otherwise engaged or otherwise inclined. She had in moments of real despair considered if there was any temporary solace to be found with the female staff. Had even toyed with the idea of Miss Sparrow. Very quickly she decided that it was one thing to toy with the idea of Miss Sparrow. Quite another to toy with the lady herself.

Then David St Aubyn arrived. It mattered very little to her that he was young for his age. All public schoolboys were young for their age but the majority of them grew up quite rapidly in their final teens and early twenties. He was not particularly good-looking: thinnish and with that slightly spivvy black hair, slicked back in the greasy way she associated with old boys of Stowe (and Harrow). She really couldn't have cared less. He was young, male and, after a certain predictable diffidence, extremely willing. A week after his arrival he had invited her to see *Brothers-in-Law*, the Boulting Brothers lampoon of the legal profession, which was showing in Taunton. They had both thought Ian Carmichael jolly funny, although most of the jokes were incomprehensible to Helen. Afterwards they had rather daringly had a drink at the Castle Hotel (he a brandy, she a crème de menthe) and kissed, excitedly, in the car park. They had kissed again in the Hillman when he said good night and dropped her off at West Hill.

Since then they had attempted, with mixed success, to keep the affair secret. There was, of course, no question of Miss Battersby coming to the Chummery; nor of Mr St Aubyn visiting the junior matron in her tiny bed-sitting room in the big house. There was always the cinema, however. And the car. And on a fine evening there were the gardens, the park, the countryside.

By the weekend of the St Christopher's match the couple had progressed from the first, rather tentative, car-park kiss to moderately heavy petting. St Aubyn was inside her blouse but not yet her knickers. It scarcely occurred to him that he would progress that far. The whole relationship had taken him by surprise and he was more than happy to spend the evenings lying entwined in Miss Battersby's lissome limbs, kissing her accommodating mouth with occasional breaks for a cigarette and not too much talk. They talked hardly at all, which, he acknowledged privately, was just as well. There was no question of either of them being in love, but neither could think of a better way of spending a warm evening than lying kissing and cuddling in long grass.

Recently they had discovered the Lake District. For some reason the Lake District was not much used. Occasionally the Scouts would stage some form of water exercise down there and from time to time the CO would dragoon a party of boys into carrying out a Lake District clean-up, dredging, burning and generally scurrying around. Otherwise it was a decorative no-go area, out of bounds unless accompanied by a member of staff. The CO was afraid of boys drowning.

In the days when West Hill was still privately owned, the family had obviously used the lake. There was a now dilapidated Victorian boat house and inside it a skiff. The skiff was called the *Earwigo* and although its cushions were motheaten and split, they were soft and comfortable and the boat itself pondworthy. When the weather was fine David and Helen would take a flagon of cider or a bottle of beer down to the boat house, row into the middle of the pond and lie there fondling each other. It had almost become a routine. When they got bored, which was not often, they would row back in and explore the woodland by torchlight. Neither knew what they were looking for but it was curiously exciting. Once they surprised a badger.

On Monday evening, the night after Fieldhouse and Stack had seen the moving light from the windows of Auchinleck and Wolfe, the two teenage lovers went once more to the Lake District.

'It's there,' said Fieldhouse, 'look!'

It was ten o'clock and the three boys were standing at the window of Wolfe. Alfred's windows faced the wrong way, so Porter had been fetched to Stack's dormitory to verify this second sighting.

Porter peered sceptically.

'It's probably a firefly,' he said at last.

Stack snorted derisively. 'Since when have there been fireflies in Somerset?' he said.

'Oh, all right.' Porter squinted. '*Qu'est-ce que c'est*, then?'

'It's obviously someone with a torch,' said Stack. 'You don't have to be PC Forty-Nine to see that.'

'It could be a bicycle,' suggested Fieldhouse.

'I don't know what's the matter with you two.' Stack's whisper was tetchy in the darkness. 'It's obviously someone with a torch and if you ask me it's whoever put those pigs' heads in the dingle. In other words, the oikery.'

'You could be right,' Porter was still tentative.

'Well, you're not going to give me a lot of rubbish about

the Mekon and a whole lot of Treens landing in the West Hill Lake District.' Stack's remarks were aimed at Fieldhouse, who had been canvassing the outer space theory earlier on. Fieldhouse was an avid reader of the *Eagle*. Stack claimed to have grown out of it. He disliked its goody-goody quality; suspected it was thinly disguised grown-up propaganda.

'I don't see why you have to be like that, Stack,' said Fieldhouse. 'I happen to think there is some sort of life on other planets.'

'Prove it.'

'You know I can't prove it.'

'You can't prove it because it's not true.'

'There are lots of things you can't prove but it doesn't make them less true.'

'Like what?'

'Like God, for instance.'

'Well, I'm not so sure I believe in God anyway,' said Stack.

'Oh, do shut up, you two.' Porter was snappish, playing his head-monitor role. 'I really don't think God has much to do with a light in the Lake District. Whatever it is, or whoever it is, obviously shouldn't be there. They're trespassing.'

'So what do we do?' asked Fieldhouse.

'What we decided,' said Porter, 'tell the CO.'

'I think that's pathetic,' said Stack. He had wanted to play Davy Crockett. 'A real funk.'

Telling the CO required more courage than any of them had quite realized. The other side of the green baize door was forbidden ground. The door divided the Burnams from their boys just as decisively as it had once divided upstairs from downstairs, family from servants. Normally, if a boy wanted to see the headmaster about something, he went, during school hours, to the headmaster's study and knocked. He only knocked, of course, if the little traffic light above the door shone green. That meant that the CO was available. If it was red, he was either out or engaged. There was no amber and therefore no unnerving ambiguity.

All this was understood, part of the routine and ritual of school life. One was always intimidated by having to knock on that heavy oak door because the CO was a figure of

123

authority who frightened small boys, even monitors. And one seldom knocked under happy circumstances. Masters did not often tell you to take your work to the CO because it was so good. Matron did not send you with a 'note for Mr Burnam' if you had a well-made bed or a tidy dormitory. In both cases the reverse obtained. Nevertheless, it was *usual*; it came within the scope of everyday experience. Disturbing the CO at night, in his own private bedroom, did not. There was no knowing what the consequences might be.

Porter, as head boy, did the knocking, rather timidly at first, but then, when there was no reply, a little louder, so loud that to their apprehensive ears it sounded peremptory, cheeky, an invitation to headmasterly anger.

'Porter! Whatever is it? It's after ten o'clock.' The CO stood in the doorway, imposing even in dressing gown and pyjamas and newly roused from sleep.

'Please, sir,' said Porter, wilting, 'there's a light in the Lake District. I . . . we . . . thought, well, sir, you did say we should tell you at once if anything suspicious . . .'

Somerset Burnam closed the door behind him very softly.

'A light,' he said, 'in the Lake District?'

'Yes, sir. Fieldhouse couldn't sleep and went to get a mug of water. You can see the Lake District from Auchinleck. And he saw this light. So he came down to tell me and Stack, sir.'

'Show me,' said Burnam.

Together they walked back along the corridor, through the green baize door, out onto a landing where the window faced south.

'We should be able to see it from here, sir,' said Porter.

They stood peering out towards the Lake District.

'Yes, sir! Look, sir! There, sir!' It was Stack who saw the light first. The CO stared thoughtfully. Privately he was both alarmed and perplexed, but it was a cardinal rule that one always put on a good show in front of the chaps. 'Never blub in public' was the saying.

'Right,' he said at last, with that decisive 'OK, carry on, you chaps, I'm in charge now' look which had helped earn him his nickname. 'Thank you very much. You did the right thing. Now cut along to bed and get some sleep. And thank you again.' The boys mumbled acknowledgement and

124

trouped off, slightly deflated. His outward show of strength overcame the inner uncertainties and Burnam was, for once, as decisive as he appeared. He went briskly back to the bedroom and telephoned Constable Taylor on the bedside phone. The constable sounded a little blurred and put out, but he knew his duty and he knew his place. He promised to come round as quickly as possible. The CO said he'd meet him at the lodge gates in fifteen minutes.

Clarissa woke during the phone call.

'I'll take the Land-Rover and Muggins,' he said from the dressing room, pulling on socks. 'I imagine it's the village children again. We'll give them something to think about this time.'

'Please don't do anything silly.' Clarissa was agitated. She did not enjoy her husband's mock Churchillian-bulldog moods. 'Don't get yourself hurt.'

'I'll take the twelve-bore.'

'Oh, don't be ridiculous,' she almost shrieked. 'That's exactly how you'll get yourself hurt. If it *is* poachers or burglars or something and they see you with a gun, then they're just as likely to shoot you as you are to shoot them.'

'One has an obligation to defend one's property,' he said stiffly. He came back into the bedroom, pulling on a Fair Isle sweater.

'You'll have the police with you. That's quite enough. I'm sure Constable Taylor would be horrified if you were armed.'

'Well, what do you suggest then? I'm certainly not tackling dangerous criminals when I'm unarmed.'

'Oh, darling, do stop being so melodramatic. You said it was the village children. Why ever should they be armed? And if they *are* armed, the only thing they'll be interested in shooting is rabbits. Who on earth would want to shoot *you*?' Her unintentional emphasis of the 'you' made this final remark sound gratuitously insulting.

'I don't understand your attitude,' he said, 'but since you insist, I shall take a stick.' He shut the door noisily behind him.

In Wolfe the three monitors were having a council of war. Fieldhouse was for going back to bed as the CO had ordered.

Stack was for nipping out of the back door and stalking down to the Lake District to observe the action. Porter was havering. All this was in character.

'Why can't we just watch from the window?' suggested Porter.

'Because we're too far away to see anything. Also because he's quite liable to look up at the windows and see us peering out. He's much less likely to see us if we're stalking in the bushes.' Stack was quite breathless.

'But if he does find us outside he'll go berserk.' Fieldhouse was also tremulous, though for different reasons. 'I don't want the cane. And I certainly don't want to be expelled.'

'Oh, you're such a goody-goody,' said Stack.

'Well, if that's what you think, too bad,' said Fieldhouse. 'I'm going to bed.' And he went, shoulders hunched, slippers scuffing across the floorboards, a study in rejection.

'What about you? Are you going to be a goody-goody too?'

Porter was stung by the jibe. He could see that Fieldhouse was inclined to drippiness, though he also felt that Stack was unfair to him. He liked Fieldhouse. Quite. He could see that Fieldhouse's parents created problems for him. Some were genetic; others, more subtle, were to do with expectation. Overtly at least, Scatty and Dorothy Travis-Gunn seemed to expect nothing whatever of Stack and this helped to make him a free spirit. The Fieldhouse parents had the obvious, fussy desire for their boy to 'do well' that inspired neurosis. Porter supposed that the Commander and his mother came somewhere in between and that this tolerant pride allowed him to be the moderate, normal person that, in a rather priggish way, he considered himself. It was helped by their being in Malta. The Commander could make a certain amount of a nuisance of himself by Forces airmail letter card. *Vide* the matter of the booze and fags. But he could not come bowling up the drive in his Rover whenever there was a problem to discuss with the CO. The Commander liked to think he could pull strings from the Med, but he was an indifferent puppeteer and the strings were long and loose.

To preserve his self-respect as the compromise candidate between Fieldhouse's Fotherington-Thomas and Stack's burgeoning Molesworth, Porter tried as far as possible to avoid taking sides. When forced to be partisan he attempted to take turns so that by being on first one side and then the other he could be if not all, at least most things to most men. There were dangers in this. He was beginning to recognize that as people grew older they developed a 'he that is not for me is against me' attitude. This upset Porter's Laodicean inclinations. Stack, in particular, was beginning to push him, to ask 'Whose side are you on, anyway?' This time Porter decided to side with the Mighty Atom. He could see no fence to sit on.

'You know perfectly well I'm not a goody-goody.'

'OK,' said Stack, 'prove it.'

'All right.' Porter smiled tightly. 'I'll see you by the back door in five minutes.'

'Wear gym shoes,' said Stack practically. He was inwardly triumphant. And a little surprised.

At the Chummery O'Rourke and Oily Watkins were playing out the final moves of their chess game. O'Rourke would have his partner in check in a couple of moves, mate in half a dozen, so he was irritated when the phone rang. No one responded. After a few rings he said irritably, 'Can't one of the others answer it?'

Oily, frowning at his few remaining pieces, said that Roberts and St Aubyn were both out. It was his move and he sat still. Eventually he said, 'They're not going away. You'll have to answer it.'

O'Rourke swore and went out to the hall where he picked up the receiver, said, 'Sorry, wrong number!' replaced it, re-entered, sat down heavily and lit a cigarette.

'Was it a wrong number?' Oily Watkins took one of O'Rourke's pawns with a rook, thus making the rook vulnerable to O'Rourke's queen.

'Didn't give them time to find out,' said O'Rourke, dragging deep on the cigarette and regarding the board with satisfaction.

The phone rang again.

'Your turn,' said O'Rourke.

'I just moved. I took your pawn.'

'No.' O'Rourke frowned. 'The phone. Your turn for the phone.'

127

Watkins went out. Through his concentration O'Rourke heard him answer with the effusive unctuousness which was why the boys called him Oily. Then the grease turned to concern. Alarm even.

O'Rourke only heard some of the words. Not that there were very many. Watkins was merely reacting to whatever was being said on the other end of the line. He did little more than cluck until, just before putting the phone down, he said, 'Yes, yes, we'll come at once.' He sounded like the Flying Doctor.

O'Rourke took Watkins's rook and raised his eyebrows as he came back in.

'That was Bert at the Plume of Feathers,' he said. 'I'm afraid Roberts is in there making a nuisance of himself. Bert says if we don't come and bail him out he'll have no alternative but to hand him over to the police. It's almost closing time.'

O'Rourke ground his cigarette into the cheap tin ashtray and looked at the ceiling in supplication.

'How bad a nuisance?'

'Bert said he'd been sick over someone,' said Oily.

Oblivious to the gathering storm, St Aubyn and Miss Battersby returned from a torchlight meander through the woods and embraced in the shadow of the boat house. The moon was bright now and there were few clouds. No need for a torch outside the thick undergrowth, especially, thought St Aubyn as his tongue roamed Miss Battersby's mouth, at moments like this. He turned the torch off and removed his tongue for a catch of breath. Miss Battersby nibbled at his earlobe. For some reason St Aubyn was not reminded of Romeo and Juliet or Tristram and Ysolde; rather of the Light Programme's Glums. Not 'me Tarzan, you Jane', but 'me Ron, you Eth.'

'I say,' she said, releasing her hold on his ear and whispering into it instead, 'do you think the water's awfully cold?'

'Feel it,' said St Aubyn. 'I shouldn't imagine so. It's had a fair bit of sun on it. Here.' He disentangled himself and knelt on the bank, dabbling his hands in the water. It was almost lukewarm. She knelt down beside him and rinsed her hand

as well. There were reeds growing in the water, and bul-
rushes. A little farther out lily pads.

'David,' she said, in a soft, teasing, daring, lover's voice,
'shall we go for a swim?'

'A swim?' St Aubyn was genuinely surprised. 'It'll be
awfully muddy. And it's not *that* warm. Besides we haven't
brought costumes.' He felt *just* like Ron Glum.

She nuzzled against his cheek. 'I know,' she said, 'that's
half the fun.'

St Aubyn's mouth dried and he was suddenly very aware
of his pulse. It was the same sort of reaction that Porter had
to Stack's recent behaviour and suggestions. He was excited
but alarmed. He was not ready to go this far.

However, before he could say anything at all, Miss
Battersby had started to undress. It took remarkably little
time for her to remove blouse, skirt and shoes. Stockings
followed quickly and, after a scarcely perceptible hesitation,
bra and knickers. St Aubyn, terror and lust vying frantically,
remained quite immobile looking away towards the middle
of the lake while wanting, desperately, to see as much as he
could of the junior matron's body. Seconds later he was
aware of white back and buttocks as she lowered herself off
the bank into the water and waded through the reeds.

'Eek!' she exclaimed, giggling, 'it's all squidgy.' She did a
sort of half bellyflop and started to breaststroke away from
him. After a few yards she stopped swimming and stood up.
'It's quite deep here,' she called to him, 'I can only just stand.'

He peered out, hoping to see moonlit breasts, but realizing
with some chagrin that they were covered by the water. It
almost came up to her chin. 'It's lovely,' she called again,
'come on in. Don't be such a cowardy custard. I won't peek.
Promise.'

St Aubyn stood up. It was absolute madness. He knew
that. But if he didn't swim, he would lose face. And if he lost
face, he'd lose Miss Battersby. He stood and began to
unbuckle his belt. His compromise was that he would not
remove his Aertex underpants.

The Plume was officially shut by the time O'Rourke and
Oily Watkins got there, but the lights were still on and when

they entered the public they found Bert and one of the overripe barmaids polishing glasses. Bert was large and florid, in braces and what had once been a white shirt designed to be worn with a stiff collar. The stiff collar was not attached and probably never had been. Bert jerked his head towards a high-backed pew which ran along a wall underneath a couple of Surteesian hunting prints and a copper warming pan, badly tarnished.

'All yours, gentlemen,' said Bert.

O'Rourke took in the smell of vomit mingling with the other more familiar public-house smells at about the same moment that he saw the remains of the sick clinging to Roberts's shirt and trouser front. Sight and smell struck him simultaneously.

'I'm awfully sorry, Bert,' he said. He delved for his wallet and found a tatty ten-bob note which he put down on the bar counter. 'I hope that'll pay for the cleaning and buy a beer or two to make amends.'

'Very kind of you, sir,' said Bert, 'and I know it's not your fault, but I'd be obliged if you could keep 'im away from 'ere in future. I'm not serving 'im and that's a fact. And if he comes in 'ere drunk and using bad language and all, I'll call the law.' There were times when O'Rourke wondered if Bert consciously modelled himself on the BBC 'Mummerset' of the Archers. Too Walter Gabriel by half.

'I quite understand, Bert.' O'Rourke decided that in the circumstances it might be better to double the ten shillings. He found an even tattier brown note and put it beside the first. Bert's smile became a little less forced. He nodded but said nothing.

'Swearing, was he?'

'Somethin' shockin',' said Bert. ' 'E were four sheets to the wind when 'e came in round nine o'clock. I wouldn't 'ave served 'im myself but I were out at the time and Betty thought she oughta give 'im what 'e wanted before 'e caused any more trouble.'

Oily Watkins had advanced on Roberts's pew during this conversation and was staring at his inebriated colleague with an expression of dismay and distaste. O'Rourke joined him.

'A pretty low form of life, I agree,' said O'Rourke.

'And after the warning we gave him,' said Watkins, 'after he fell under the bus.'

'Pity he *didn't* fall under the bus. He'd be better off dead and buried.'

Oily smiled dreamily. 'He does look as if he's been dead and buried anyway.'

This was not far from the truth. Roberts's complexion was codlike at the best of times, which in his case was around mid-morning. If one could imagine a cod with acne. And dandruff. But now, as he sat slumped and comatose in his pew at the Plume of Feathers, his face was moving from cod to verdigris. His mouth sagged. And he stank.

'What was he drinking?' asked O'Rourke.

'Guinness and gin,' said Bert.

'Good heavens.' Oily, who liked a dram himself, gulped. 'Not mixed together, surely?'

' 'e was chasing one with t'other,' said Bert. *'Plymouth* gin. Neat. 'e was very particular about the Plymouth.'

'And what was he saying? Was he even remotely intelligible?' O'Rourke was puzzled by the delusions and obsessions which apparently fuelled Roberts's alcoholism. The other night after the bus incident he had been talking religion of an apocalyptic sort. The Second Coming was evidently imminent and Roberts had some special but, to his listeners, unfathomable part to play in it. O'Rourke wondered if he was single-minded about this or if, in drink, he battened on to whatever fancy happened to be passing.

'Lot of stuff about India and the Empire,' said Bert. 'Kept talking about "wogs". That wog Gandhi, that wog Nehru, that wog Nasser, them Mau Mau wogs.'

O'Rourke shrugged and grimaced at Watkins. 'I suppose,' he said, 'we'd better get him home. Bert, could you be extremely kind and let me have some old newspaper? I'm buggered if I'm having him soiling the upholstery.'

The MG had leather seats of which O'Rourke was absurdly proud. He polished them once a month with saddle soap. He was a real-life model for the Leather Institute advertisement: 'A car with leather upholstery never looks its age'. With a sharp intake of breath and resolute expression the two sober West Hill masters took an armpit each and half dragged, half carried Roberts outside.

131

'Phew, what a pong!' said Watkins as they manoeuvred him through the door held open by Betty who used the other hand to pinch her nose.

The car was a two-seater but there was space in the back for a third occupant sitting sideways. Somehow they manoeuvred Roberts into it, then settled into the front seats. O'Rourke had the lid down and as he gunned the car along the silent village street the warm night air wafted away the smell of alcohol and vomit. Behind him Queenie Roberts started to sing in a quavering high-pitched apology of a tenor voice:

> 'I'll sing you twelve O
> Green grow the rushes O
> What is your twelve O?
> Twelve for the twelve apostles . . .'

Astonishingly he was word perfect.

Porter and Stack took the quickest route to the Lake District, which was across the lawn with the three copper beeches, over the ha-ha, and across the park in a straight line, until they reached the iron railings which sealed off the lake and adjoining woods. Halfway across the park they heard an engine on the drive and sprawled headlong in the grass.

'CO's Land-Rover,' said Stack as they watched the vehicle trundle over the cattlegrid and on down the drive about fifty yards to their left.

'He didn't see us, did he?' Porter whispered, just like Stack. It was instinctive.

'He wouldn't be looking. Any case, we were lying down by the time he came round the corner.'

They remained prone while the Land-Rover continued down the slope and until the rear lights disappeared over the brow of the hill. Then gingerly they stood, dusted themselves down, and waited until the engine cut out and all was quiet again.

'Is it safe to walk?' Porter was not moving at all, as if statuesque immobility would somehow guarantee invisibility.

Stack started to move on, one pace at a time, feeling out the ground so that he did not transfer his weight from one foot to the other until he could be sure he was not treading on a twig or a cowpat. 'We can walk a bit longer,' he hissed. 'Just get ready to duck. We'll crawl the last part.'

A few yards farther on they saw the Land Rover's lights illuminating the white of the front gate posts. The gates themselves were open. Like the Windmill Theatre, they never closed. The CO was standing in front of them with Muggins on the end of a lead. He was watching the main road and waiting. The boys saw him glance at his watch and then start to pace impatiently. They dived quickly and started to crawl.

O'Rourke liked to drive fast. Before the war he had had a big black Velocette motorcycle and he regarded the MG as a concession to middle age. At this time of night in the middle of Somerset there was little chance of meeting another car, so he cornered fast, enjoying the skids and the shrill of burning rubber on the tarmac. A hundred yards short of the main West Hill gates, however, they encountered another vehicle, namely the bicycle of PC Taylor who was proceeding steadily to his rendezvous with Somerset Burnam. O'Rourke swerved to avoid the bike, corrected the slide almost nonchalantly, and accelerated away. He had once driven at Brooklands.

'That was the police,' said Watkins nervously.

'Only up to a point,' O'Rourke's smile was so fast and thin that it was hardly more than a tic, a split second's contraction of the facial muscles. 'Constable Taylor and the police are not really the same thing.'

Seconds later they were in the straight that led past the main gates. O'Rourke pushed his foot hard on the accelerator and almost as quickly removed it and braked. He had seen the lights of the Land Rover beaming across his path at right angles. Also man and dog.

'It's the CO and Muggins,' he said. 'What in the name of hell are they doing?'

'You can't stop with Roberts in the back.' Watkins, unlike O'Rourke, was intimidated by Burnam. He was not confident of getting another job should Burnam turn nasty and fire him. Therefore he was more than usually anxious to keep his nose clean.

Roberts was no longer singing. He had presumably gone back to sleep. O'Rourke calculated that if he pulled up sufficiently far away from Burnam he wouldn't notice the smell. In the darkness the drunk man's form was so slouched into the car's interior that Burnam would never spot him. Besides, he presumably had something else on his mind and O'Rourke was curious to find out what it was. He stopped the car and got out quickly, followed by a more lethargic Oily Watkins.

'Evening, headmaster.' O'Rourke was at his most brisk and official. 'Anything wrong?'

'I believe we have interlopers in the Lake District.' The CO spoke in the sort of voice used by Richard Dimbleby on state occasions.

Muggins sniffed rudely at Watkins's fly and the CO jerked at his leash.

'I'm just waiting for Constable Taylor,' he continued. 'He should have been here five minutes ago.'

'We passed him a minute or so ago, struggling on his velocipede,' said Watkins, trying unsuccessfully to be jovial and ingratiating at the same time. 'He should be here soon.'

'Can we help?' O'Rourke was sceptical but intrigued. 'Any idea how many there are? Or who?'

Burnam explained about the light moving haphazardly through the Lake District and his two employees nodded.

'More the merrier, I should say,' said O'Rourke. 'Don't want them slipping through the net. Watkins and I are game for a little French and English, aren't we, Watkins?'

Watkins said he was, just as Constable Taylor cycled up, puffing slightly, dismounted and took off his bicycle clips.

'Evening, Constable,' said Burnam rattily. 'I thought we said quarter of an hour?'

'Got 'ere as fast as I could, sir,' said the policeman. O'Rourke thought he was going to add something about being almost knocked over by a Mr Toad in an open sports car. The law, however, knew its place and made no comment. Even though it might have liked to.

'Righty-ho, then,' said Burnam, taking charge heavy-handedly. 'Constable, you and I have torches, so I suggest we take either end of the line. I'll let Muggins off the lead. He should sniff 'em out quickly enough. The rest of us fan out, about ten yards apart, and sweep west towards the lake. Any questions?'

He really ought to have been in the Army, thought O'Rourke, grinning silently. Though not too near the front line. He pulled out a cigarette and began to light it.

'No smoking, if you don't mind,' said Burnam. 'We don't want to give our position away.'

O'Rourke dropped the cigarette and ground it with his heel gracelessly.

'Don't you think the torches might perhaps give us away?' he said mutinously.

From the brief pause that followed, it was clear that the CO hadn't thought of this, but he rallied quickly.

'No torches until Muggins has found them,' he said. 'As soon as he's on to something, we light up and give chase.' He waved his stick for emphasis. 'Righty-ho, then. Off we go!'

It was, as O'Rourke knew it would be, an almost total shambles. The only real professional apart from himself was the dog. They stumbled and cursed and the CO kept hissing 'Ssssh'. O'Rourke reckoned any half-competent poacher or burglar would have done a bunk ages ago.

At their vantage point on the slope of the park, Porter and Stack looked out from either side of a hollow, lightning-crippled oak, and giggled.

'PC Taylor must have brought half the Somerset police with him,' said Stack.

They were still more than fifty yards from the lake. A compromise, naturally. Stack had been all for climbing the railings and infiltrating the Lake District, not in the least scared of what they might find or of what might find them. Porter would have preferred to have stopped as soon as the Land-Rover came in sight. Hence the blasted oak. While waiting for the CO to organize his troops, they had divided their attentions between the gates and the lake. They had seen O'Rourke's MG, though not identified it. O'Rourke had parked well short of the Land-Rover's headlights and extinguished his own at once. They had watched the arrival of the police, observed the conference and heard the clumping footsteps and not very muffled voices as the search began. Their view of the lakeland goings-on was less certain. At first, seeing no light, they assumed there was no one there. Then they had heard a splash and a definitely female giggle. More splashes. A male voice. But, strain though they might, they could identify neither the voices, nor the words. To make it worse, clouds had appeared and dowsed the moon. They could not see the source of sound.

'It's a man and a woman, swimming,' said Porter.

Stack did not disagree but could add nothing.

Any half-competent burglar or poacher *would* have done a bunk by now, but Miss Battersby and David St Aubyn were not and had not. They had heard the Land-Rover but paid little attention. Also the MG, to which ditto. The water was pleasant. They swam a little. They came ashore for a cuddle which David St Aubyn found almost uncomfortably erotic until, just as he was on the verge of losing all control Miss Battersby, quite naked and laughing softly, disengaged, told him not to be naughty and re-entered the water. This process was repeated more than once. It was hardly surprising that they were oblivious to the advance of Burnam's men.

'Oh, bloody hell!'

Oily Watkins's shout lit up the silent night like an oral Very light. He had trodden in a fresh cowpat and, as he was wearing heavy duty Clark's sandals with no socks, the cold sludge of ordure encased almost naked skin. It was one thing to put your wellington boot in cowdung; quite another to put your foot in it. So he called out.

Moments after the shout Muggins started to bark. Porter was reminded of the pigs in the dingle. The bark had the same strident insistence, aggression mixed with fear. Muggins had something cornered but wasn't sure what it was. Canine savoir-faire told him it might be bigger than him, might have sharper teeth. So he stood off at a safe distance, hackles raised, and shouted. There was no longer any point in Burnam and Co. trying to preserve their fragile anony-

136

mity. The CO and the constable snapped on their torches and the foursome began to run towards the dog's barking, the CO shouting the same sort of encouragement that he roared from the touchline during rugby matches. The beams of the torches arced haphazardly over the landscape, revealing nothing but trees, bushes and railings until one of them found Muggins. He was standing with his feet planted firmly apart, head down, tail wagging. Beside him on the bank was a pile of what looked, even to the boys by the hollow oak, like abandoned clothing.

'Maybe it's suicide,' suggested Stack, biting his thumb. 'Gosh, I bet Fieldhouse'll be sorry he missed this.'

The four men converged on the dog, with Watkins bringing up a dejected rear. As the other three scanned the lake he rinsed his foot in the water and continued swearing under his breath.

'We know you're there,' shouted the CO. 'The game's up. You're not going to be able to get away. The police are here. Come on now . . .' As he shouted, he and PC Taylor continued to move their torchbeams across the surface of the water, lingering over each reed and lily pad, until O'Rourke saw what they were looking for. Towards the middle of the lake, among the lilies, the football shape of a human head.

'There, swing your torch back left,' he instructed the constable. 'No. Left. Left. Down a bit.' The head had gone but there was a telltale circle of wash. 'There. Hold it there, man, and wait.'

They did not have to wait long. Seconds later the head broke the surface, spluttering slightly and blinded by the light of the policeman's torch.

There was a stunned silence. Eventually the CO said, 'Good Lord! St Aubyn! What on earth do you think you're doing?'

'I was just having a swim, sir, as a matter of fact.'

'Changed sex by the look of it too,' Watkins, sitting down on the grass, the better to bathe his foot, had discovered Miss Battersby's bra. He held it up as a curious Burnam shone his torch on it.

In an unexpectedly plaintive tone Burnam said, 'I think you'd better get out of the water and tell us exactly what you've been up to.'

137

St Aubyn began to swim towards them as, from under the boughs of a weeping willow tree, there came a stifled and very obviously female sob. Instinctively two torches swivelled to the spot, revealing for a moment the pneumatic form of Miss Battersby knee-deep in the pond and clinging to a branch for support.

For a moment the torches illuminated her, and then, from the other end of the lake, the one nearest the park gates, came the evening's final surprise. First there was a loud splash. Then, a cracked, flat, squeaky and unmistakably drunken voice carried across the suddenly silent night. The two torches swung away from Miss Battersby's nakedness and swiftly found their target.

'O all ye Works of the Lord, bless ye the Lord,' sang Batty Roberts in the spotlight, 'Oh ye Waters that be above the Firmament, bless ye the Lord, Praise him and magnify him for ever.' He sang with his eyes closed, his hands clasped before him, and his head raised to the sky, and as he sang he processed, if a single supplicant singer can be said to process, into the still waters of the lake. 'O ye Showers and Dew, bless ye the Lord; O ye Winds of God, bless ye the Lord; praise him and magnify him for ever.' Slowly, slowly he moved on into the lake, the water rising around him. 'O ye Dews and Frosts, bless ye the Lord; O ye Frost and Cold . . .'

'It's Queenie Roberts,' whispered Stack gleefully, 'singing the Benedicite.'

'And trying to walk on water.' Porter hugged himself with amazement and joy.

'Without much success.'

'Without *any* success.'

'And did you see Miss Battersby?'

'Starkers!'

Together, they giggled hysterically, aware that in the glorious adult chaos below them no one would notice them, and that if they did no one would care.

'Starkers,' repeated Stack.

'Starkers,' said Porter.

And together, uncontrollably, 'Absolutely starkers!'

* * *

The CO's post mortem was painful and essentially solitary. He discussed the scandals of the Lake District with Clarissa and with O'Rourke. Separately. And in a sense perfunctorily. It was not so much that he found their views uninteresting but irrelevant. Smedley's analogy with feudalism was accurate. There was nothing democratic about West Hill. At staff meetings, it was true, members of staff were, technically speaking, free to give their views. Monitors, it was also true, were given authority over younger and usually smaller boys. Delegation was essential, but it did not mean dereliction. The CO was aptly named. The buck stopped at his big mahogany desk in his intimidating study just as surely as the buck had stopped in President Truman's Oval Office a few years before. Very occasionally, on questions of health or hygiene, he deferred to matron, but otherwise his decisions were taken on his own and, once taken, were final. It was his belief that a headmaster who changed his mind was losing and that a headmaster who was seen to change his mind was lost. That was what he told Clarissa whenever she accused him of intransigence. He was, under his well-calculated veneer, a quite weak and uncertain character, but he did have the self-knowledge to realize it. He understood that only a genuinely strong man could afford to appear weak.

Under normal circumstances, therefore, Messrs Roberts and St Aubyn and Miss Battersby would have been on the first available train to Paddington. But, as Somerset kept repeating to himself, these circumstances were not normal. Far from it.

7

Obviously Roberts would have to go. O'Rourke conceded that the man had a drinking problem, but so far Roberts had not been drunk in school. Burnam would not be writing him a reference; indeed he would be sending a stiffish note to Gabbitas, Thring and Co. They liked to boast, on the front page of *The Times* no less, that their expertise was based on eighty-three years' 'personal acquaintance with many headmasters and headmistresses'. Very well then, this was one headmaster who would be using his acquaintance to see that no one else employed the inebriate Roberts. But Roberts was going anyway at the end of term, and in the meantime Burnam needed a history master. Far too late to get another. He personally, though O'Rourke disagreed, was inclined to think that the shock of walking into the lake might sober the man up. It was a bad business certainly, but it had taken place outside school hours even if it had been on school property.

'Tell him to see a doctor,' Clarissa advised him. O'Rourke said he'd already done that. No use. Roberts refused to admit that he drank any more than anyone else. Only that he had a weak head. 'No doubt Dylan Thomas says the same,' muttered O'Rourke.

Burnam finally had his interview with Roberts after lunch. It did not go well. Roberts, though fortified with Alka Selzer, was clearly not himself. It was apparent from his response, or lack of response, to Burnam's opening remarks, that he remembered nothing of the previous night. Burnam obligingly filled him in, whereupon Roberts went an even whiter shade of pale.

'It's not good enough,' said Burnam, flexing a ruler in his hands and fixing the victim with one of his stares.

'No, sir.'

'I should be perfectly justified in dismissing you forthwith.'

'Yes, sir.'

'Is that all you have to say?'

'I'm very sorry, sir.'

This was the sort of conversation Burnam was used to having with small boys. It was disconcerting to have it with a grown man. He found himself wishing he could deliver six of the best, shake hands and forget the whole thing. He even, fleetingly, had the feeling that if he suggested it, Roberts would agree.

Instead he said, 'It won't do, you know.'

'No, sir.'

'Do you have any explanation?'

'I must have had too much to drink, sir.'

Burnam sighed. A long throaty exhalation of despair, both genuine and histrionic.

'I know you were drunk,' he said. 'I saw you walking into the lake singing the Benedicite. You wouldn't have done that if you hadn't been drinking vast quantities of gin and Guinness, would you?'

'Probably not, sir. '

'*Probably* not? What do you mean, *probably* not?'

'No, sir, of course not.'

Roberts did seem gratifyingly cowed, though the CO realized that it might have as much to do with hangover as penitence. Burnam made a show of consulting papers on his desk, pushing his glasses up and down his nose, frowning, giving an impression of deliberation, as if he had not yet made up his mind, and Roberts's fate was still in the balance.

'Your employment here is only until the end of term,' he said, still pretending to read.

'Yes, sir,' agreed Roberts. He was obviously in the mood to agree with anything the headmaster said. He would have said 'three bags full' given the chance.

'Which means five more weeks.'

'Yes, sir.'

The CO appeared to be doing some serious thinking. At length he said, 'You do realize that you've put me in an

141

extremely difficult position?' This, though phrased as a question, was obviously rhetorically intentioned because he continued before Roberts could acquiesce. 'If you were a permanent member of the staff here, I should sack you at once. However, the fact of the matter is that you were brought in here as a temporary stopgap to help out in an emergency. There is a job to be done here and unfortunately you're the only man available to do it.'

Burnam wondered if he was laying it on a little thickly. Roberts's attitude was unnervingly meek.

'You do understand that I will not tolerate drunkenness in the school?'

'Yes, sir.'

'Nor exhibitionism?'

'Yes, sir.'

'And that by making an exhibition of yourself in the Plume of Feathers you've severely damaged the relationship between the school and the village?'

Roberts nodded.

'I set great store by a satisfactory town and gown relationship,' Burnam went on, 'and I simply will not have it jeopardized by any silliness. Especially by a *temporary* master. So I must ask you to give a solemn undertaking not to patronize either of the village's two public houses. Do you agree?'

Roberts said yes.

'Now, I'm prepared to allow you to stay on here according to our original agreement, provided,' and here he paused for another of his stares, 'provided,' he reiterated, 'that there is no repeat performance of last night's shocking behaviour. Is that understood?'

Roberts nodded and said, 'Yes, sir.'

After which there was nothing left to say. It was not, the CO conceded, satisfactory. Not in the least satisfactory. But it would have to do. Roberts was not the easiest person to communicate with and Burnam was not sure his message had got through. Odd fish, Roberts. Burnam had a hunch he'd be put away before too long. Or even do something drastic like throw himself under a train. He only hoped it wouldn't be on the Taunton–Minehead line during term-time. The school would never live it down.

* * *

142

It was easier to cope with St Aubyn. With him he could be paternal, almost literally. St Aubyn's father and he had shared digs during their last year at Cambridge and rowed in the same eight. The college third eight. Not a very distinguished one.

'I'm extremely disappointed, David,' he said, 'I'm afraid you've let the side down very badly.'

Secretly, so secretly the CO could not admit it even to himself, he was jealous of the younger man. He had never gone swimming with a naked woman. He had always been far too inhibited, though Clarissa, had he known it, would have been perfectly amenable, at least while she was still proud of her figure. The CO would have liked to have swum with Miss Battersby himself. He would like to have university and the Army before him. With his experience he would make a far better job of being young than David St Aubyn would ever manage.

'I'm sorry, sir. I'm afraid we got rather carried away.'

'It's not what I expect from a member of the West Hill staff. You're supposed to set an example.'

'Yes, sir. It won't happen again, sir.'

'I ought to send you home, you know. And tell your father why.'

St Aubyn flushed, but something about the CO's tone and the way he had phrased the sentence suggested that it was a threat he was dangling but not about to execute. He was sharp enough to know what his own lines should be.

'I'd be awfully grateful if you wouldn't, sir.'

Burnam went through his 'obvious thinking routine', even rising and staring out of the window towards the scene of the nocturnal frolics, as if carrying on a difficult internal debate with himself. In fact, he was thinking that young St Aubyn was not a patch on his father and had a weak face. Also that he tied a bad tie. It was always slipping below the top button of his shirt. He was afraid that far from being a chip off the old block, which was what he had hoped, David was actually a bit of a drip. Eventually he turned back and sat down again.

'How old are you, David?'

He knew perfectly well how old he was. St Aubyn knew that he knew.

'Eighteen and a half, sir.'

'You have your whole life before you. You do realize that, don't you?'

'Yes, sir.'

'You do realize that if what happened last night got back to the dons at Magdalen it would scupper your chances of going to Oxford altogether.'

St Aubyn had not considered this and had no idea if it was true. He suspected not. Nevertheless he hung his head.

'Yes, sir.'

'And I don't expect your regiment would be exactly thrilled either.'

St Aubyn doubted this even more. He had already heard titillating tales of the officers' mess, stories of sexual initiation ceremonies for newly arrived subalterns, what chaps got up to on foreign postings.

He kept his head down. 'No, sir, I suppose not.'

'Now,' said Burnam, 'I don't want your career ruined before it's even started any more than you do. So I'm going to do my best to see that none of this gets out. However, I'm afraid I have to take some steps to make sure that it won't happen again, which means that for the rest of the term I'm going to impose a curfew on both you and Miss Battersby. From now on you'll have to be in the Chummery by eight o'clock in the evening. And no going out afterwards. If there are special reasons for being out late you can come and ask my permission. I'm not going to be unreasonable about this.'

'That's very kind of you, sir. I do appreciate it. And I'm very sorry about last night. It won't happen again.'

Burnam smiled and nodded.

'Now, listen.' He assumed an expression of complicity which suggested that they were both men of the world, all chaps together. He cleared his throat. 'I know you probably think I'm a pompous old buffer, but I quite understand that for a red-blooded bloke of eighteen Miss Battersby's a jolly attractive prospect. She's a jolly attractive girl.'

St Aubyn blushed. 'Yes, sir,' he whispered.

'And no one's going to object if you enjoy being with each other and having fun. I mean, you can play tennis or go riding and what-have-you. It isn't as if there's nothing to do.

144

But I absolutely will not have any hanky-panky. Quite apart from any question of morality. And I'm sure you realize that I feel very strongly on the question of morality, no matter what the young today think. I don't want any of that John Osborne nonsense here at West Hill. Besides, Miss Battersby's still very young.' It was the CO's turn to turn puce. 'I do hope,' he said, 'that there hasn't been . . . I mean . . . you haven't . . . there hasn't been any hanky-panky, has there?'

St Aubyn, also very red, said he was sorry but he didn't understand.

'What I mean, er, David, is . . . well, not to put too fine a point on it, there's no possiblity of Miss Battersby becoming pregnant, is there?'

'Good heavens no, sir.' St Aubyn seemed shocked at the suggestion.

'No,' said the CO, 'good. I only ask because she was . . . well, as you know, she's very much under our care and protection here. Mrs Burnam and I are *in loco parentis*. As we are with you too.'

He got up to signal the end of the interview and put out a firm if fleshy hand. St Aubyn shook it.

'Righty-ho, then.' The CO was back in command. 'We'll start again with a clean slate. Home by eight and no objections to your being friendly with Miss Battersby. But absolutely no hanky-panky. Understood?'

'Understood, sir.'

St Aubyn grinned.

Mr Burnam grinned back.

They understood one another.

Clarissa and Somerset agreed that, in the circumstances (as they both kept repeating), it would be better if Somerset did not conduct the interview with Helen Battersby.

'In the circumstances,' said Clarissa, flicking absent-mindedly through the unchanging pages of *Country Life*, 'I think it might be best if I talked to the girl. Women's talk. There are things I don't think a man can say to her.'

'In the circumstances, I dare say you're right.' Somerset was gruff. 'I think it might come better from you.'

Clarissa smiled a little sadly. As far as sex was concerned Somerset was rather a mufferoon and so gauche with women other than his wife (and arguably matron) that he might as well be back in the sixth form at Canford.

'That's settled then.' Clarissa slapped the magazine shut and looked at her husband. 'Confined to barracks after eight and a serious warning.'

At seven after supper Helen Battersby came to Clarissa's little sitting room, a feminine stronghold which no one, not even her husband, entered without invitation. Clarissa sat in an armchair working at needlepoint. She was trying to re-cover the dining-room chairs, but it was like painting the Forth Bridge. By the time she had finished the eighth, the first would be worn out or soiled beyond repair. The design was geometric floral with pointy fleurs-de-lys and angular daisies. She was not sure she liked it but it was too late now. The third chair was halfway to completion.

'Helen,' she said, looking up and smiling, 'thank you for dropping in. Do come in and close the door. I won't keep you a minute.' The girl was alarmingly nubile. Clarissa herself was still an attractive woman, arguably more so in early middle age than in her teens and twenties. Then she had been thought gawky and flat-chested. Now people said she had good bones. Also she had acquired a serenity which appealed, at least to the older man. But Miss Battersby was an early bloomer: blonde, busty, with sulky pouting lips. Her pulchritude would, guessed Clarissa, be barmaid's flab by the time she was thirty. But she wasn't thirty. She was a just ripe sixteen with sex on her mind.

Clarissa went on with her needlepoint. 'It's about last night,' she said.

Miss Battersby said nothing. Just sat, glowering. Sulky little madam, thought Clarissa, but she kept on with her needlepoint, apparently absorbed in its gentle repetitive rhythms.

'Do you want to tell me about it?'

'There's nothing to tell.'

Her needle dipped in and out of the cloth. The grand-mother clock seemed to tick in time. Clarissa bit back irrita-tion. Despite her thirty-six-inch bust, Miss Battersby was only a child.

'Helen, dear,' she said coolly but not quite unkindly, 'we both know that's not quite true, don't we?'

Miss Battersby pouted, but the lips remained sealed.

'My husband says you were in the lake without any clothes on.'

Still nothing.

'It must have been cold.'

Not even a glimmer of a smile. Just that sullen, sexy pout.

'Helen, you know one of the reasons your parents sent you here was so that you'd be away from those unsuitable men you'd been seeing.'

'David St Aubyn's not unsuitable,' she said too loudly. There were tears not far away. Possibly imminent. Clarissa did hope not. 'And we weren't doing anything wrong.'

Clarissa concentrated on her hands and the work on her lap. 'Helen,' she said, 'you mustn't think I'm unsympathetic. Or stupid. I do know about men. I had boyfriends myself when I was your age. And I've had two children. I know what it's like to be in love.'

'Who said anything about being in love?'

Clarissa let this pass. She found the remark disturbingly modern.

'Look,' she said briskly, 'for myself I don't awfully care what you and David St Aubyn get up to, but as members of staff, even temporary ones, you have to maintain certain standards. This isn't the Duke of Bedford's nudist camp. Nor the South of France. It's a boys' preparatory school. My husband would be perfectly within his right to send you straight back home to your parents.' She glanced quickly at the girl and was irritated to see her wipe her eyes with the back of her hand. The eyes were wet. Miss Battersby sniffed.

'He's not going to do that,' continued Clarissa, 'because he's a kind man and he doesn't want you to get into trouble. None of us wants you to get into trouble. You do understand that, don't you?'

Miss Battersby sniffed again and a teardrop started to roll very slowly down her cheek.

'We weren't doing anything wrong,' she said.

Clarissa, very carefully, set down the needlework on the low table in front of her where it rested with a jar of hum-bugs,

Callard and Bowser butterscotch, assorted magazines, a tin of elastic bands and a bowl of flowers she had picked herself that morning in the rose garden. She was not as neat a person as she would wish.

'You think it's perfectly all right to go nude bathing with men?' she asked.

'I think people's bodies are very beautiful,' said Helen unexpectedly and with heat. 'I think we're very prudish about clothes and covering ourselves up. I mean, if God had meant us to wear clothes we'd be born wearing clothes. Look at the Greeks.'

Clarissa frowned. 'Do your parents know you think like this?'

'I haven't talked about it to my parents. They wouldn't understand.'

'What makes you think *I* understand?'

The girl shrugged. Clarissa wasn't sure whether this was because she didn't know or didn't care. She tried not to let her irritation show.

'Nudity's one thing,' she said, 'sex is another. And because we're all worried and concerned about you and sex, we've decided to make sure that you don't go out after eight o'clock at night.'

'Eight o'clock?' Miss Battersby was incredulous.

'Eight o'clock.' Clarissa spoke sensibly. 'You can read or listen to the wireless. You and I could play whist. Or Monopoly.'

'Honestly!' Not much sign of tears now. 'I'm not one of the boys you know.'

'I'd noticed,' said Clarissa, but the irony passed unobserved.

'I won't!' said Miss Battersby. 'I absolutely won't. I resign. I shall leave tomorrow. I'm sixteen years old. You can't treat me like a baby.'

'Go home to Mummy and Daddy?' asked Clarissa thoughtfully. 'And what will you tell them? Say we've been frightfully unfair just because you went for an innocent nude swim with your boyfriend?'

The pout again.

'Now, if you're sensible, Helen, and do as we ask, there's no reason for your parents to know anything about this. You can stay on till the end of term and we'll be very happy to have you. We just don't want you getting into trouble. It's for your own good.'

Miss Battersby shrugged. Defeat at last. Despite her looks she was suddenly a little girl caught playing 'Mummies and Daddies'; not a *femme fatale* in flagrante delicto.

'I don't see what's wrong with what we did,' she said. 'We were just having a bit of fun. But Daddy would kill me if he found out. I know that. Do you promise you won't tell him?'

'Promise,' said Clarissa, exuding a patience and affection she could not bring herself to feel.

'Can I go now?' she asked, 'I'd like to listen to the Glums. They're on in a few minutes.'

'Of course,' said Clarissa. 'But Helen, dear, before you go, there's just one thing.'

'Yes?' Miss Battersby had stood to go. Even in her cheap nylon yellow uniform overall she still looked stunning.

Clarissa thought what a fatal combination those sort of looks and that sort of mind almost inevitably were. 'Just a bit of advice, dear. To do with sex. It's very wrong before marriage. I'm sure we agree about that. But it is possible to get carried away, especially if you're fond of someone and you let yourself be tempted. And it would be too awful to find yourself pregnant. Do remember that. If you ever do find yourself in a situation like that, you must make sure the man behaves like a gentleman and takes precautions. Do you understand?'

Miss Battersby grinned. For the first time that evening she seemed genuinely amused. 'Don't worry, Mrs Burnam,' she said, 'I'd never let a bloke go all the way; but if I did I'd be absolutely positive he was using a French letter.' She smiled. 'Thanks awfully, Mrs Burnam.' And she let herself out, leaving Clarissa gazing at her needlework.

Young people today, she thought, before she could stop herself.

The school's equilibrium was now restored. Like most established institutions it was unexpectedly resilient. Despite the CO's dominance, it had a life of its own so that, like Parliament or *The Times*, the Church of England or Yorkshire

County Cricket Club, or even the country itself, it seemed to survive internal feuds, drunkenness, incompetence, sexual irregularity, debt and any number of other handicaps which would have quickly accounted for a mere individual. Routine was a useful anaesthetic, and not just the routine of morning inspection, breakfast, prayers, French, maths, break, Latin, English, lunch, rest, geography, divinity, cricket, tea, prep, bed. *Amo, amas, amat, amamus, amatis, amant* was wonderfully conducive to peace, quiet and a lethargic acceptance of the status quo. Just as *genou, hibou, joujou, pou*. Or the twelve times table or the kings and queens of England. Even Hillard and Botting or *Kennedy's Latin Primer* with 'Latin' inkily altered to 'Eating'. Learning by numbers was part of the West Hill drill, and learning by numbers led, eventually, to life by numbers. Hence equilibrium. The power of incantation. The hypnotic quality of rote. Familiarity breeding an assurance that the world had fixed points to which you could cling, especially when you were under thirteen years old.

To the very small boys, all those under eleven say, the boat had never appeared to rock. Pigs' heads in the dingle, the felling of Prideaux, the drunkenness of Queenie Roberts and the public nakedness of Miss Battersby – none of these interfered with the essential immutability of life, any more than the death of Commander Crabb or the nastiness of Colonel Nasser or the menace of Lindwall and Miller or the rudeness of *Look Back in Anger*. Even if they were aware of these things, which on the whole they were not, they were peripheral. Real life was the classroom, the dormitory, the public baths in Taunton every Thursday lunchtime. Sweet coffee, Cornish pasties, the flick of damp towels. Real menace was the CO or Mrs Hildersley in a bate. Real terror was being caught eating blotting paper in prep. Real pleasure was a bag of rosebuds or Sharp's toffees on a Sunday afternoon.

The older boys, most obviously Porter, Fieldhouse and Stack, were less certain of the calm. They still argued contentedly about the relative speeds of Lindwall and Trueman, Mike Hawthorn and Stirling Moss, the latter decidedly suspect because he drove a nasty foreign Maserati while Hawthorn patriotically drove a BRM. 'Brrm, brrm, brrm, BRM,' boys would chant as they ran down the school corridors. 'Bags I Hawthorn,' they would shout as they raced their new Jetex cars along the changing-room floor. 'You can be Fangio.' Just as, roller skating, they would insist, 'I'll be Chataway, you can be Kuts'. Even Porter, Fieldhouse and Stack played these games, though never too obviously and never in front of newbugs and small fry. They brewed nettle soup in the half-restored dingle. They played some card cricket. They ploughed through the whole of *The Pickwick Papers*, the whole of *David Copperfield*, relaxed with Buchan and Conan Doyle, returned to serious reading with Thackeray and George Eliot, curled up illegally with smuggled copies of the *Eagle*, *Hotspur* and the *Rover*.

Their part in the ritual of the place helped them relax. They beat the gong for meals; they called rolls; read lessons at prayertime; were instructed in the monotony of leadership. An outsider, even one skilled in the observation of people, might have concluded that the boys were happy, content, normal. If anything was preying on their minds, such an observer would have concluded, with some justice, that it was the imminent scholarship exams.

These certainly had the effect of reducing other worries to scale. For all three boys they were the first great watershed. Entry to West Hill was not by examination. It was determined by parental choice and parental ability to pay – an ability subsidized, in the case of Porter, by the Royal Navy. (The Navy was not prepared to see its officers' sons educated at grammar schools in Valetta or Gibraltar.) Less privileged children like Gavin and Chrissie in the village took their first exams two years earlier and their eleven-plus had a much more ruthless effect on later life. The eleven-plus which Gavin and Chrissie passed ensured that they went to the grammar school from which, in due course and with due luck and application, they could expect to go to university and thus what O'Rourke referred to a little disdainfully as 'life's officer class'. Failure would have meant the secondary modern and an almost inevitable relegation to 'life's other ranks'. For Porter, Fieldhouse and Stack, their exam did not have quite the significance of the eleven-plus. Not even very stupid West Hill boys like Edge-Foxhunter or Boad II failed common entrance more than once. In their cases they failed Shrewsbury and Rugby, where academic standards were high, but managed to get to Milton Abbey and Ellesmere, where they were rather less rigorous. Edge-Foxhunter and Boad II were clearly not destined to leave a very deep or lasting imprint upon life, but they were obviously members of its officer class. It was just that they weren't going to get beyond major. Porter, Fieldhouse and Stack did not come into this category. It was felt by Burnam and others that all three, if not necessarily 'fit for field marshal' (another O'Rourke phrase, ironically intended), were capable of advancing to the sort of level where you had red round your cap and an AT driver who saluted. They were certainly capable of passing the common entrance (a special and separate exam was required for Winchester) to what Burnam called 'one of the great public schools'. (The rest he described as 'a perfectly respectable school', though he did not, usually, believe it.) Whether they were capable of passing in as scholars was another matter. A scholarship to any of their three chosen schools was definite evidence of real academic potential recognized by cash and, in the case of Winchester, a place in a segregated 'College' inhabited exclusively by scholars. A scholarship was not essential. Some scholars burned out early and became chartered accountants; some who merely scraped through the common entrance went on to achieve the field marshal's baton. At their age, however, Porter, Fieldhouse and Stack did not realize this. For the first time in their lives they were being put under real pressure. This was not done cruelly. Or not consciously so. Parents and staff were scrupulous in their attempts not to impose too great a burden of expectation.

'Whatever the result,' wrote Commander Porter from Malta, 'I know that you will be a credit to yourself, your parents and the school.' Porter knew this was not true.

'I'm not asking you to come top,' said Burnam in his pep talk, 'I'm only asking you to do your best.' The manifest hypocrisy appalled them.

Even O'Rourke terrified them. 'Just because they come from the Dragon or Summerfields or Horris Hill,' he told them, 'doesn't mean to say they're any brighter than you. Nor, I need hardly add, better taught. They just think they are. So don't go in there with an inferiority complex. There's no need.' They didn't believe him.

Only Scatty Travis-Gunn exuded genuine nonchalance. 'Never had a lot of time for scholars when I was at school,' he confided to Donald. 'Too pleased with themselves and useless at anything except work. There's a lot more to life than books.' Donald didn't believe him either.

The shocking antics of the Lake District were, naturally, discussed in bated breath. Miss Battersby's nakedness and Batty Roberts's drunkenness were unprecedented.

Stack, precocious as ever, spent an enjoyable ten minutes describing the scene to a blushing and disbelieving April Burnam, who would have liked to confirm the story with her mother but, for a variety of reasons, did not quite dare. Gradually the facts, progressively garbled as they spread through the school, came to be vaguely known by all. But as nothing official was ever said and as there was no sign of punishment for the offenders, the affair's significance seemed slowly to wane.

Interest always waned at West Hill. The boys were so fickle in their enthusiasms that fashions were always known as 'crazes'. That summer there was a craze for model aeroplanes. The previous term it had been a game called Jacks. Before that it was marbles. Card cricket and conkers were seasonal but ephemeral. *L'affaire* Roberts and *l'affaire* St Aubyn–Battersby were exciting, exotic, even momentous, but by the middle of the following week they were as stale as yesterday's national news. Commander Crabb was superseded by an EOKA terrorist outrage in Cyprus which was in turn overtaken by the latest threats from Colonel Nasser. The St Christopher's match, the Lake District shenanigans and the scholarship exams were their West Hill equivalents.

The staff, relatively elephantine as far as memory was concerned, was less inclined to forget, let alone forgive.

'Eight o'clock,' hissed Helen Battersby at a hastily contrived rendezvous in the rose garden during break, 'what can I do between eight o'clock and bedtime? She wants me to play cards with her. Silly cow. Kiss me.'

St Aubyn kissed her, lust tempered by the terror that someone might come through the rose-garden gate and catch them. Miss Battersby's teeth ground against his and he pushed her away.

'They're probably right,' he said wetly.

153

'What do you mean, right?'

'Well. You know.' He straightened his tie which had suffered during the junior matron's latest attack.

'I don't know anything,' said Miss Battersby, 'but I'm not going to let the Burnams ruin my love life.'

St Aubyn said nothing. He was hopelessly torn between carnal desire and the nagging fear that one more false step would remove him from the officer class and consign him to life's sergeants' mess or worse. Cavalry to Catering Corps; merchant banking to the hotel business. He shuddered, then looked at Miss Battersby and let her kiss him.

The hours after eight had certainly been the most sexually productive for St Aubyn and Battersby. In a sense they were pioneers – emerging from an age in which sex, like alcohol, was taboo before dusk. The relationship was relegated temporarily to the back burner where, like Miss Battersby, though unlike the more tepid St Aubyn, it simmered. It was possible to hold hands before lunchtime; possible to kiss in the rose garden during break, and neck in the long grass before the sun was over the yardarm. But for the time being they went no farther. There was a tacit understanding between them that there would only be a repeat of the Lake District, which counted, they both reckoned, as 'heavy petting', either when it was dark or when they had more than a pint of shandy to drink. St Aubyn, in particular, was not ready for the reality of sex in the sober light of day.

Batty Roberts stayed away from the Plume of Feathers but not from the bottle. O'Rourke and Oily Watkins watched with dismayed resignation. He was never drunk during school hours, but never entirely sober, coming down for breakfast breath heavy with peppermint and alcohol, like, thought O'Rourke who produced the analogy from a fertile imagination rather than first-hand experience, a tart hung over on crème de menthe. In the evenings, despite the other men's efforts to involve him, he simply retired to his room and, as far as they could see, drank himself into a stupor. They tried bridge, but neither Roberts nor St Aubyn were able to concentrate. They tried hiding bottles, but he always found them and then, with alcoholic cunning, hid them himself so efficiently that no one else discovered them and he sometimes forgot. O'Rourke found one under the bonnet of his MG; two in the lavatory cistern.

And the religious obsession remained. In the evenings from his room they could hear him apparently reading out loud from the psalms, or playing Gregorian chants on his gramophone. O'Rourke tried several times to engage him in philosophical debate but with unsatisfactory results. It resulted either in a rambling monologue based on the imminence of the Second Coming and peppered with quotations from the book of Revelation, or in a superior silence which meant he would not demean himself by discussing God with pagans.

Roberts continued to refuse to take professional advice over his drinking but O'Rourke thought he might be persuaded to listen to a professional over religion. There was no point in having anything to do with the local Church of England padre, a whey-faced bigot and monologuist who would have had no sympathy and no understanding, but O'Rourke sensed that Roberts's Christianity, though muddled and unorthodox, was more Catholic than Anglican and he was also friendly with Father Hegarty, the Jesuit who ministered to the relatively small Catholic congregation in that part of Somerset. Father Hegarty was a worldly fellow who liked a jar and was fundamentally better disposed towards sinners than the righteous. O'Rourke drove to Taunton one day, found poppadums and mango chutney, and invited the priest for curry. Roberts, however, took one look at Father Hegarty and retired to bed complaining of stomach pains. He did not emerge until morning.

The situation could hardly, therefore, be described as satisfactory. O'Rourke counted off the days until the end of term as eagerly as any homesick newbug. But, despite the tension, there were no real eruptions. The threat was always there, but as one overwrought day succeeded another, O'Rourke became lugubriously optimistic. That summer he was due to stay with his married sister in Oughterard, County Galway. There would be salmon fishing. Later he was treating himself to a brief trip to Tangier, if funds allowed. He tried to concentrate on these two pleasing prospects and to get through the West Hill days on automatic pilot. Next term there would be no Roberts, no St Aubyn, no nubile matron. Normality once more. Meanwhile it was best to daydream and pray.

Burnam, however, fretted. This was natural. Not only was it in his nature, he was the boss, the CO, the managing director. It was his school. If things fell apart and the centre failed to hold, it was his life which suffered. Schools could be killed by scandal. The word got round disturbingly fast. Parents removed their offspring and they talked to other potential parents.

'West Hill?'

'Going through rather a bad patch, I hear.'

'Really?'

'Burnam's judgement seems to have gone. Hired a dypsomaniac temporary master who turned out to be some sort of religious freak. And on top of that, another of the staff was found fornicating with one of the matrons in the garden.'

'You don't mean it?'

' 'fraid so. Freddie Baskerville's taken his boy away and sent him to King's Taunton Junior.'

The thought of this conversation taking place in the nation's officers' messes and wardrooms, in churchyards after matins, worst of all, in the senior commonrooms of public schools, kept Burnam awake at night. Perhaps he should have sent them all packing. It would have meant much more work for the survivors but it would also have meant safety. On the other hand, he couldn't have sacked the history master just before the scholarship exams. And having St Aubyn meant that he himself no longer had to take any of the junior classes for divinity or general knowledge. And he was terribly useful for lower-school games. Mrs Hildesley could have done without Helen Battersby, but it would have put an unnecessary strain on her and Miss Sparrow. Clarissa would have had to stand in on Mrs Hildesley's days off.

And, and, and. But, but, but. The CO lay awake, fidgeting with the sheets, counting sheep, plumping the pillow, irritated beyond measure by his wife's light, contented snore. He cursed Gabbitas, Thring; he inveighed against Cambridge for being the instrument of his meeting with St Aubyn *père*. He found himself lingering over Helen Battersby's nubility and tried prayer as a mental cold shower but with only partial success. Finally he fell asleep only to wake early and tired and as short-tempered as the people in the Horlicks advertisement.

Despite their apprehensions, therefore, all concerned found the scholarship exams, when they came, a welcome relief from a less than usually happy ship. The waiting itself had been a strain but, now that it was upon them, all three candidates were surprised to find themselves quite exhilarated and even mildly optimistic.

'It's like the chap in the barrel, going over Niagara Falls,' said Stack on the morning of departure for their various schools.

'What on earth do you mean?' asked Fieldhouse. 'I don't feel in the least like a man in a barrel.'

'It's a simile, silly,' said Stack impatiently, 'poetic licence. What I mean is, if you were in a barrel bowling along towards Niagara Falls, you'd feel jolly nervous. Sick probably.'

'Ugh,' said Porter, grinning. 'Think of the pong, being sick in a barrel.'

Stack persevered. 'The point is,' he said, 'that waiting to go over the falls is worse than actually going over them itself.'

'Unless the barrel breaks and you're drowned,' said Fieldhouse reasonably.

'No, but I mean, you wouldn't know much about it. It would all be over so quickly.'

'You can't tell me,' said Porter, 'that thinking about being drowned in Niagara Falls is worse than *really* being drowned.'

'That's not what I said.'

'Yes, it is.'

'No, it isn't.'

'Yes, it is.'

'I don't see,' Fieldhouse butted into this impasse with more sweet reason, 'what all this has to do with the scholarship exams.'

'It's got a lot to do with it.' Stack was the epitome of his nickname. A mighty atom on the point of fission. 'Stupid. We're all in our barrels waiting, waiting, waiting, and now it's over. Niagara's here.'

157

'I shouldn't try that simile in your English essay,' said Porter, 'I don't think they'd understand it either.'

'Oh,' Stack subsided, 'what a relief it will be next term to be surrounded by real brains and not a lot of dumkopfs like you lot.'

Dorothy Travis-Gunn drove Stack to Winchester; his parents took Fieldhouse to Sherborne; and the Burnams themselves chaperoned Porter on his excursion to Marlborough. Somebody had to do it since the Commander and his wife were away on Her Majesty's Service. An aunt could have been found to do the job, but the Burnams volunteered happily enough. It gave the CO a chance to cement his old-boy network of useful connections among the Marlborough housemasters and it gave both of them a much needed break. They would only be away for a single night because Marlborough had promised to get Porter to the railway station in Newbury for the return journey. Someone from West Hill would meet him in Taunton. The school would be in O'Rourke's care for a couple of days and O'Rourke would have Mrs Hildesley as his formidable adjutant. Between them they would be more than a match for the staff's three potential troublemakers. A more imposing team, Somerset ruefully half admitted, than Clarissa and himself.

Not that he ever thought of himself as a bad headmaster, but as he passed on through middle age he was less comfortable with his career. When he had first bought West Hill the idea that he was buying himself a job which he might not have achieved on his merits had never occurred to him. Now, increasingly, it haunted him. He consoled himself with the thought that he had turned West Hill from an indifferent, slothful dumping ground of a school into an efficient and effective supplier of well-mannered, well-educated thirteen-year-olds to the public schools. That was no mean achievement.

And yet it was not enough. He envied other men their progress. He was embittered by the way his contemporaries climbed the ladders of their chosen professions, their achievements recognized in rank, title, pay and perks. *He* could only look forward to another twenty or so years of the same, after which he would sell the school, invest the capital and retire with Clarissa to a cottage with wisteria on the walls and roses in the garden. Not for him the imperious ascent from colonel to brigadier to general to field marshal or from third to second to first secretary and then ambassador. Because prep schools were little family businesses, privately owned cottage industries, he could not even, like a public-school head, move from headmaster of a minor school to a major one. A public-school headmaster could at least aspire to Eton, but there was no way a prep-school head could aim for the top job at the Dragon. That appointment was spoken for.

There was a way out, of course, and he acknowledged to himself if to no one else, not even Clarissa, that he took it more and more. He still had a genuinely altruistic commitment to traditional values and standards, all the more so in what he perceived as an uncertain world where change was becoming a virtue and no one, whether they were wogs, like Nasser, or oiks like this John Osborne beast, seemed to know their place any longer. But whereas his boys had once been little more than pawns in his life game, they were now becoming the game itself. Like a parent who suddenly realizes that he has passed his hopes on to his children because, realistically, he can no longer entertain them for himself, so Burnam was beginning to live vicariously through his boys. Through his daughters too, naturally, but for him girls were different. He was ambitious, ruthlessly so, for their future happiness, but he was traditional in those ambitions. He wanted them to marry well and live happily ever after, just as their mother had done.

But his aspirations for the boys were now the fierce ambitions of his youth. *He* had wanted to be fit for field marshal, needed to score a hundred before lunch at Lord's; to win at all costs. That was no longer possible for him but it was for them. *They* still had the chance of a future and so, without quite realizing it, he began to live through them. In the old days when a boy went to Winchester or Sherborne or Marlborough to take the scholarship, they had gone as his champions, representing himself and the school, in the hope that they could return and lay the award at Burnam's feet as a farewell tribute. Now when they went off to compete, he went with them. This term, for the first time in his life, he *was* Stack and Porter and Fieldhouse, and he willed them to win because he himself was past winning. The baton was theirs now and he knew it. *His* youthful promise was broken – *theirs* was still intact.

The getting-up bell had not yet rung but West Hill was already stirring. In the kitchen Elsie was busy burning the porridge on the Aga; Miss Battersby, woken early by bird-song, was turning the pages of a Barbara Cartland romance; her superior, Mrs Hildesley, was preparing pills and therm-ometers for three boys in the sickroom with strep throats; Clarissa Burnam was puckering her lips at the mirror and wondering if she had overdone the cherry red. In his study her husband's wireless set gave news of the British capture of EOKA terrorists in Cyprus. Most important, a boy on a scarlet bicycle had just come from the village, bearing three yellow envelopes.

Somerset Burnam sat at his desk and looked at them.

'What do you think, Muggins,' he said eventually, 'dare we open them?'

The dog stared at him, then turned away and lowered its head onto its paws with a heavy sigh.

Burnam continued to gaze at the envelopes for a few seconds, then shook himself like a man waking and picked the paperknife from a little tray of office equipment neatly arranged on the desktop. He knew it was good news. The schools sent the bad news by letter. At least that was what they usually did. The custom might have changed. If it was very bad news it might be telegrammed. If they had failed to even get a place. But no, that was not possible. Finally he selected one of the envelopes, slit it with surgical dexterity, opened, read, and smiled. Good news, not spectacularly so, but still good. Better, if he was honest with himself, than he had expected. He opened the second and his smile widened. Now that *was* good. Not fantastic. Not incredible. But an awfully good show. Already this was the best academic year since '51 when Bockett got the Pye-Smith at Eton.

160

Two down and one to go. He paused and swallowed.

'Well, Muggins,' he said, 'fingers crossed.' But the dog did not look up. The CO hesitated a second, knife poised, then cut and removed the final telegram.

'Oh,' he said out loud, 'now that does call for some sort of celebration. Mighty Atom indeed! It certainly is a great day for the Irish.' Not that Stack was in the least Irish.

Muggins raised his head an inch or two and looked at him from one eye. He did not seem impressed.

The CO told Clarissa first, then went to the dormitories, Wolfe first, then Alfred, and finally Auchinleck. Descending order of academic achievement. A Winchester scholarship, fourth place on the roll, for Stack; a minor scholarship at Marlborough for Porter; and an exhibition at Sherborne for Fieldhouse. It was an unprecedented West Hill hat trick. Probably also a fair reflection of the boys' abilities, though Burnam had reservations about Stack and he wondered if Marlborough were not undervaluing Porter. He personally thought Porter more mature; a better college man. It was why he had made him head of school. He had doubts about Stack. There were flaws there. The St Christopher's match had demonstrated that. But the scholarships were awarded for academic achievement not character. A pity in some respects, but that was the way they arranged these things. It was ludicrous to quibble. West Hill had scored a triumph. Better than beating St Christopher's. Compensation for the night of the naked matron. He would mark it with a whole day's holiday and a school excursion to the Quantocks with a picnic for all.

'Worth a day off, wouldn't you say?' The Mighty Atom's freckled face was dancing happiness. '*Three* awards. That's a record. Aren't we clever!'

The three winners were sitting on Porter's bed in Alfred. A procession of other boys passed in and out.

'Congratulations, Stack! Well done, Porter! Terrific effort, Fieldhouse.'

'Lucky Queenie Roberts did all that stuff on Henry VIII,' said Stack, 'we all got a Henry VIII question, didn't we?'

161

'I got one but I didn't do it,' said Fieldhouse. 'I did the building of Stonehenge instead.'

'Queenie gave us that too,' said Porter.

Fieldhouse smiled. 'He said they'd both come up and they did. I don't think he's as barmy as he makes out.'

'Fluke,' said Stack.

'Have it your own way.' Fieldhouse was always anxious to give credit, due or not. 'But it's a jolly interesting coincidence.'

'I really thought I'd made a mess of the Latin translation,' said Stack, 'it was only boring old Caesar but there was one sentence I just couldn't get.'

'I know I did badly on the French prose.' Porter pulled a face. 'I just couldn't remember what the French for owl was.'

'So what did you put?'

'I put "*oiseau*".'

'Oh, well,' Stack giggled, 'at least you didn't put "*genou*".'

'I really didn't think I'd have got anything,' said Fieldhouse. 'I mean, I'm sure I could have done much better. And an awful lot of the others looked terrifically bright. You should have heard them swanking afterwards. I didn't think I had a hope.'

'It's much better not to think you've done well,' said Stack. 'Scatty's always telling me that. He said during the war that was always when things went wrong. You'd think you'd got the Jerries on the run and suddenly there'd be reinforcements, or you'd run into an ambush or something. It doesn't pay to be pleased with yourself.'

'Well,' Porter disagreed, 'I'm pleased with myself now. And the CO's obviously pleased. And I bet all our parents will be pleased.'

'No, but you know what I mean. Of course we can be pleased now but we couldn't earlier.'

Porter laughed. 'Like going over Niagara Falls in a barrel.'

'Oh, very funny. Ha, ha.' Stack was too elated to take genuine offence but self-respect demanded some reaction. He hit Porter with a pillow before scampering off to get dressed.

* * *

162

West Hill only went through the motions of work that day. The bush telegraph had spread the news to everyone by breakfast, but the CO had to make the formal announcement at prayers together with the news that a whole school holiday with an expedition to the Quantocks would commemorate the happy event. Date to be announced later. Like other victorious commanders after battle, he also acknowledged the God who had been so evidently on the West Hill side.

'We thank thee, O Lord, for looking kindly on our scholarship candidates. On Donald Stack at Winchester, on William Porter at Marlborough, and on Adrian Fieldhouse at Sherborne. Continue to aid us, we beseech thee, to guide us daily in all our endeavours at both work and play that we may always serve thee in our thoughts and in our deeds, striving always to please thee, not wasting our lives in evil thoughts or idle pastimes. We thank thee for these and all thy other blessings. Through Jesus Christ Our Lord.'

Short pause and a properly united 'Amen'. The CO was extremely adroit at the instant prayer to suit any occasion. Very important attribute of the successful headmaster, indeed of the leader and public figure of all kinds and in all walks of life, though not something that was taught at West Hill, except by example. It should be recorded, however, that Donald Stack was only just able to suppress an irreverent titter. 'What's God got to do with it?' he asked Porter afterwards. 'Personally I'd sooner say "thank thee, O Queenie Roberts!" '

Before the morning was ended all members of staff had shaken the scholars by the hand and expressed congratulations according to their individual style.

'*Bon effort*,' from O'Rourke to Stack, 'in fact, *un très bon effort*. I suppose now you'll go from unbearable to insufferable. Formidable.' He pronounced 'formidable' *à la français*, as he put it.

'Thrilling,' said Helen Battersby to Porter, 'too thrilling for words. I bet your parents are pleased.'

Roberts clasped Fieldhouse's hands, looked him a little rheumily in the eyes and declared, 'The headmaster was quite right when he asked us to thank God. If you put your trust in the Lord, you can move mountains.'

163

Fieldhouse looked down at the floor and said, 'Yes, sir.' Later he said to the others, very seriously, 'I think Queenie Roberts is bonkers. I mean seriously.'

St Aubyn was actually a little peeved, since he had never won a scholarship or an exhibition anywhere.

'It must mean a great deal to you,' he said to the three of them as they drank their breaktime milk.

'Three hundred pounds a year, sir,' replied Stack, beaming with cream-rimmed lips, like Coco the clown.

David St Aubyn did not laugh, but this was not a day for discipline.

'You realize,' said Stack later on after all three had been ceremoniously 'bumped', like Tom Brown in the blanket, by their fellow members of the cricket team (another piece of informal but traditional West Hill ritual), 'that term's over as far as we're concerned. We don't have to do a stroke. We don't even have to obey the rules.'

'Come on.' The three of them were lying on the grassy bank in front of the pavilion, waiting for the CO to come and conduct First XI cricket practice. Porter split the blade of grass he had been chewing and blew through it with his hands clasped. It made a muted shriek, a victim screaming through an attacker's hand. 'We may not have to do much work,' he said, throwing the grass away, 'but we still have to stick to the rules. By the way, do you say Compton like "from" or like "lump". "Frompton" or "Lumpton"? "Compton" or "Cumpton"?'

'Does it matter?'

'The CO says "Cumton",' said Fieldhouse meditatively.

'He would,' said Porter. 'I wonder what Compton says.' He pronounced it like the CO.

'Bound to say Compton,' said Fieldhouse, pronouncing it like 'romp' rather than 'rump'.

'Why?' Porter picked up another blade of grass and began to tear it too down the middle.

'Because,' replied Fieldhouse, 'it's the non-U way. And you can tell Compton's non-U because of the Brylcreem advertisement.'

They all laughed.

'Have you smelled Brylcreem?' asked Stack. 'I got some out of a machine once, in the loo at Waterloo Station. It's foul.'

164

'And definitely non-U.'

'Miss Sparrow said "serviette" yesterday,' said Field-house. 'She told Bosanquet to put his serviette back in his table napkin ring.'

They all laughed again, giggling, carefree. It was fun to be lucky thirteen.

'Seriously though,' Stack put on a different voice, an octave or two lower, to demonstrate the degree of seriousness intended, though his monkey face and ink-stained blue Aer-tex shirt made it difficult to take too seriously (unless evidently you were a Winchester examiner), 'we *could* break the rules and get away with it.'

'What's that got to do with Compton or Cumpton?'

'Or U and non-U?'

'Oh, come on, you two,' Stack showed signs of becoming peevish, 'I'm trying to be serious.'

'But not doing too well at it.' Porter was determined to be frivolous. The day demanded it.

'Oh, let him be serious if he wants to be,' Fieldhouse was placatory as so often. 'I disagree. Seriously. I don't think we can break the rules just because we've finished our exams.'

'The CO's never going to do anything to West Hill people who've just won scholarships. We're too precious.'

'I wouldn't bank on it,' said Porter.

'All right,' said Stack, 'suppose he came up here and found us smoking. What do you think he'd do?'

'Beat us,' Fieldhouse spoke with an earnest certainty, 'or expel us.'

'Expel us!' Stack pulled a daisy out of the bank with unexpected violence. 'Can you imagine that? Spoil everything. For one of the few times in his life he has the chance to gloat over that horrible old humbug, Ormsby-Percival, at St Christopher's. Do you imagine he'd throw that away just because he found us smoking?'

Porter scratched the back of his head. He was inclined to scurf. 'Are you talking about theory or practice?' he asked.

'Both,' said Stack. 'But I'm more interested in the practice than the theory. What I reckon is that the CO's pathetically anxious to get through this term without any trouble – otherwise he'd have sacked at least three of the staff after that night in the Lake District. If he didn't sack them, then I don't think it's likely he'll sack us. Whatever we do.'

'They're all temps. They're leaving at the end of term anyway.'

'So are we.'

'That's different.'

'No.'

They sat for a moment's thought, chewing grass with bovine concentration.

'That's still theory,' said Porter at last. 'What about practice? What have you got in mind? You're obviously up to something.'

'Yes,' said Stack, grinning, 'I'm up to something. I'll tell you later though. The CO's coming.' And he was. Muggins lolloped up the bank and licked Stack's face as they heard the headmaster's shout: 'Come on, you chaps. Wakey, wakey, rise and shine.'

As it was, Stack did not confide his plan until the day of the scholarship holiday that Thursday. For the whole week the debate about their exemption from punishment continued, largely inconclusively. Neither Fieldhouse nor Porter found it particularly interesting since both were natural conformists to whom the keeping of rules came more naturally than the breaking of them. They thrived, too, on authority's approval, much preferring the CO's carrot to his stick. Stack seemed not to mind one way or the other. He cared a little what his mother thought of him, and perhaps about Scatty's opinion; but really the only person he respected enough to kowtow to was his father. Which was convenient. Stack VC, being dead, was an easy ikon to please. Whatever Stack decided was right could be justified with the thought that his father would have wanted it that way and approved. These endorsements were obviously a fiction and as Stack grew older so the fiction became more farfetched. Eventually the father of his imagining would have justified anything provided his son wanted it. This was a curious perversion of parental influence but it did help to explain Donald's relative indifference to authority.

The sun shone on the holiday, which was a blessing but not an essential one. Little boys were perfectly happy in mud and rain. They just got dirtier than in sunshine. The weather

166

never spoiled a day on the Quantocks, though precisely what it was that boys so enjoyed was never entirely clear to the adults. Perhaps it was just the illusion of freedom – the same appeal as the dingle. There was nothing to 'do' on the hills. You could walk or run or lie about in heaps. You could look at the views and smell the bracken and the mustiness of last year's leaves. In autumn you could harvest whortleberries for straining through handkerchiefs (to matron's outrage) and turning into 'wort wine'. You could sometimes find deer.

But these were Fotherington-Thomas pleasures. 'Hello, birds. Hello, sky.' Small boys were supposed to be boorish Molesworths, not the sort of people to enjoy mooning about the countryside communing with nature like Lakeland poets. Yet in a robust, exuberant, small-boy manner, that is what they did. No Wordsworth and Coleridge plotting of ballads and epic verses. If there was chatter it would be the usual Stirling Moss/Mike Hawthorne and Lindwall/Trueman argument; high-spirited fantasy about walking across the Sahara or favourite meals of all time. Usually, however, they did not say anything much; just absorbed the sights and the smells of Somerset; the quilt of arable below them to the south and the misty outlines of Flat Holm and Steep Holm in the muddy Bristol Channel to the north. Perhaps there was some magic in the hills, an echo of Arthurian England at Tristram Stone above the dusty quarry or even of opium-drugged Coleridge hiking from his cottage at Nether Stowey to William and Dorothy at Alfoxden. Whatever the reason, West Hill boys enjoyed the Quantocks with an innocent simplicity which encouraged their teachers as much as it surprised them.

'Do you think we should buy some ciggies at Old Ma Giles?' asked Stack as the bus strained up Cothelstone Hill. The diesel-powered coach, driven by the younger of the coach company's owners, managed the gradient quite well; the older bus, prewar and petrol drinking, coaxed on by the senior partner, coughed and hacked like a pensioner.

'You know it's out of bounds,' said Porter primly, as the elder bus crunched gears and threatened momentarily to roll back towards Nether King's Compton, 'besides she'd never sell them to us.'

'She might.'

'I don't know why you're so keen to break rules. You don't even like smoking. They made you sick in Malta.'

'That was the beer, not the smoking.'

Porter shrugged. 'You can try if you must,' he said, 'but I'm not having anything to do with it.'

The buses took them to a point at the edge of a wood. There the tarmac gave way to the dirt track which ran along the spine of the hills almost as far as Minehead. The CO and family were waiting for them by the Land-Rover. They had come on ahead. The CO held a heavy walking stick and had a khaki army surplus waterbottle slung over one shoulder. Clarissa wore shoes as sensible as her husband's but no stick. The girls were in the school games uniform of shorts, light Aertex shirt and Clark's sandals. They exuded an air of happy family that was catching.

'Righty-ho, then,' said Burnam when everyone had disembarked and gathered round. 'You all know the drill. Everyone must stay with their group. I don't want anyone larking off on their own and getting lost. Remember to shut gates behind you. No litter. No fires. And everyone meet over there,' he waved his stick up the track towards the black remains of a tree, 'by the blasted oak at one o'clock sharp. OK. Have a good morning.'

A babble of excitement and the school, split into prearranged parties of three and four, scurried off in all directions. Porter, Fieldhouse and Stack naturally comprised one group.

'Let's not go too far,' said Stack. 'I want to talk to you both.'

'Sounds exciting,' said Porter.

'No, seriously.'

'Oh, boo to "seriously",' said Porter. 'I want to be silly.'

'Do we have to have a serious talk?' Fieldhouse sounded petulant. 'I think Winchester's gone to your head. You're always having serious talks. Can't we just enjoy ourselves?'

Stack shrugged. 'You don't have to listen,' he said. 'No one's forcing you.'

'Too late now,' muttered Fieldhouse sulkily. 'No larking off on your own was what the CO said. I have to stay with you.'

'Oh, balls,' said Stack. 'We've been through all that. The

168

CO doesn't mean *us*. We can do as we like. The rules don't count. That's what I want to talk to you about. Seriously.'

For about a quarter of an hour they walked the track, flicking at persistent flies with switches of bracken, until they came to the head of a combe. Fifty yards below they could see a stream sparkling out of the hillside, cutting a path through the undergrowth until it acquired a fringe of scrubby trees and bushes before disappearing into thick woods.

'Let's sit by the water,' said Stack, and led the way downhill, running, leaping, watchful for rabbit holes, hidden boulders and other hazards.

'Righty-ho, then, as our beloved headmaster would say,' he began when their descent was complete and they were sitting, shoes off, feet dangling in the brook.

'Let's be serious!' chorused the other two.

Stack ignored them. 'I spoke to Diggory this morning,' he said flatly.

It was very quiet on the Quantocks. The only sound was the water gently trickling down towards Nether Stowey.

'How?' asked Porter. He seemed suddenly apprehensive. 'And why? You're not going to tell me you're serious about that ridiculous idea of the pig and Eifion Hughes.'

'One question at a time, if you don't mind. Fieldhouse, you don't know anything about this, do you?'

Fieldhouse shook his head.

'In answer to your first question, I used the electric telephone. As you may have noticed, there's a call box about a hundred yards from the back gate. I rang him at six this morning.'

'What if you'd been caught?'

'No one's up at six in the morning, stupid.'

'Supposing they were?'

'I'd have made something up. Said I had to call Scatty before he went out milking. Almost true. And as I keep telling you idiots, the CO would have smiled and looked the other way.'

'It doesn't matter,' said Fieldhouse. 'He obviously got away with it. The point is, what were you ringing Diggory for? And what *is* all this about Eifion Hughes and a pig? I'm lost.'

Stack picked a pebble from the bank and threw it

169

downstream. 'It's simple,' he said. 'My stepfather's sow has a new litter. He can afford to lose one piglet. Diggory's bringing it over in the van on Saturday evening and we're going to paint it blue, grease it up and slip it into Eifion Hughes's meeting in the village hall. That'll teach those yobbos to put their wretched pigs' heads in the dingle.'

When Fieldhouse spoke again he sounded hushed to the point of flabbergast. 'You're not serious.'

Stack laughed. 'I don't understand why you two are so unconvinced by my seriousness. Of course I'm serious. What's not serious about it?'

'But you can't.'

'He can,' said Porter grimly.

'You'll never get away with it.'

'You mean,' Stack was very much the leader suddenly, '*we*'ll never get away with it. This is *our* operation. We're all in it together. If the CO won't stand up for West Hill and what's right, then we jolly well have to.'

'No, but . . .' offered Fieldhouse lamely.

'It needs all of us,' said Stack. 'I'll hold the pig because I'm used to them. Neither of you is going to be much cop at doing that and it would be an awful waste just to have him run loose down the High Street. Diggory's our getaway driver. He'll have to stay in the van and keep the engine running so we can make a quick escape. There's a side door by the boiler house. Donald, your job is to open that up for me so I can throw the pig in. Then we do a bunk back to the van and off we go. Adrian, you keep cave for Constable Taylor or anyone else who's lurking about. OK?'

'Of course it's not OK,' said Porter. 'We'd never get away with it.'

'Give me one reason why not.' Stack set his jaw.

'You just can't do it. For a start, they'll see you putting the pig through the door. They may be communists but they're not blind.'

'No, they won't. They'll all be looking the other way, drinking in the gospel according to St Eifion. We'll wait until he's been talking for five minutes or so, got them under the spell of his Welsh wizardry, then bung in the porker when they're all in a trance.'

'But they'll chase you . . . us.'

'Don't be ridiculous.' Stack sensed victory. 'They'll be far too busy trying to catch the pig. You tried holding one the other day. You know how difficult it was, even without a coat of Vaseline. It'll be charging about the place squealing and knocking people over like skittles.'

'Look,' said Fieldhouse, who had gone rather white, 'it's not the war and we're not Marine Commandos or Para-troopers. It's just not on. You can't do that sort of thing. Not in Somerset in 1956.'

'They put the pigs' heads in the dingle,' objected Stack.

'That's different.'

'It's not.'

'Yes, it is.'

'No, it isn't.'

' 'Tis.'

' 'Tisn't.'

'Oh, bloody hell!' shouted Porter. 'Stop being such babies. You're behaving like a couple of newbugs in nappies. Honestly, we're supposed to be monitors. And scholars. Surely we can discuss this sensibly.' He stood up and swatted a fly. 'What do you think would happen,' he said slowly, 'if we *were* discovered? I'm not suggesting we would be, but we might as well look on the gloomy side.'

'That's what I've been getting at all week,' said Stack. 'I don't think anything would happen.'

'Oh, come on.' Fieldhouse also stood up. Then sat down again.

'Nobody was punished for the dingle business.' Stack spoke evenly, with a sense of subdued outrage.

'Hardly anyone knew about the dingle business,' said Fieldhouse. 'But putting a pig into a political meeting's public. The press will be there. It will be all over the *Western Gazette*. It *is* different.'

'It's not a crime,' said Stack. 'It's tit for tat. A reprisal.'

'That's what General Grivas says when EOKA shoots British soldiers in the back.'

Stack flushed. 'Don't be ridiculous,' he said. 'Sometimes I don't think you know whose side you're on.'

Porter intervened again. 'If,' he reasoned, 'only the CO and a very few others knew – or suspected – we'd done it, then you could be right. But Fieldhouse has got a point.

171

Suppose we were found out and our names got in the papers, then the CO *would* have to sack us. "West Hill boys plant pig in meeting. 'Hooligans' says leading MP." Can't you see it? He'd have no option.'

Stack frowned and looked thoughtful. 'Maybe,' he said. 'But I think a lot of people would be on our side. Especially if the dingle story got out. I mean, look at that business when they kicked Aneurin Bevan down the steps of that club, White's. They didn't get expelled from the club. In fact, I bet they got stood free gin and tonics because all the other members thought Bevan got what he deserved. It would be the same here.'

'I doubt it,' said Porter. 'Let's suppose you're wrong. Just for the sake of argument. What chance have we got of being found out? Realistically.'

Stack splashed his feet in the stream and sighed. 'Practically none,' he said. 'As far as I can see, the only way would be if someone happened to be passing. But they won't. They'll all be either in the boozer or the hall. And if there *is* anyone around, we wait till they've gone.'

'How long will it take?'

'About as long as it takes Fieldhouse's friend Grivas to throw a grenade into a café in Nicosia. Diggory drives up, parks the van by the hall, we nip out with the pig, you open the door, I chuck it in, we hot-foot it back into the van, Diggory speeds off, and we're back in bed in a jiffy and Bob's your uncle.'

'That's another point,' said Fieldhouse, 'and, incidentally, you know perfectly well I don't like Grivas any more than you do – how can we be sure the CO or someone won't catch us leaving or coming back? Or realize we aren't in our beds.'

Stack was very self-assured about this. 'No one ever comes into the dormitories after lights-out unless they hear someone talking,' he said. 'We can leave some spare clothes and pillows bundled up under the sheets as a precaution, but it's very unlikely. As for catching us on the way out or back, it'll be dark enough and we'll just have to go really carefully. But we managed on the night of the Lake District thing. None of them are terribly observant, you know.'

Despite the no-messing-around, robust Church of England Christianity that had characterized their upbringing both at West Hill and at home, none of the boys appeared to be concerned about the ethics of the proposal. Even Fieldhouse, the most cautious of the trio, was only concerned with the likelihood of being found out and the severity of the consequent punishment. In so far as there were principles involved, one was the Old Testament notion of eye for eye and tooth for tooth and the other was that socking it to working-class yobbos of left-wing persuasion was, *per se*, a Good Thing. Confronted with these motives the boys might have demurred, but only because they disliked the pejorative tone. They would have dressed up their justifications. But their real reasons were much simpler. All of them, Stack in particular, found the scheme exciting and, in some ill-focused way, funny. And Porter and Fieldhouse were afraid of being thought cowardly. Especially by Stack. It was this that clinched the decision.

'Of course,' said Stack loftily, 'if you two wanted to funk it, I'll go ahead on my own with Diggory. Won't be as easy but it can be done. Or I suppose I could try to find someone else.'

After which there was no further argument, and conversation turned to cricket and some colourfully inaccurate speculation about the mechanics of sexual intercourse.

They were still discussing fornication (the Bible, at this stage in their lives, was a prime source of information and terminology) as they walked to the blasted oak for the picnic lunch.

'I suppose it's fun,' Porter remarked wistfully, 'but it must be rather uncomfortable. Does the man *have* to be on top?'

'Yes,' said Stack authoritatively, 'it doesn't work otherwise. It's like nuts and bolts. They only fit if you get the angle right. If you see what I mean.'

'How do you know?' asked Fieldhouse sceptically.

'I just do,' said Stack, whose knowledge was based on observations in the farmyard, some lurid conversations with Diggory and a vivid imagination. 'That's why women don't enjoy it as much as men. It's not as comfortable for them because they're always under the man and, of course, the man's usually heavier.'

'*Don't* women enjoy it as much as men?' asked Fieldhouse.

'Of course not, silly. That's why you have to have harlots.'

'Do you remember that time in Bible reading when you asked the CO to explain what a "woman taken in adultery" meant?'

'And he went bright pink.'

'And Porter creased up.'

'I did not.'

'Well, you sneezed in a jolly funny way.'

'It was just a sneeze.'

'Jolly funny sneeze.'

'Hey, look! Do you think she's been taken in adultery?'

It was St Aubyn and Miss Battersby, newly emerged from the bushy undergrowth, still entwined and walking slowly along the path ahead of them.

'Coo,' said Porter, 'do you think they've . . . I mean, you know? I mean, do you think they've been doing it?'

'Fornicating?' said Stack.

'Well, yes.'

'I bet you sixpence,' said Stack, 'that if they haven't been fornicating this morning they'll be fornicating after lunch.'

'OK,' said Porter, 'I'll take you on. But how do we prove it?'

'We follow them and watch, of course,' said Stack.

Burnam had driven the Land-Rover over the rough ground to the oak and it now stood in its shade with the back open. Inside the cream-coloured urns, paint chipped with age, familiar from a hundred team teas, were filled today with cold Idris orange juice. ('I drink Idris when I's dry,' said the piccaninny in the advertisement. No one considered it in the least offensive. The word 'racist' did not yet exist.) Already boys were queuing in orderly lines for drink, before moving across to trestle tables sagging under the weight of sliced white-bread sandwiches filled with Marmite, sandwich spread, spam and corned beef. The CO, half-consumed sausage roll in his right hand, was supervising food while Clarissa kept an eye on drink. There was scarcely any need because the school was sufficiently well disciplined to help itself in an orderly, well-mannered fashion, each boy knowing instinctively what was his fair share, never barging in front of another and above all never complaining, at least not out

174

loud. No West Hill boy would ever have flouted convention when it came to food and drink. Mealtime manners were vital in distinguishing them from oiks and yobbos.

'Please, sir, I want some more.'

'Now Twist,' the CO would have said, pleasantly but firmly, 'we wait until we're asked, don't we?'

Burnam was smug. His paternal view of the school was most justified at moments like this. His boys were being a credit to himself and West Hill. They were celebrating a family success with the sort of understated enthusiasm that he wanted. No raucousness; no shouting and charging about; nothing indecorous; just a well-mannered pleasure in the English countryside, in each other's company, in Marmite sandwiches and Idris orange juice. He moved slowly from group to group as they ate and drank, heard about the deer that had been spotted over towards Bicknoller and the dead rabbit someone found at the head of Holford Combe. He identified a couple of very old bird's eggs and an abandoned nest. If there was the slightest cloud on his horizon, it was the observation that both St Aubyn and Miss Battersby had grass stains on their clothing. Nor did he care for the slightly feverish expressions on their faces.

'I wondered, dear,' he said to his wife sotto voce, 'if it might be an idea to get young St Aubyn and Helen Battersby to tag along with us this afternoon.' He nodded towards the couple who were sitting apart from the main body of picnickers, obviously engrossed in each other. Clarissa followed his gaze and smiled.

'Don't be such an old spoil sport, Somerset,' she said. 'They're very sweet. Try to remember what *you* were like when you were their age.'

As far as the CO could remember, which was no farther than absolutely necessary, he was just like he was now when he was their age. But all he said was, 'Very well, darling. But don't blame me if they get up to anything silly.'

'If they get up to anything silly,' said Clarissa rattily, 'that's their business. Your responsibility only goes so far. You can't watch them every hour of the day and night. Besides, it's a holiday. Let's just enjoy it.'

Somerset Burnam sighed. 'Yes, dear,' he said and, withdrawing his eyes from the not altogether pleasing prospect of the young matron and her beau, he allowed his gaze to wander benignly over his boys.

'*My* boys,' he said to himself.

The afternoon began, like the morning, with a brief instruction from the CO about the need for shutting gates and synchronizing watches. Then the school dispersed in its little groups, fanning out to all points of the compass, eager in the effervescence of the moment. Porter, Fieldhouse and Stack were among the last to leave the picnic site, though they were careful to keep St Aubyn and Miss Battersby within stalking distance. The latter had set off in the advance guard, self-consciously careful not to hold hands, but still walking close enough to each other for Stack to feel confident of winning his sixpenny bet.

'OK,' said Stack, just as their quarry was about to disappear into dead ground, 'let's go!'

To begin with it was scarcely a stalk. The main path along the Quantock spine was littered with mini-platoons of West Hill boys, so the idea of anybody 'following' or 'being followed' was ridiculous. After a while these walkers began to disperse, peeling off into combes and copses, until only St Aubyn and Battersby, and Porter, Fieldhouse and Stack were left. The stalking group was cautious. They hid behind trees, crouched behind bushes, lay prone in the bracken and sometimes even crawled. All versed in Grandmother's Footsteps, they alternated between frantic, gambolling scampers and immobile freezes without so much as a twitch of the nostril. By standing very still they seemed to think they could make themselves invisible as an ostrich with his head in the sand. They need not have bothered. St Aubyn and Miss Battersby had eyes only for each other. They never looked back, and if they had they would have seen only idyllic English hillsides and idyllic English skies. As far as they were concerned, they were the first, last and only people on the Quantocks that afternoon. In a few moments, when they found a suitably secluded spot, they were both rather hoping that one thing might lead, as it were, to another. Which was the main reason, *pace* the scholars' fieldcraft, why they did not notice their three pursuers.

176

Whether or not they were going to move beyond 'heavy petting' was something neither St Aubyn nor Miss Battersby knew. The fervour of the morning's activities had surprised both of them since it was quite light and they were entirely sober. That they might 'go all the way' was always at the back of Miss Battersby's mind, if not farther forward, since sex was her major preoccupation. It must have occurred to St Aubyn too because a few days earlier, while having a short back and sides at a barber's near the bridge over the River Parrot in Taunton, he had noticed an advertisement for Durex contraceptives and purchased a packet of three condoms, just, he told himself, 'to be on the safe side'. He had no serious expectation of using them, but you never knew. And while actually to have carnal knowledge of Miss Battersby might be very heaven, to get her with child would be very hell. Chaps, in 1956, were still inclined to do the decent thing and a lifetime of Miss Battersby other than in bed could scarcely be contemplated. Miss Battersby did not (yet) know about this secretive purchase of rubber goods, but she was fed up to the teeth with virginity, had experienced a feeling of extreme deprivation since the imposition of the curfew and, after this morning, was very inclined to go all the way, Durex or no Durex, consequences or no consequences. She just hoped they could find somewhere a bit softer to lie on. This morning had been bumpy and, for reasons (St Aubyn's) of secrecy and discretion, they had been rather in among the bracken.

'Ooooh,' she said, and crashed her teeth against St Aubyn's in a paroxysm of frustration. Petrified, St Aubyn stared past her ear, looking for voyeurs. Seeing no one, he shut his eyes and let her get on with it.

Porter, Fieldhouse and Stack watched gleefully from prone positions fifty yards back, and continued to follow as the two unclinched and moved on towards their trysting place. Because of Miss Battersby's insistence on comfort, this turned out to be more exposed than the earlier one. She refused to lie on bracken and the first small patch of grass was sprinkled with rabbit pellets. Finally, however, they settled on a rough miniature lawn, an oasis in the middle of a sand of whortleberry and bracken. Lust made junior matron reckless. She sank on to the grass without a thought. St

177

Aubyn looked around nervously. The boys had thrown themselves flat on their stomachs. There was no one in sight.

'Suppose someone finds us,' said St Aubyn. 'It's a bit exposed.'

'We'll hear them crashing through the bracken,' said Miss Battersby. 'Come and lie down.'

He looked round once more, feeling inexplicably uneasy, but there was still no one to be seen, so he did as he was told and allowed himself to be attacked by eager limbs and lips.

'I think they've started,' hissed Stack, shading his eyes against the sun, 'but it's difficult to see. Let's get a bit closer.'

They were still fifty yards off.

Fieldhouse hesitated. Porter equivocated. Stack slid through the undergrowth like a seal on rocks; sinuous but awkward.

'Shh. For heaven's sake, go slower,' whispered Porter.

Stack obliged.

After a few yards Porter crawled alongside. 'How do we know where they are?' he asked. 'We might as well be in the jungle. We're going to look pretty silly if we suddenly crawl into them in the middle of . . . well . . . you know.' Stack gingerly got to his knees and peered out of the greenery.

'Still some way away,' he said. 'Listen.'

All three listened hard.

'I can't hear anything.' Fieldhouse had drawn level too.

'Heavy breathing and grunts,' said Stack. 'It's like animals. You should hear sheep.'

'I still can't hear anything,' complained Fieldhouse. 'Can you see anything?'

'I think,' said Stack, squinting, 'I can see the bracken sort of shaking, but I can't actually see them. Tell you what though, there's a tree just ahead. If I climb it, I should be able to get a good view.'

It was a hawthorn and immensely old, to judge from its size. The usual hawthorn was little more than a shrub but this was unquestionably a proper tree. Its gnarled twists and forks made it look climbable though it was also, as is the way with hawthorns, prickly. The three boys crouched at its foot and looked up.

'You can't climb that,' said Porter.

178

Stack considered the tree with a professional's eye, like a mountaineer plotting the safest way up the North Face.

'Yes,' he said at last, 'I can climb that.'

'You'll tear your hands to shreds. And your shirt. Matron will have a fit.'

'Oh, bollocks,' he said, 'not if I'm careful.' He was the school's best gymnast. The facial features were not his only simian characteristic. On the ropes under the cedar by the front drive he could play like a baby gorilla, shinning up them in seconds and then swinging from one to another with apish arms and legs almost double-jointed, fingers, huge and prehensile, like elastic carrots. The hawthorn had no terrors.

'Won't they hear you?' Fieldhouse whispered, even more softly than the other two. He was unhappy, not just because he was afraid of being discovered but because he instinctively disliked the role of voyeur. He was also embarrassed by the thought of what he might see.

'They'll be much too busy to bother with me. Besides, they'll assume I'm a bird or a squirrel or something.'

'Supposing they look up,' said Porter. 'Since when did birds and squirrels wear Aertex shirts?'

'They won't look up.' Stack spoke with authority. 'They're far too busy looking at each other.'

The first few feet were easy enough. The other two watched him move carefully upwards, testing each foot and handhold gingerly before committing his weight. The tree seemed solid.

'I can see them,' he called down when he was about six feet up. He was still whispering but so loud that it seemed to Porter and Fieldhouse that every human on the hills must have heard. But there was no reaction from the loving couple, who were, as Stack had surmised, engrossed in each other to the point where the outside world would not interrupt them unless it announced itself very loudly indeed. Miss Battersby's bra was unhooked and her dress had ridden up around her thighs. She had undone all but the bottom button of his shirt. Both pairs of hands were exploring naked flesh, though both were still, just, above the waist. Their legs were entangled, their mouths pressed close together, apart from an occasional pause for breath, and they moved with a passionate restlessness from side by side to Miss Battersby on top to St Aubyn on top. Stack, mesmerized and dry-mouthed with prurience, considered his sixpence as good as won.

Unfortunately his excitement, like the lovers', made him careless. His view of them was adequate but not perfect. Occasionally they rolled out of sight. Bits of bracken kept getting in his way. He climbed another foot or two, but he still could not see them as well as he would have liked. He was keen to witness every detail.

From below, Porter and Fieldhouse watched with increasing anxiety. He was at least ten feet up.

'Stack,' whispered Porter, 'for heaven's sake, be careful. Don't go any farther.'

Stack did not listen. There was a long branch sticking out in the direction of St Aubyn and Miss Battersby. It was not terribly thick but, he reckoned, if he lay flat along it and inched his way forward, testing as he went, it would probably hold. As soon as it started to give, he would stop or retreat. He could see that master and junior matron were getting really serious. St Aubyn's shirt tails were out of his trousers. Miss Battersby's dress had ridden higher, so high that he could see the white of her knickers. She seemed to be trying to cross her legs behind St Aubyn's back. Stack inched farther along the bough, willing the dress to rise still farther, remembering the glimpse of Miss Battersby's nakedness in the Lake District, the excitement of it. Surely, surely those so white knickers would not stay on much longer . . .

And then he fell. The boys below could see it coming. They tried to warn him, but he was so absorbed in his vicarious sex that he failed to notice the ominous bending of the bough beneath him; couldn't see how thin it had become; didn't hear until much much too late the ominous creak of tortured hawthorn; didn't hear it until the first tentative sighs of breaking wood became a shriek, a crack, a horrid irreversible rupture which sent him falling, falling. And then the pain.

A stuck pig wasn't in it, thought Porter, even though he had never heard a pig being stuck. The noise was dreadful. Scarcely human. Not intelligible. A weeping falsetto of anguish and torment.

For a second both boys continued to lie where they were,

too shocked to do anything but stay rigid and hope that somehow what had happened would reverse itself and unhappen, leaving Stack up in the tree, the lovers in each other's arms and legs, and all right with the world. But the screaming continued, and from its incoherence there began to emerge the barely discernible word 'Help!' repeated again and again almost as if it was being offered as a panacea, the word itself a relief to the pain.

'Come on!' Porter knew it was a mindless command, even as he uttered it. 'We must *do* something!'

There was obviously no future in trying to hide their presence from St Aubyn and Miss Battersby now. The boys stood hurriedly and rushed to the side of their fallen comrade. He was lying on his side with his right leg twisted under him at an angle so unnatural that even Porter, inexperienced as he was, knew that it must be broken. A half-forgotten fragment from *Scouting for Boys*, bolstered by a long ago first-aid lesson from Oily Watkins, warned Porter that the one thing one must never do was to move the patient. If you did there was a danger of haemorrhaging. A cup of tea was a good idea but the nearest cup of tea was probably five miles away in Nether Stowey. He dimly remembered Oily Watkins teaching them to tie a tourniquet. You ripped your shirt up and wrapped it very tightly round the injured limb. But that was to stop bleeding, not mend breakages.

Five years of West Hill had prepared them for the scholarship exam but not for this. Both boys stood above Stack for a second or so, totally nonplussed. Then Fieldhouse bent down and asked, in a terrified but oddly matter-of-fact voice, 'Are you all right?'

'Of course he's not all right. He's bloody hurt. What the bloody hell do you think you little bleeders are bloody well doing, anyway?'

St Aubyn, dishevelled, puce with rage, embarrassment and frustrated passion, burst out of the bracken, closely followed by Miss Battersby, hastily hooking her bra with one hand and smoothing her dress with the other. She too was a high colour.

'It's broken,' she said, kneeling beside the victim. 'Poor little sod. I bet it hurts.'

'Serve him bloody well right,' said St Aubyn. 'You realize

181

what they were bloody well doing? They were bloody spying on us, that's what they were bloody doing.'

'Oh, do stop swearing and do something useful.' Frustration did not improve Miss Battersby's temper. Really, when all was said and done, David was just a child. Oh for an older man.

'Such as?' St Aubyn glowered. Stack continued to cry on the ground, the full-blooded screams having given way to a softer though persistent whimper.

'Oh, stop snivelling, you pathetic little tick.' St Aubyn looked as if he might have kicked the boy.

Miss Battersby, in turn, looked as if she might kick St Aubyn. The boys appeared to have impaired a beautiful relationship, even if only temporarily.

'He has broken his leg,' she said, with an unnerving deliberation, 'and if you had broken your leg I've no doubt you would be lying there snivelling, as you so charitably put it.' Her magnificent breasts heaved. 'Now, for Pete's sake, go and find Mr Burnam and get him to bring the Land-Rover as near as poss so we can get him to hospital.'

St Aubyn's lip twitched wetly but he said nothing, simply turned and hurried away at a limp trot.

'And you boys,' she turned her attention to Fieldhouse and Porter, 'if you run down there,' she pointed in the direction of their alfresco double bed, 'you'll find Mr St Aubyn's jacket. And while you're at it, take your shirts off. He mustn't catch cold. Bring the jacket back while I cover him up with the shirts.'

The boys ran off, impressed by the unsuspected authority in the junior matron's demeanour.

'You're going to be all right, Donald dear,' she soothed, arranging the flimsy Aertex shirts over his legs and arms as best she could. 'You're going to be all right. Just don't try to move.' She took his hands in hers and held them very tightly, letting him squeeze with his fingernails so hard that she almost cried out herself. Donald sobbed. But later he would fantasize about this scene all through adolescence.

It seemed an eternity before help arrived, but it was actually only half an hour later that they heard the throb of the Land-

Rover high on the hill, followed by Muggins's bark and the staccato commands and queries of the CO in his most commanding-officer mood.

They could hear his 'Righty-hos' echoing across the combe, peremptory, authoritative, gentlemanly; an expression of officer-class Englishness in emergency; the sort of noise that sprayed the globe pink. As they came closer, a softer counterpoint could be discerned. Docile wife and cowed subordinate mooed acquiescence.

Miss Battersby relinquished Stack's hands and stood, waving to attract attention. The rescuing party waved back, CO in the lead. Burnam's waterbottle still hung at his side, strap across his chest like a Sam Browne. He hacked at the bracken with his stout stick: a Quantock Livingstone, a West Country Baden-Powell.

'Righty-ho,' he called, 'everyone keep absolutely calm. St Aubyn and I'll chair-lift him up to the Land-Rover and we'll have him into Taunton General in a jiffy. There's no need to panic.'

Then, arriving, he knelt beside the injured boy and thrust the mouth of the waterbottle between his lips, gently but firmly, and certainly not asking if he was thirsty.

'Righty-ho,' he said, 'everything's under control, Donald. You're going to be all right. Just keep a stiff upper lip and bite on the bullet.'

Porter, standing a yard behind the kneeling CO, caught Miss Battersby's eye and could not suppress a giggly, cheeky grin.

Miss Battersby winked.

8

Stack's plaster cast and crutches were objects of both merriment and admiration. There was something undeniably comic about the energetic, athletic little boy limping and lurching about West Hill. Stack thought it quite funny himself. But they were also symbols of pain endured and therefore of courage.

'Gosh, Stack, did it hurt dreadfully?' asked the boys in his dormitory. Stack managed to convey the impression that it had indeed been painful beyond belief, but that he had obeyed the CO's injunction about stiffening his lip and biting on the bullet. He did not say it in so many words, but this only enhanced his status. At West Hill it was bad form to blow one's trumpet. Understatement was the preferred option, and Stack's self-deprecating little smile, slight shrug of the shoulders and 'Well, it was a bit painful, actually' was well calculated. He was more of a school hero than ever. The entire staff, with the exception of David St Aubyn, signed his cast.

The official reaction bore out his suggestion about rule-breaking and its consequences. Nothing was said. Not that, strictly speaking, it was against the rules to climb trees and break your leg, but under normal circumstances it would have been held to be 'contrary to decency and common sense', as the school prospectus put it. Privately, the CO reckoned that breaking the leg was sufficient punishment in itself. A beating would have been superfluous and the pain trivial by comparison.

Spying on courting couples was definitely 'contrary to decency and common sense', but if the CO did realize that this was Stack's reason for clambering up the hawthorn, he did not let on. Even to himself.

'Why did you climb the tree, Donald?' asked the CO.

'Because it was there, sir,' he replied, quick, he later boasted, as a flash.

The CO seemed both amused and satisfied. If the answer explained Mallory's death on Everest in 1924 it would certainly do for Stack's broken leg in 1956.

It was agreed between the interested parties that the sixpenny bet was off. Stack maintained that, had he not fallen from the hawthorn, fully fledged fornication would have taken place, but he did concede, quite gracefully, that that was not what the bet was about.

'There's no such thing as a certainty,' said Porter, whose father, the Commander, liked a flutter now and again, 'until they've passed the winning post. That's what betting's about. I mean Devon Loch was a certainty in the Grand National. If you'd stopped the race after the last fence it would have won. But it went and tripped over its own feet.'

'Silly filly,' said Stack.

'The point is,' said Porter, 'you never know how things are going to turn out until they've actually turned out.'

'The point is,' Stack demurred, 'that I don't owe you sixpence and you don't owe me sixpence.'

Stack's accident was a threat to the success of Operation Piglet. To the reluctant Porter and the very reluctant Fieldhouse the broken leg seemed a perfect reason for abandoning the whole terrifying enterprise. Not to Stack. Stack said that he would sit in the back of the van as lookout man, while Fieldhouse would be the door-opener and Porter the pig-carrier. Porter pointed out, reasonably enough, that whereas Stack obviously had a way with pigs, he, Porter, had no such a rapport or experience. Stack, half accepting this, wondered whether Diggory's girlfriend Scarlett might be enlisted, but this was quickly vetoed. As was the idea of recruiting another West Hill boy. There was no one else they could trust. The conspiracy was large enough already. There was nothing else for it. Porter would have to carry the pig.

* * *

185

O'Rourke had a ticket for the Eifion Hughes address at Nether King's Compton Hall. He had heard him once before, in the '45 election. Hughes had come down to Caterham, home of one of the Guards depots. O'Rourke and one or two brother officers had gone to heckle and stayed to cheer. Well, if not cheer, at least to applaud respectfully. O'Rourke had followed Eifion Hughes's career ever since and had, in general, approved its maverick quality, its reluctance to conform, and its adherence to principles which he did not always share but could usually understand. When Odstock, over a pint in the Plume, had said that Hughes was speaking that Saturday, O'Rourke had bought a ticket there and then. Odstock was secretary of the local ward party and just happened to have some in his pocket.

The tickets could scarcely be said to have sold like hot cakes. Despite the wretched working conditions of men like Gavin and Chrissie's father, the rural proletariat showed a tiresome reluctance to kick over the traces. No matter how Odstock tried in the pub and at the cricket ground to explain that they were the victims of a capitalist system, an oppressed class labouring for the benefit of an idle squirearchy, the message never seemed to get through. Sometimes he felt that the Tolpuddle Martyrs were the exception that proved the rule. The rule being that country folk resembled the animals they husbanded. Whenever Odstock asked if they didn't think they were entitled to bigger wages, better housing, shorter hours, a higher standard of living, a more rewarding quality of life, they simply grinned at him and said they didn't mind if they did have the other half, thank you very much. It had not always been like this. There had been a time when peasants revolted. Indeed, Odstock had written an article entitled 'What price Wat Tyler now!' only to have it rejected with a printed slip from the *New Statesman*. He did think Kingsley Martin might at least have had the courtesy to write personally.

'The next generation will be different,' he told himself, willing Gavin and Chrissie to become the rural revolutionaries of the sixties and seventies. But even as he said it, he knew he was wrong. For every Gavin and Chrissie he saw through the village school, there were thirty or more Gavin and Chrissie's mums and Gavin and Chrissie's dads.

186

And grammar school and university would ensure that adult Gavin and Chrissie would never stay in feudal Somerset, unless by some horrid irony they came back as school-teachers to fight the same sort of unequal struggle that preoccupied him. Much more likely that they'd be urbanized. Maybe even absorbed. The British upper and middle classes had an insidious habit of assimilating clever rebels, of turning them into parodies of Cheltenham man, of transforming them into Homo Tunbridge Wells. He hoped that times had changed. The other day he had been to London to see the new play, *Look Back in Anger*, that everyone was writing about. That, it seemed to him, had a tempered fury that would not be allayed by bourgeois placebos. No way a playwright like Osborne, surely, would ever succumb. That was a true revolutionary's voice. Odstock envied it.

For the moment, however, he had to accept reality; and reality was that there were no John Osbornes in Nether King's Compton and precious few who would sympathize with his view even if they could understand it. That translated into distressingly few tickets sold for the Eifion Hughes meeting on Saturday.

'I don't know,' said O'Rourke, stuffing the blackthorn under his arm and looking quizzically around the grimly functional little auditorium. 'If you can persuade the troops to stop lurking in the shadows, you may create the illusion of a crowd. Not a full house I grant you, but a degree of respectability.'

'It's very disappointing.' Odstock's dejection was visible in the way he drooped, hands sunk deep in the pockets of his green corduroy trousers.

There were about thirty people in the hall, most of them sitting in the two rows of uncomfortable slatted wooden seats, in the English fashion at the very back. Chrissie and Gavin, lolling, selfconsciously casual and pseudo-adult in the front, were exceptions. Otherwise the assembled bashful consisted of two easily distinguished groups. One was Odstock's lot, farm workers and local tradespeople, shop assistants, and even one of the girls from the Plume, looking singularly out of place with her peroxide beehive hair-do and mauve-painted nails. The others were the local middle-class Fabian tweedies: the Misses Peebles, spinster ladies of

187

advanced years and vegetarian inclination; a Quaker couple from Norton Fitzwarren; a large bearded man from Bishop's Hull who was said to be a potter; and a scattering of other well-intentioned worried allsorts.

'There'll be quite a Hughes bandwagon,' said Odstock. 'Journalists. Things like that. The candidate.' He paused morosely. 'You didn't manage to persuade any of your colleagues to come?'

O'Rourke shook his head.

'Not even curious?' asked Odstock.

'Not even curious.'

Odstock shook his head and ascended the platform, which had been draped in red cloth for the occasion. He clapped his hands for attention and asked if ladies and gentlemen would come a little nearer the stage.

'The Member for Machynlleth has one of the loudest voices in Parliament,' he said, 'but I think it would be nice if, for once, he didn't have to use it. If we all gather round, he'll be able to be a little more conversational. Which would be nice for us and a change for him.'

There was a scattered titter and the Quakers and the Misses Peebles came forward timidly, though the bearded potter sat his ground.

O'Rourke decided that, despite Odstock's injunction, he would retreat if not to the very back, at least halfway, to the door marked 'Fire Exit'. If proceedings became unexpectedly dull he could always nip out for a fag. In fact, come to that, he had time to nip out for one now. There was plenty of time before Hughes was due.

It was a warm clear night and O'Rourke enjoyed his five-minute smoke. The stars were bright enough to remind him of North Africa though the silhouette of the parish church was a potent antidote to that sort of daydreaming. He regretted the war. Common purpose, camaraderie, the spice of daily danger, above all, the removal of trivial worry. He had never been concerned about income-tax returns or athlete's foot or the risks of cigarette smoking when living with the constant possibility of violent death. Now all three were permanent, nagging worries. From being a sharply focused, single-minded drama, life had turned into a diffused, aimless light comedy. He was often mildly amused by the happen-

188

ings at West Hill but scarcely moved or motivated. It was a peripheral sort of existence and he felt like a twig on the river caught in a slow drift to death. He would get there in the end, but meanwhile he was bumping aimlessly along the banks, spinning in languid eddies with no real purpose. He envied Burnam his certainties. Burnam was a mainstream log, bulldozing along in the centre of the current, never deflected. They would both reach sea or waterfall, or whatever lay at the end, at much the same time and in much the same way. Meanwhile Burnam had his certainties, and he had his doubts. Nothing he could do about it though. The die was cast when he stopped being a Guards officer and became a prep-school beak. Perhaps. Perhaps it was the difference between war and peace. Or just a question of temperament. Perhaps, in maturity, he would always have found life a dubious proposition.

He ground the cigarette butt under his heel and re-entered the hall. There would be plenty of certainties from Eifion Hughes. No doubt about that at least. He suspected that politicians were given to private doubt as much as most men, but no one was as committed to public certainty as your average MP.

The audience had swollen to perhaps forty by now with the advent of a few more Fabians and a darts team of red-faced, beer-bellied men in braces. O'Rourke sat down by the fire exit and tried to compose himself into a half-comfortable position. He was still failing in this endeavour when there was a flurry by the main entrance. Two men, obviously journalists, one armed with a heavy camera, entered, followed by half a dozen others in down-at-heel shiny grey suits. The suits could only have come from Burtons. Officials of the local party, O'Rourke presumed. They had the look of cut-price commissars.

Eifion Hughes, Odstock and the candidate followed at once, bustling with self-importance. Hughes was smaller than O'Rourke remembered: a tubby five-footer with scarlet tie and matching face framed in thick white curls. He grinned and waved at the audience, not apparently the least crestfallen by the turnout. The three went to the platform and the candidate and Hughes sat on chairs as upright and uncomfortable as the audience's. Odstock said the customary few words to introduce the candidate and the candidate said the customary few words to introduce the Member for Machynlleth. O'Rourke's attention wandered.

Odstock's introduction was a drone and the candidate's a rant, but both were brief. Hughes was on his feet within five minutes. 'Comrades,' he began, 'the Bible tells us "They shall beat their swords into plowshares, and their spears into pruning hooks; nation shall not lift up sword against nation, neither shall they learn war any more." '

He gripped the sides of the lectern and peered round with a fierce beam. Then, removing his right hand, he waved it at the ceiling, jabbing a stubby finger as he repeated, louder, ' "Nation shall not lift up sword against nation, neither shall they learn war any more." ' The hand was replaced and the grim smile passed over his audience again like the Angel of Death. 'When I was a little boy . . .' he said, in an altogether softer, melodious and almost absurdly Welsh lilt.

O'Rourke half smiled, half sighed. It was like a conjuring trick. The rising and falling of the voice; the theatrical gestures and cadences. The sort of thing Burnam tried to do in school prayers. He was surprised he had found Hughes so impressive on that earlier occasion. Perhaps it had been real that time. Perhaps repetition and frustration had given it the inner emptiness O'Rourke noticed now. It was predictable stuff: family of eight, father out of work; walking five miles to school in wooden clogs; silver and servants up at the 'Big House'; Winston Churchill and the business at Tonypandy; natural bellicosity of ruling classes; oppression by force; now inevitable dissolution of Empire resisted by killing innocent natives; Colonel Grivas very nice chap; Colonel Nasser not wog but highly civilized person; Mr Kenyatta, Dr Banda and friends not monkeys but intelligent graduates of British universities; British ruling class fascist, imperialist thugs maintaining own disgusting riches at expense of poor working class, native peoples at home and abroad; Conservative Party political expression of that thuggery; and so on. O'Rourke hated the language of hatred, but never more so than when it was counterfeit. He could not help feeling that some of Hughes's best friends were probably Tory pit owners.

'Comrades,' shouted the politician, 'Comrades, do not be

190

duped. Some members of this government, you may say to yourself, seem decent enough sorts of men. Some members of this government may not seem the sort of men who would rob the working man of his last penny, who would take the last slice of bread from the working man's child. But be not deceived. The leopard cannot change his spots.'

It was as Hughes said this that O'Rourke was aware of a sound at his side. Looking up, he saw the doorhandle of the fire exit begin to turn. Then the door opened and he found himself looking into the eyes of a small boy holding a bright blue piglet. The boy wore a handkerchief over the lower half of his face but he was in the casual uniform that West Hill wore for games and 'mucking about'.

Even if William Porter had not been in uniform, O'Rourke, who had been teaching him for five years now, would have had no difficulty in recognizing him, handker-chief or no handkerchief. For a second the two stared at each other in surprise and bewilderment. Then, suddenly, Porter dropped the pig and disappeared as the door slammed shut behind him.

The effect of the pig was much as expected and desired. At first Eifion Hughes, bowling along before the Force 9 of his own rhetoric, was not aware that anything was amiss. The audience were quicker on the uptake and reacted according to background. The Nether King's Compton folk, to whom pigs were a part of everyday life and whose sense of humour was rudimentary not to say basic, chortled happily and slapped their thighs like Austrians in the *Schuhplattle*. The Fabians, mostly townspeople with a somewhat insipid Fotherington-Thomas attitude to the country, found the pig a matter of concern and even alarm. Unfortunately the King's Comptonians, who could have dealt with the pig speedily and efficiently, were not particularly disposed to do so, and the Fabians, who wanted the pig dealt with immedi-ately, were too alarmed and inexperienced to manage it.

For at least a minute therefore the pig was free. It shot across the hall, down the aisle, back up it, turned left and bolted down a side aisle, all the while squealing and whim-pering. Coming rapidly towards the stage a second time, it decided to ascend the steps and charge across the platform where it relieved itself on the run leaving a stream of urine

191

immediately in front of the speaker's feet. The man from the *Western Gazette* took a photograph but the flash alarmed the pig still more and it shot back across the stage into the body of the hall.

By now even Eifion Hughes was forced to recognize the piglet. With a characteristic parliamentarian's weakness for the speedy ad lib, he fixed the animal with the sort of baleful expression he usually reserved for the Prime Minister at question time and said, 'Aha, I see a Young Conservative in thin disguise.' This vastly amused those of the audience who were still listening and gave the man from the *Western Gazette* his best quote of the evening. But it did nothing to solve the problem of the pig. It was the candidate, obviously dismayed by the imminent disintegration of the meeting and the disruption of his finest hour, who removed his jacket, rolled up his sleeves and advanced purposefully on the piglet. Eifion Hughes, resigned to the fact that this confrontation had, momentarily at least, proved more interesting than his speech, stopped talking and watched along with the rest of the crowd as the candidate lunged at the pig, appeared to get a grip and then lost it again as the animal slipped straight through his hands and charged into the Quaker wife, bouncing off, and leaving a thick blue stain on her off-white skirt.

'It's greased!' shouted the candidate. 'They've greased the pig!'

It took at least ten minutes to trap the wretched piglet and it was only done when one of the farmers stopped laughing long enough to go out and procure a sack into which the animal was finally induced to run. By the time this happened most of the Fabians had departed for home and the majority of the others had used the diversion as an excuse for a return to the Plume. The candidate and Hughes and Odstock agreed that there was no sense in attempting to continue with only a rump of what had in any case scarcely constituted a quorum and the meeting was adjourned in disorder. 'It was,' said Hughes, who seemed able to see the funny side of it, 'the only time in my entire political career that I have *ever* been prevented from finishing what I had to say. Lucky there aren't more Tories of that calibre.'

For Fieldhouse, Porter and Stack the operation was thrilling, petrifying and almost flawless. Stack had become quite manoeuvrable on his crutches and managed the stealthy journey to and from the rendezvous with Diggory surprisingly easily. After some brief but intensive coaching, Porter succeeded in holding on to the pig quite securely until the moment of release. All traces of blue paint were removed by turpentine before they left the van.

There were just two snags.

The first and relatively trivial one was that anticlimax set in almost at once. They could not brag about their achievement for fear it would get back to the CO. Nor did they have the satisfaction of seeing the effect of their efforts. If only they could have hung around the hall long enough to hear. If only they could have risked a peek through one of the windows. But Diggory had been adamant. A speedy getaway was essential. The risk of being caught blue-handed was just too great.

There was some consolation the following morning when they saw the *Sunday People*. The men from the *Western Gazette*, recognizing a good story when they bumped into one, had the good sense to make a few pounds on the side, and the *People* ran a large photograph of the piglet bolting across the platform in front of Eifion Hughes. It was captioned (of course) 'Young Conservative in thin disguise' and, on Monday, prompted some angry and ribald exchanges in the House of Commons.

Normally they would not have seen the *People* since boys were only allowed to read *The Times* and *Telegraph* on weekdays and the *Sunday Times* and *Observer* on Sundays. And herein lay the second of their snags: it was O'Rourke who showed them the photograph and caption. O'Rourke, as they had feared, knew.

9

O'Rourke accosted them after morning service, an apparently casual encounter by the cedar. The three boys were gossiping nervously, speculating on the consequences of the piglet episode, consciously willing O'Rourke to ignore it, when they saw him meandering with selfconscious aimlessness across the weeping beech lawn. He was hacking at the occasional daisy with his blackthorn and there was a tightly rolled newspaper under the other arm. It was too late to flee.

'*Eh bien*,' said O'Rourke in his upper-class Anglo-Irish accent, '*comment ça va*, Stack?' He prodded the boy's plaster cast with his stick. 'The leg. Mending nicely?'

'Yes thank you, sir.'

'Good. I'm glad to hear it.'

A long uncomfortable pause, then O'Rourke said, 'Eifion Hughes was speaking at the village hall last night. The MP for Machynlleth. Quite a character. Pity you boys couldn't have heard him. You might have learned something.'

None of the boys spoke. Porter swallowed hard.

'Unfortunately,' O'Rourke smiled a touch grimly and took a whack at one of the climbing ropes, 'he was interrupted before the end of his speech. Someone inserted a piglet into the meeting.'

Stack snorted, then suppressed the laugh ineffectually behind the back of his hand. O'Rourke glanced sharply at him and removed the paper from under his arm. 'The piglet made the national press,' he said, handing it to Porter. The other two crowded round. The 'story' was no more than a deep caption and it contained no clues about who might have been responsible. It just said that 'practical jokers' had painted and greased the animal and pushed it into the hall halfway through the MP's speech. For all three the sight of their endeavours in cold and public print was oddly shocking. An unprecedented collision between their world and the one outside.

'Gosh, sir!' said Stack when he had finished reading. 'Who on earth would do a thing like that?'

O'Rourke stared hard at all three and all three felt the same prickling sensation around the base of the spine, the same dryness of mouth, the same reddening of ears and face.

'I think,' he said eventually, 'that we all have a very sound idea of who on earth did a thing like that, don't we, Porter?'

Porter became still redder, stared at the ground and shuffled his sandals.

'Don't we, Porter?'

'Um, er,' Porter was whispering, 'yes, sir.'

'Bloody silly thing to do.' O'Rourke hit the rope again. Harder this time.

Two heads hung. Not Stack's.

'Please, sir,' he inquired, 'why silly, sir?'

'Don't be naive, Stack.' O'Rourke was snappy. 'You're supposed to be a Winchester scholar. Don't insult your own intelligence.'

Stack persisted. 'No, sir,' he said obstinately, 'I don't see what's silly about it. I mean, when the village oiks put the pigs' heads in the dingle, no one said it was silly. If that wasn't silly, I don't see what's silly about putting a piglet into the village hall. It was a Labour meeting, after all, sir.'

'Some sort of revenge, I suppose?'

'Sort of,' conceded Stack, 'but I don't see what's wrong with that, sir. I mean, if the law wasn't going to punish whoever beat up the dingle, then someone else has to do it, don't they? They shouldn't have been allowed to get away with it.'

'And what sort of world do you imagine it would be, Stack, if everyone thought like you?'

'Jolly sight better if you ask me, actually, sir.' Stack bristled.

'I see.' O'Rourke looked disdainful. 'Eye for eye, tooth for tooth. Law of the jungle. Every man for himself. Is that it?'

'No, sir.'

'Then *quoi*, pray?'

'I'm only saying, sir, that if the law doesn't work, then it's

195

up to the citizen to make it work. It's like a citizen's arrest, if you see what I mean.'

'Frankly, no, Stack, I don't see. If you repay one act of hooliganism with another, then you simply have two acts of hooliganism. Two wrongs, as the good book says, don't make a right.'

But Stack persisted. 'You have to stick up for what's right, sir. If the law won't do it for you, then you have to do it yourself. It's like Hitler. If we hadn't stuck up for ourselves, we'd be German and all in the Hitler Youth. That's what my stepfather says. The law was the League of Nations and a fat lot of good they were, sir.'

'Oh, do put a sock in it, Donald.' Porter found Stack's 'serious' monologues increasingly irritating. They had become markedly worse since the scholarship and were all, *he* reckoned, at least 90 per cent piffle. He turned back to O'Rourke. 'Please, sir,' he said sycophantically, 'do you think anybody else knows? Has anyone been told?'

'At this precise moment,' O'Rourke picked his words carefully, 'I'd be surprised if anyone knew for certain. But I'm quite sure that everyone is going to have suspicions.'

'They won't be able to prove anything,' said Stack sulkily.

'Don't be such an ass.' Porter was really angry now. He could see Stack talking them into real trouble. He guessed O'Rourke wanted to avoid it, but the more Stack went on arguing and being generally truculent, the more likely it was that O'Rourke would turn them in. 'You know perfectly well there was a witness. Someone was spotted. If the police have a witness, then that's curtains. They'll have an identity parade and all that kind of thing.'

O'Rourke pursed his lips. His feelings about the incident were hopelessly ambivalent. It was harmless enough in itself and had far less malice in it than the despoliation of the dingle. But it was still the sort of offence which, had it been perpetrated by Gavin and Chrissie, would have attracted heavy penalties. Whereas the bench would dismiss little toffs like Fieldhouse, Porter and Stack with a caution. When undergraduates at Oxford and Cambridge had too much champagne and went on the rampage, it was 'youthful high spirits'; when their proletarian counterparts had too many pints of bitter and sang in the streets, it was called being

196

'drunk and disorderly'. Rich wot gets the pleasure; poor wot gets the blame. Fact of life. The West Hill boys would have been guilty of nothing more than a 'prank'; the children of Nether King's Compton would have committed a 'crime'. If only for educational reasons O'Rourke wanted the boys to understand something of this. And yet he could not bring himself to turn them in. The law might let them off more lightly than it would Gavin and Chrissie, but the middle-class world might well be stricter, unofficially. Like cricket, there were laws and there were conventions.

It could be a black mark for life. 'Young Stack? Left West Hill under some sort of cloud, I believe. Something to do with a pig.' And there was the good name of the school. An absurd notion perhaps, but still real. Burnam would be mortified. O'Rourke was not overly concerned about that, but there were commercial considerations too. Parents took their boys away for far less. And those parents would dissuade others. 'No discipline. Gone to the dogs. Boys in and out at all hours. Wretched business with a pig and some Member of Parliament chappie.'

So O'Rourke had determined to deal with his private knowledge in his own private way.

'Have any of you three ever met anyone whose parents didn't send them away to boarding school?' he asked, apparently shifting ground.

All three said yes in an aggrieved but puzzled way, not sure what he implied, not certain what answer was expected, and doubtful too of what their own response really meant.

'I'll rephrase it,' said O'Rourke. 'Do you have any friends who don't go to prep school?'

More awkward. What did he mean by friend? They all *knew* people who went to state schools, whose parents were poor. Stack and Fieldhouse knew village boys. Women who 'did' had children; so did farmhands. They knew them but they didn't know them. They were civil, agreeable, sympathetic but not intimate. Their social intercourse went just so far. Porter, Stack and Fieldhouse knew their place; the rest knew theirs. It too was like cricket: Gentlemen versus Players; amateurs with their initials before the surname; professionals with their initials after. You could play in the same team but you hobbed with different nobs, or even if you hobnobbed together you did so on clearly understood terms. Somerset Burnam, for example, played in the same cricket team as one of the gardening 'boys'. After the game the two men would drink beer together and pore over the day's finer points. Burnam would call Sam Sam. Sam would call Somerset Mr Burnam. And neither of them ever forgot. Life was like that. A game of cricket.

The three boys shuffled their feet, grimy toes caressing the leather origami of Thomas Clark and Son's scuffed brown leather.

'Not really, sir, no, sir.'

'Rather a shame, wouldn't you say?'

More foot shuffling. No eye contact.

O'Rourke pressed on. 'Don't you feel it's rather limiting only to know people like yourselves? You're part of a tiny privileged minority. The English themselves are a tiny privileged minority in a world where most people's lives are pretty bloody, frankly.'

Still the boys stayed silent as O'Rourke raked them with another interrogatory stare.

'You're in a minority which is in a minority which is in a minority ad infinitum,' he continued, 'and it's a privileged minority. You're fantastically bloody lucky to have been born where you were and to whom you were. I don't think you fully realize that and I don't think you properly understand why other people might resent your luck. You've been well educated in a very particular way but it's been a very limited sort of education. There's more to life than books. Life out there,' he waved his blackthorn towards the ha-ha, 'is pretty bloody rough. *Pas gentil*. And most people out there aren't like you. In fact, they're not only not like you, they don't like you either. And they have their reasons. You don't know any more about the working class than Eden knows about Egyptians, do you?'

'They don't know anything about us either, sir.' Stack was still surly and defiant. 'It's just as much their fault. I don't mind knowing those kind of people but they don't exactly go out of their way to be nice, do they, sir?'

'All right,' said O'Rourke, finally getting to his point, 'maybe they don't know you any better than you know them, but it takes two to tango, don't you think?'

The boys stared up at him blankly, not understanding what the tango had to do with anything.

'I think it *is* time you met some children who don't have your advantages. I think you might learn something. Don't *you*? They're not all illiterate bolshies out there. Even in Nether King's Compton there are children of your age who are every bit as clever as you are. Do you realize that?' He was surprisingly angry.

'With respect, sir,' said Fieldhouse, 'if they were as clever as us, then how come they don't get scholarships to places like Winchester or Sherborne? Anyone can enter. There's nothing to stop them.'

O'Rourke looked at him contemptuously. 'It's because you can ask questions like that,' he snorted, 'that I want you to meet some other people of your own age. People who don't have your advantages but have to fight to get to the top.'

The boys looked back at him now, incomprehension mingling with shame.

'I take the view,' said O'Rourke, 'that the piglet was the product of ignorance rather than malice. And since the task of the pedagogue is to banish ignorance, I propose to arrange a meeting between you and two of the brightest village children. You shall all have tea at the Chummery and learn how the other half lives.'

10

The plan failed.

It did not founder on the misgivings of the West Hill boys because they were governed by discipline reinforced by threat. None of them had the slightest wish to take tea with the village yobbos, but even near the end of a final term, authority was ultimately too alarming to be flouted. Stack sulked, but although he came nearest to rebellion, he trekked along to the Chummery at 4.30 one afternoon, hair uncharacteristically neat, for a round-table tea with the enemy. For half an hour they sipped strong sweet Indian tea and listened apprehensively while O'Rourke told them tales of sergeant majors he had known. At five the phone shrilled and then they could hear O'Rourke's disappointed monosyllables as he listened to Odstock's explanations and excuses.

Odstock bowdlerized Chrissie and Gavin's objections and gave them an adult gloss. He did not say, as they had said, 'Go up there and have tea with those toffee-nosed little bleeders, you've got to be joking?' or 'Talk to them? What have we got to talk to them about? Be nice to them? What have we got to be nice to them about?' much less 'I hope they choke on their bleeding scones.' Instead he told O'Rourke that he was afraid Gavin and Chrissie were being truculent and unreasonable, though he could understand why, and that in the circumstances he thought a meeting might be counterproductive. Besides, unlike O'Rourke, he couldn't give orders. At least not with the same certainty.

'In the circumstances,' O'Rourke concurred. 'Circumstances' were a wonderful catch-all excuse. He used them himself all the time.

'In the circumstances,' he told Porter and Fieldhouse and Stack, 'they've decided not to come. I gather they're still very angry about the piglet. So much so that rational debate is *hors de question*. Mr Odstock and I have decided to call it off.'

So they ate their scones and departed.

Limping up the hill, Stack said, 'I never did think they'd turn up. They're just funks, really. Wet.'

'I'm quite glad they didn't come,' said Fieldhouse, 'actually.'

'Jolly bad manners,' said Porter. 'After O'Rourke had gone to all that trouble, and Oily Watkins cooked those scones.'

'No manners, and no guts,' said Stack.

The sands of term were running out and boys and masters alike were counting the days. Some smaller boys did it literally, down to the last minutes.

'Fifteen days, seven hours, thirty-seven minutes and forty-two seconds.'

'You can't do seconds – they go too fast.'

'It's thirty-seven seconds already.'

'Thirty-five.'

'I think we should stick to minutes.'

A restless lassitude gripped the school; a steamy wait for release. Outside the gates the world rumbled ominously as the Suez Canal continued to flow through the Prime Minister's drawing room and terrorists murdered British soldiers in Cyprus and East Africa. The Test series against the Australians, however, was the main focus of outside interest for the boys of West Hill. In free time they would gather around the huge walnut-encased wireless set in the library and listen to Rex Alston and John Arlott describing the action ball by ball, visualizing the drama of Trueman versus Miller, Lindwall versus Compton, Statham against Harvey, Miller against Hutton. They had seen photographs of the men from Down Under in their baggy green caps and some had been taken by parents to the Oval and Lord's, had actually seen English heroes in the flesh.

'Ten days, six hours, thirty-two minutes.'

'Nine if you don't count Sunday.'

'Why don't you count Sunday?'

201

'Because there's no work on Sundays, stupid.'

'We're still here though.'

Even during lessons there was little more than an apology for study. Scholarship and common-entrance exams were over for the year so there was no longer the same compelling reason for struggling through Xenophon or wrestling with the time it would take to fill a tank with water if the cubic capacity of the tank was thirty-two gallons and A minus B equalled whatever Oily Watkins said it equalled. Instead, masters set general-knowledge tests or let them read more or less improving novels or reminisced about the summer of '48 or told them travellers' tales of the Orient Express or hiking in the Tyrol. They regaled them with memories of their own childhoods when, always, the life of the schoolboy was nasty and brutish and would have been short too if the nastiness and brutality were really to be believed.

'Exactly a week.'

'I make it six days, twenty-three hours and fifty-eight minutes.'

'Your watch is slow.'

'Yours is fast.'

'Mine's Swiss. It's got real jewels. It can't be fast.'

'What's special about that? The best watches are made in England.'

'They aren't.'

'Are.'

'Aren't.'

As the days ticked by pleasantly and idly enough in the July heat, with its morning haze and smell of lawnmower clippings, there were still breaths being held, especially among the staff.

'I don't mind admitting,' conceded Burnam, in a rare burst of confidentiality to O'Rourke, 'that I'll be glad when term's over. Must be getting old. Too much excitement.'

O'Rourke merely smiled encouragingly and sympathetically. It was just as well, he reflected, that the CO did not know the truth about Eifion Hughes and the piglet. That episode had proved little more than a one-day wonder and was locally attributed to 'high-spirited' Young Conservatives or Young Farmers or most likely both. Official efforts to find out for certain were dilatory, not least because Labour

202

party indignation was tempered by the speedy response of their champion. 'Young Conservative in thin disguise' became a catchphrase for party speakers around the country, provoking immediate and automatic mirth among the faithful. Not even they were particularly interested in seeing the jape's perpetrator brought to book and fined 10s for a breach of the peace. Nevertheless, the knowledge that O'Rourke knew made the three scholars nervous and it made O'Rourke himself surprisingly fidgety as well.

He was apprehensive too about Batty or Queenie Roberts. It was not that Roberts was behaving badly. Quite the reverse. His behaviour was sober, even exemplary, and he made no mention of religion to boys or colleagues. To colleagues, indeed, he made no mention of anything much, confining himself to curt social niceties which remained scrupulously if marginally short of calculated rudeness. He said little more to the boys, allowing them to read or 'get on with their own work', while he himself stared morosely and blankly and silently out of the window. It was obvious, at least to senior and perceptive boys like Fieldhouse, Stack and Porter, that he was not looking at anything outside but was engaged in a more introspective contemplation.

O'Rourke, watching Roberts with the concern and attention of a conscientious zookeeper, could only guess what the good behaviour was costing but sensed that it was only a matter of time before the dam of self-control broke. When it did, he guessed the metaphor would prove all too accurate. There would be a dam burst: drama and disaster. He had similar apprehensions about Helen Battersby. St Aubyn's reaction to the cessation of necking and petting was one of relief as much as frustration, but Miss Battersby's sexual appetite was altogether more voracious. Abstention caused her anguish. In her case, however, there was no obvious solution close at hand. O'Rourke pitied her parents when the holidays began but guessed she would hold out somehow until term ended. As with Roberts, however, it was only a question of time.

'Five days, nineteen hours and one minute.'

'Seven hours if you're a car person.'

'I'm a train person.'

203

'I'm glad I'm a car person. I'm at home while you lot are still here in your dormitory.'

'The last night's not like the rest of term. Matron doesn't mind if we talk after lights-out. You can have pillow fights.'

'We always have roast chicken and ice cream on the first night home.'

'You can eat sweets in bed on the last night if you're a train person. I've got a gobstopper specially saved.'

'Five days, nineteen hours exactly.'

'*Seven* hours for us.'

Somerset Burnam always gave a leavers' talk before term's end. It was a rite of passage, a recognition of passing out, a ceremonial washing of hands. It was also supposed to impart information, and advice.

The CO enjoyed the main part of this talk, which was about character, leadership and the role of the Old West Hillian in contemporary society. He talked about obligations and the ideal of service to the community, to the country, to the Church and to one's fellow Old West Hillians. 'You are not,' he told the rather awed fourteen who were passing on to public school in September, 'just the future leaders of the nation, you are boys who have been educated at West Hill. That will make you *special* men with *special* duties and *special* qualities. In later life we at West Hill expect you to set an example to those less fortunate than yourselves. Being a West Hillian is something to be proud of, but not to be smug about. It means that you must work harder than others and play harder than others and that, above all, you must not rest on your laurels and waste the time that God has given you.'

Without the slightest sign of selfconsciousness he then recited Kipling's 'If', a poem which he regarded as the prep-school headmaster's creed and which he had known by heart since he was twelve or thirteen himself. As he recited he glared at each boy in turn until, reaching the final four lines, he threw his head back a little, fixed moist eyes on the ceiling and declaimed in full, resonant, barrack-square baritone:

'If you can fill the unforgiving minute
With sixty seconds' worth of distance run,
Yours is the Earth and everything that's in it,
And – which is more – you'll be a Man, my son!'

It would be wrong to suggest that there was not, at this point, a dry eye in the house. Sadly, the CO's were the only wet ones. The attitude of the West Hill graduating class of '56 was such that not one shed even a suspicion of a tear and the overwhelming emotion was embarrassment. Middle-aged men are far more romantic than small boys.

The CO disliked the second part of his speech as much as he relished the first. As the last echoes of Kipling vanished into the woodwork he removed his spectacles and coughed. When he resumed speech, his voice had left the Old Vic and was back to conversational.

'Next term,' he said, beginning to perspire lightly, 'you will no longer be big fish in our little pond here, you will be back at the beginning again, and you will find that you are no longer in a world of boys but a world of men. At about your time of life very remarkable physical changes take place. Your voices will break. You'll have to start shaving. And, most important of all, there will be a sudden enlarging of your private parts.'

He was definitely sweating now. How he disliked having to talk about the facts of life. He seldom thought about these alleged facts, taking them for granted and not allowing them to interfere with the real business of living. As far as the sex act was concerned, he had with a minimum of trial, error and help from his wife, discovered the missionary position. This was a position he could (and did) now take up with his eyes shut every Friday night except when Clarissa had the curse. As a young man, he had assumed the responsibility for contraception but Clarissa had soon said that she would prefer to take her own precautions in her own way. He was far too prone with shock ever to ask how this was effected, but it appeared to work since there had been no unplanned pregnancy. It seemed to him unnecessary and mildly dis-tasteful to know too much about the functioning of the human body and he had only the haziest idea about the mystery of birth. As far as he was concerned, it was quite enough to know that nine months after being impregnated Clarissa went to hospital and produced a baby. As for his part in the process, he thought it much overrated; not unpleasant but mildly disgusting. He could perfectly easily do without.

He recognized, however, that this disinterested attitude was regrettably rare; also that young adolescent boys could become not just disconcerted but positively preoccupied by sex. Above all, he was aware that most middle-class parents were just as reluctant as he was to instruct their offspring in the 'facts'. They opted out of the task by sending them to schools like his. When the cards were truly on the table, the relationship between himself and the boys' parents was brutally commercial. He was paid to get them into public school, to teach them good manners and, alas, to instruct them in basic sex.

'Some of you,' he continued, 'will already have noticed these changes beginning. Others may have to wait a year or even more. What happens is,' he took a deep breath, before spitting out the forbidden words, 'that your John Thomas gets longer and your balls drop.'

The boys were much more interested in this than in the uplifting lecture on civics. They at least were no longer embarrassed and they were avid to learn.

'When that happens,' the CO battled on, 'your body starts to manufacture seeds and it is these seeds which combine with the, er, eggs in the female and eventually produce babies.'

A dim boy from 2B who had just squeaked into Milton Abbey raised an inky paw.

'Yes, Bagge?' said the CO.

'Please, sir, how?'

'How what?'

'How do the seeds combine with the eggs, sir?'

The CO flushed. Someone tittered. The CO glared.

'Please don't interrupt, Bagge,' he said. 'You can ask questions at the end.' He inhaled again and continued. 'The actual business of mating needn't concern us in detail because, obviously, it's not going to matter until after you get married.' He ventured a watery smile. 'Those of you who live in the country will probably have a better idea than you town boys.'

206

Stack glanced at Porter and grinned. Nothing new so far. As an observant and interested country boy, he was beginning to wonder if he didn't know as much about procreation as the CO, though admittedly there was fairly firm evidence that the CO had the advantage of first-hand experience.

'If you're breeding horses, for instance,' said the CO, 'you wait until the mare comes on heat. Then the stallion mounts her and the seed, the sperm as it's called, is transmitted from one to the other. Then the seed fertilizes the egg and eventually the mare gives birth to a foal. That's what breeding is about. Yes, Stack, is something funny? May we all share in the joke?' He stared at Donald, one eyebrow cocked, privately thankful for the chance of a diversion.

'No, sir. Sorry, sir.' Stack was pinkly contrite.

'Now,' said the CO unhappily, 'as far as you're concerned, there *are* one or two things you need to know. One is that because God gives us too many seeds to start with you will soon have "wet dreams". This means that some of the seed will come out of your John Thomas while you're asleep. It's not at all the same as bed wetting and there's no need to worry about it. It happens to everyone.

'The second is that you may sometimes find you're tempted to play with yourself.' He disliked this bit almost as much as having to explain the mechanics of copulation. It had to be done though. 'If you feel this urge coming on, there are various things you can do. If you have the chance, a cold bath or shower works jolly well. Or even a cold flannel. Or just try to think of something else. Whatever you do though, don't give in to the temptation. The Victorians used to think it sent you blind and although modern doctors aren't sure about that any longer, there's no question, it won't do you any good whatever. You'll feel very off colour and you'll also come out in some unpleasant spots. Besides which, if you're discovered, you'll almost certainly be expelled. It's not only physically dangerous, it's also a sin. In fact, it's as bad in its way as fornication or adultery.'

All fourteen boys had begun to enjoy masturbation. All fourteen experienced an anxious moment. More than one wondered if his problems with the small print of Hillard and Botting could have anything to do with failing eyesight.

207

'Now . . .' The CO felt he was over the worst unless there were awkward questions. Usually there were no questions at all. 'One final problem you're going to have to face up to is older boys.'

The silence assumed a greater, almost tangible, depth. Not even Stack was expecting 'older boys'.

'In any public school,' said the CO, 'there will always be one or two older boys who take an unhealthy interest in their juniors. You will find that there are a number of rules to protect you from advances from seniors, but even so you must be very careful. If an older boy starts to take an interest in you, then you must tell your housemaster at once. You may think it seems perfectly innocent at first, but it's not natural. You will choose friends from your own age group. Otherwise the only seniors you may have anything to do with are prefects.'

The CO wiped his forehead with the paisley handkerchief from his sports jacket pocket.

'I think that's all I have to say. You are about to pass out of childhood into what we call the age of "puberty". It is not always an easy age, but I'm quite sure that with the background of a West Hill education to build on you'll manage well. Righty-ho. Any questions?'

Shoe shuffling, subdued giggles, surreptitious glances, then inevitably Stack's was the hand that rose.

'Please, sir,' he said, 'I don't quite understand. What exactly must we look out for? I mean, with older boys. What do they want to do to us that's so wrong?'

'I don't think there's any point in going into too much detail.' The CO was not quite panicked but he was distinctly fazed. 'The point is that they're not just interested in your, er, mind. They're interested in . . . well, they're interested in, er, playing with your John Thomas and having you do disgusting things to them too. Later on in life those boys will very often become what are called "homosexuals", and they'll spend most of their lives in prison. If you should allow yourself to become involved with an older boy, that could happen to you too.'

The CO removed his glasses again and peered around. He was about to halt proceedings when Stack's hand went up again. 'What exactly *is* a homosexual, sir?'

208

This looked like a safe enough half volley, though the CO did not trust Stack to ask anything straightforward.

'It's someone who prefers their own sex to the opposite one.'

'But, sir,' Stack protested, 'there aren't any of the opposite sex at public school.'

The leavers began to giggle but the CO snapped in sharply, 'Don't be disgusting, Stack.' He raked them with a peremptory frown, blond eyebrows beetling impressively.

'Righty-ho, then,' he said. 'You can cut along now. But remember what I said: once an Old West Hillian always an Old West Hillian. We expect you to uphold the honour of the school all through your life.'

Outside in the corridor, when they were out of the CO's hearing, Porter said to Stack, 'The really amazing thing is that the CO and Mrs Burnam must do that every week.'

Fieldhouse joined them. 'What?' he asked.

'You know,' said Porter, 'sex and things.'

'Plug in their connections.' Stack sniggered.

'Don't be disgusting,' said Porter.

They discussed the CO's talk throughout the rest of term. Not the Kiplingesque passages of moral exhortation; that was adult flannel. The sex instruction, however, was found fascinating by all school leavers, even though it failed to answer those questions (mainly mechanical) which most intrigued them. The matter of blindness naturally worried them, particularly as none of them could understand why blindness should strike down the self-abuser and not the righteously married man. From a medical point of view, it seemed to them that there wasn't a lot of difference. All agreed, however, that it must be important to wash your hands. All were also appalled at the idea of being interfered with by older boys; and Porter, Stack and Fieldhouse were much struck by the CO's so obvious embarrassment. None of them were quite sure why private parts had to be quite so private or why sex attracted such taboos. The CO's talk had excited them with what it implied rather than what it revealed. Not his intention at all.

'Three days, six hours, fourteen minutes.'

'This time next week I'll be in Malta.'

209

'I'll be in Hong Kong.'

'Chinese food! Yuk.'

'We don't eat Chinese food. Cook does English food, just like home.'

'We're going to the Norfolk Broads. My father's teaching me how to sail.'

'Three days, six hours, eight minutes.'

'Unless you're a car person.'

Although the fag end of the summer term was mostly a balmy anticlimax, it always managed to pull itself together in time for a final valedictory *feu de joie*. The very last day was given over to sports in the morning; and prize-giving in the afternoon followed by a speech. This was delivered by the most distinguished visitor the CO could conjure up. Then everyone had a nice cup of tea and the 'car people' went home with their parents, leaving the 'train people' one last night in captivity before they took the bus for Taunton station the following morning. Most years the bigwig visitor was a local worthy of limited interest or stature, but this time the CO had excelled himself by netting West Hill's most distinguished living Old Boy, General Sir Lendrum Winthrop, Deputy Chief of the Imperial General Staff. Sir Lendrum had been at Arnhem, which, though unpleasant at the time, had been no disadvantage to a number of notable military careers. He was almost as famous outside West Hill as he was within. In the CO's plans for modernization and enlargement, there was a new dormitory which he was intending to christen 'Winthrop' in the general's honour. West Hill could bestow no greater accolade.

The theory behind this terminal celebration was that it stopped everyone mooning around and getting into trouble. Heats had to be run for the sporting events. The school buildings and grounds had to be chamfered up and so did the boys. It was best-behaviour day; everyone and everything on show; one final effort before the summer hols.

Preparations this time ran smoothly enough. A running track was marked in whitewash around the First XI pitch and although some of the less athletic were eliminated, the overriding principle was that although all could not win prizes, all should be allowed to compete in the final of something; even if it was only the sack, the obstacle, the slow bicycle or the egg and spoon, Joe Soap must have his turn.

This meant that fond parents would have some evidence that their child was participating and perhaps excelling. The evidence might be slight, but it existed. It enabled Somerset Burnam to ward off any criticisms with a cheery 'I thought Freddie put up an awfully good show in the slow bicycle' or 'I *am* sorry Brian dropped his egg' when meeting his paymasters. Not that many parents had criticisms. It was generally acknowledged that Burnam and Co. did a good job and they were in any case pathetically grateful for the chance of being childless for threequarters of the year. It kept them young. Or so they thought.

It was not just the visit of General Sir Lendrum which made this particular Founder's Day different. In many ways it proved to be the most memorable in the school's history, and if, later, those who were present had difficulty in placing it, they were always able to do so by remembering that it was the day Colonel Nasser seized the Suez Canal.

'He's done it, then,' said O'Rourke at breakfast in the Chummery.

St Aubyn had got to the table first and commandeered the *Telegraph* which he held open in front of him. O'Rourke was scanning the front page across his coffee cup and the blue contrail of his first cigarette.

'I'm sorry,' St Aubyn had only read the sport. 'I can't think why they haven't chosen Wardle for Old Trafford. Far better than Lock or Laker. And he can bat.'

'Nasser,' said O'Rourke tersely, 'he's nationalized the canal.'

'Oh,' St Aubyn did not even feign interest, 'is it really that important? I'm much more interested in the Australians than the wogs. Do you think we'll win this time?'

O'Rourke gave up. He was to hear the word 'wog' many times during the rest of the day, from both boys and their parents, for, unlike St Aubyn, most of those at West Hill that day were interested in Suez.

It was not a very passionate or overwhelming interest and certainly not significant enough to interfere with sports or prizegiving. Nevertheless it cropped up. Commander Porter,

211

pink-cheeked and pink-eyed, perched on his shooting stick by the finishing line, fingered his Army and Navy Club tie and said to Mr and Mrs Fieldhouse, 'First home leave in ages and this has to happen.'

His angular wife scanned the playing fields with binoculars, idly hoping to come across something young and virile.

'What do you imagine we'll do about it?' asked Mr Fieldhouse diffidently.

'Send in the Fleet,' said the Commander in jaunty seadog manner, 'and blow brother Gippo out of his canal once and for all.'

Mr Fieldhouse seemed a little perturbed. 'Do you really think so?'

'I shall be sorry if we don't,' said the Commander. 'Wouldn't miss it for the world. Just wish the man had waited until my leave was over.'

The Travis-Gunns were at the start where Somerset Burnam presided with a starting pistol and a panama hat with I Zingari ribbon.

'Morning, Burnam,' called Travis-Gunn. 'Watch where you're pointing that thing.'

'Morning, Travis-Gunn,' replied the CO, 'Mrs Travis Gunn.' He fired the weapon and they watched as the final of the under-eleven hundred yards trotted off up the track.

'The general still going to be able to make it?' asked Travis-Gunn, ambling over to the headmaster who was reloading for the seniors' version of the hundred yards.

'He called from Whitehall this morning,' said Burnam self-importantly, 'and said he'd be here come hell, high water or Colonel Nasser.'

'Said that, did he?'

'His very words.'

'That's my Lendrum.' Scatty laughed.

'You know him, do you?' asked the CO, wind fleetingly removed from his sails.

'We served together before the war. Briefly. India. Tough little bugger. Too pleased with himself though. If he had his way, they'd be dropping him and a battalion of paratroopers over Cairo before lunch.'

'He can't have got his way, then,' said Burnam, 'he promised he was catching the 10.30 from Paddington.'

'Which must mean he's missed the boat for Port Said.'

'I suppose so.'

Allusions to Suez were all similarly lethargic and lacking in real urgency. The mood, especially among the many naval and military men present, was essentially that of Plymouth Hoe – not so much Drake's drum as Drake's nonchalance. Even the boys caught it.

'I say, Stack,' Porter enthused, shortly after winning the 220 which Stack himself would have won with two good legs, 'is there going to be a war?'

'Not until after lunch,' said Stack, 'Scatty says.'

It was a beautiful, languid July day. The marquees flapped quietly in the breeze, as did the bunting and the pink and green West Hill pennants. The sky was azure and cottonwool; fathers had the crisp-fit, striped tie look of a certain sort of cigarette advertisement; mothers were fluffy below the neck and wore wide-brimmed Ascot-style straw on their freshly coiffed heads; their little boys wore white shorts and singlets edged in pink and green. The crack of the CO's starting pistol, well-bred shouted encouragement and then palm upon palm as the winners were clapped home: these were the sounds of the middle class at play.

Shortly before one o'clock the senior obstacle race, a scaled-down commando assault course involving tarpaulins and used tyres, was won by Peter Dunstable-Smith in a new school record (Dunstable-Smith had very strong arms – invaluable on the double bars) and everyone adjourned for lunch. This was a picnic. Richer boys with parents in elevated areas of what professional parents called 'trade' sat down on deck chairs while their parents drank vin rosé in glasses and ate smoked salmon from Fortnum's. More parents, especially those with military or naval backgrounds, spread the food and drink on groundsheets or tartan rugs. No smoked salmon for them; instead, ham sandwiches, Marmite sandwiches, cheese sandwiches, jam sandwiches, perhaps a chicken leg or drumstick. For the adults beer, usually Whitbread in pint bottles decanted into pewter tankards; for the boys Schweppes ginger beer from opaque brown bottles. The most robust meals were the local farmers' and of these the most envied was the Travis-Gunns': outsize cornish pasties made by Scatty himself and fresh raspberries from their vegetable garden. The Travis-Gunns drank their own draught cider, cool in a gallon-sized earthenware jar. Donald, and any boy who happened to be passing, drank the same diluted with fizzy orange and garnished with sprigs of borage. The borage not only gave the drink a cucumber fragrance but made it seem more grown-up.

'Lendrum should be worth the admission price,' said Scatty, who like his wife was mildly put out by Donald's inability to compete and by the consequent lack of reflected glory. A Winchester scholarship was all very well but today he would honestly have preferred the Victor Ludorum. They all would.

'The archdeacon was so dull last year,' said Donald, 'not a single joke in the whole twenty minutes.'

'No jokes from Lendrum either,' said Scatty. 'Not a joking man, the general. But plenty of fire and brimstone. He'll put the fear of God into you all. Plus love of Queen and country, Rule Britannia, sock it to the natives and all that rot.' He took a swig of cider.

'I thought you liked General Winthrop,' said his wife, gazing at him through the only dark glasses on display.

'*Like* Winthrop? You must be joking. You don't *like* Winthrop. You love him or you hate him. There's no half-way with him.'

Stack looked at his stepfather thoughtfully.

'Which do you do?' he asked.

'I'll tell you later,' said Scatty. 'First of all you'll have to make up your mind. That's what being a Winchester scholar is all about, isn't it?'

214

11

General Sir Lendrum Winthrop was surprisingly small. Tiny in fact. As he entered the tent with the CO he looked like a miniature beside him, though the CO was hardly huge, just well built. And yet, despite his size, the general looked a general. He walked very upright and his gleaming black eyes flickered as if even in the few moments that it took to walk to the rostrum he had marked down every crooked tie, every unpolished shoe and every dandruffed collar in the place. He himself was immaculate. His brown brogues glittered, his brigade tie was knotted just so, and his lightweight tweed suit was exquisitely tailored as if it had been pressed minutes before. His skin was very dark and thick, like a pigskin wallet, and his hair, by Trumpers, was black and slick. He was almost more like an Indian than a British fighting man, but you only had to glimpse him for a second to see that he was indeed a fighting man. And a fighting man's fighting man at that.

Stack, Fieldhouse and Porter sat by the entrance with the other prefects. It was their job to usher parents to seats and, now that proceedings were under way, to make sure that they were not disrupted by latecomers. As the general passed, all three experienced a frisson of something which, on later analysis, they all agreed was fear. He should have been simply a very small man in a very neat suit but there was something else. Something rather horrid.

The CO's speech was conventional enough but sufficiently full of information to hold his audience. It was a succinct summary of a successful school year, interrupted by polite clapping as he mentioned such highlights as the winning cricket team and the unprecedented number of scholarships. A brief introduction of the general (more clapping) was followed by prize-giving.

It was interminable. The Alice-in-Wonderland principle was worthy but tiresome and parental attention wandered as little boy after little boy walked up to shake the general's hand and receive his prize (a book, usually by Sir Arthur Conan Doyle, school crest embossed without, West Hill bookplate pasted within). 'Form Six French. First Prize, Watson. *Proxime accessit*, Holmes.' 'Form Five French. First Prize, Marshall; *Proxime accessit*, Snellgrove.' Form Four French, Form Three, Form Two, Form One; Form Six English Composition, Form Five English Composition, Form Four, Form Three . . . The CO intoned as if conducting morning prayer from the London telephone directory. The general smiled, inclined the upper half of his body like a marionette, shook hands, murmured a word or two, never more, of congratulation, straightened, accepted another book from the CO, smiled at the next prizewinner and repeated the performance. Again and again and again. Two, three, smile. Two, three, shake. Two, three, give. A parade-ground performance. No soul to it but infinite professionalism, ingrained from Sandhurst.

Eventually it was finished and the CO turned and thanked his guest with charm and economy, reintroducing him at the same time as 'our most distinguished of all West Hillians', as 'one of Britain's foremost men at arms' and 'the front of our front line of defence'. The general listened, unmoved and impassive, to all this and a brief summary of his career and achievements. When it was over, and only then, did he allow a crisp tightening of the lips and creasing of the cheeks. This passed in the language of his body as a smile and was gone almost before it appeared. Quick blink and you missed it.

Then he began. He had prepared a speech some days before, he said in a dry staccato clip. 'Perfectly adequate speech.' He waved a sheaf of papers. 'But out of date. Not going to make it. More important things to say. Things that need saying. Things that don't need notes because they're in my bones.'

It was Nasser, of course, and the canal. This act of 'ruthless rapaciousness and base ingratitude' was the general's pretext for a stunningly stirring evocation of the British Way of Life, the British Empire and the values which informed them. 'Take India,' said Sir Lendrum, piercing his audience with his little black eyes in order to reinforce the command. 'Before we came to that unhappy country, what was it like? I'll tell you what it was like. Chaos. Total chaos. The great historian Macaulay tells us that the native rulers were utterly corrupt. They sat about "chewing bhang" and "fondling concubines". The administration, such as it was, was incompetent and crooked. Then a handful of dedicated British soldiers and administrators took India by the scruff of the neck and imposed order. We gave them law. We gave them order. We gave them justice. And dignity. And a common language. We taught them what Western civilization was all about.

'And then what happens?' The general gazed about him, not wanting an answer but seemingly satisfied by the respectful silence of his audience. 'I'll tell you what happens. They kick us out. The native Indians suddenly decide that it's not enough to be well ruled. Not enough to be cared for properly. Not enough to be elevated to a civilized status they were incapable of attaining themselves. Oh, no. They decide they want to do it for themselves. India for the Indians.

'So then what happens? After trying to reason with the half-educated, self-appointed so-called leaders of the country, we, in our wisdom, shrug our shoulders and say "very well". And we leave the Indians to their own devices. And then what do we see? We see appalling bloodshed. We see India divided as it had not been divided since before the British came. We see a return to the very chaos that we, the British, had prevented for hundreds of years. In no time at all it is as if we had never been. Country's back in the Middle Ages. Nothing but "chewing bhang" and "fondling concubines". All because of the vanity, yes, the vanity, of men like Mr Gandhi and Mr Nehru.'

Strong stuff, thought O'Rourke. And obviously going down a treat. This was what this audience had hoped to hear. For him, however, there was a peculiar irony, for as he listened to the little general he was reminded of the words, a few days earlier, of Eifion Hughes. This was the other side of that coin. Just, to O'Rourke's equivocal mind, as over the top; just as exaggerated; and just as wrong. Just as dangerous.

217

He could sense that it was working a treat with most of the parents, but he wondered how it was working with the boys. He hoped their innate scepticism had not yet been stifled. Certainly he had done his best to cultivate it.

The general was telling everyone that it was a dangerous world in which we lived but that for all the dangers posed by fanatics like 'the gibbering Gippo' or by alleged 'friends' like the two-faced John Foster Dulles, the greatest danger came from within.

'Scarcely ten years after defeating Nazism,' said the general, 'I see the country becoming soft. Too many of us think the world owes us a living. That we're entitled, entitled; if you please, to *free* medicine; *free* education; even *free* school milk. Well, I'm speaking to you as a man of experience who's knocked around a bit and I'll tell you what I have discovered. And it's this. In this life nothing comes free. We have to fight, fight and fight again.'

Porter, Stack and Fieldhouse, sitting on the bench by the entrance, were enthralled and not necessarily unconvinced. But they also found that first fleeting fear being reinforced. They had been alarmed by the general when he had done no more than pass by. Now that he had opened his mouth, they found him terrifying. Even Stack recognized that this was someone whose orders you obeyed implicitly and, like his friends, sensed that, for all his talk of civilized values, there were no orders the general might not give.

The general was just launching into a description of how and when people should be taught a lesson they wouldn't forget, when the boys at the back of the tent heard a noise from outside. It was laughter.

Fieldhouse looked at Stack, Stack looked at Porter. Porter, after a moment's consideration, pulled aside the tent flap and, on exaggeratedly tippy toes, went out to investigate.

'Shhh,' he said as soon as he was out in the sunshine, 'Shhh.' This was pure reflex. He had assumed it was simply latecomers who did not realize that the general was in full flight. He was certainly not prepared for what he saw.

Some yards away, arm in arm, a man and woman staggered giggling towards the tent. Even without the bottle, which looked like gin, that the man clutched in his free hand, it would have seemed probable that they had been drinking. Even without the disarrangement of dress – shirt buttons undone, a coming-adrift at the waist, not to mention a general dishevelment and untidiness of hair – it would have seemed equally probable that some form of sexual congress had been taking place. It was an improbable combination, one born of desperation, an inability finally to repress what came naturally: Miss Battersby and Mr Roberts.

Porter was appalled. So much so that for a moment he was rooted immobile to the spot. Behind him he could hear the general's staccato phrases rasping on, obviously not about to come to an end. In front of him he could see two mindless drunks lurching inexorably towards the marquee. The collision was too frightful to contemplate.

Porter advanced to meet them. 'Please, sir,' he said in a loud, urgent whisper.

Roberts beamed at him: a hideous inebriated leer. 'Good afternoon, Porter,' he said. 'Miss Battersby and I are off to debate with the general.' His breath reeked. Porter blanched.

'Miss Battersby,' Porter whispered even more urgently, but even as he addressed her, he realized that there was no point in appealing to the junior matron. Her eyes were glazed, her face slack. She might as well have been sleep-walking.

'Have a drink,' she said.

'Stand aside boy,' said Mr Roberts, adding portentously, 'The Day of the Lord is at hand. He cometh with clouds and every eye shall see him.'

'Oh, cripes!' said Porter. But he stood aside and the odd couple passed on towards the tent. As he fell in behind them, Miss Battersby looked back and winked.

Only a few heads turned as they entered. The general had them captivated, mesmerized, impervious to interruption.

'Behold a pale horse,' shouted Roberts, words slurred, 'and his name that sat on him was Death.'

This time people did look round. There was a collective 'shushing' noise. The CO observed Roberts and hastily whispered to O'Rourke, sitting on his left. O'Rourke slipped out of his place and began to move towards Roberts. The general did not look up, nor did he falter.

219

'There are times when men of honour must stand and be counted,' he was saying.

'I myself,' shouted Roberts, 'have seen the ungodly in great power: and flourishing like a green baytree.'

Several parents now turned angrily. One puce-faced man called out, 'Sit down and shut up.' Others hissed. O'Rourke had almost arrived by Roberts and Miss Battersby. The general still did not look up.

'On all sides,' he said, 'British honour is being insulted, British reputation sullied, British generosity rejected.'

'Gilead is mine, and Manasses is mine!' bellowed Roberts. 'Emphraim also is the strength of my head.'

O'Rourke was alongside now.

'For God's sake, Roberts,' he said, 'shut up and come outside.'

'The very name of Britain is at stake,' rasped the general, finally beginning to sound irritable.

Miss Battersby started to giggle.

'Judah is my law-giver,' called Roberts as O'Rourke took him by the arm and attempted to steer him out. 'Moab is my washpot.'

O'Rourke seemed to be making very little impression on Roberts. To O'Rourke it was all horribly reminiscent of the evening in Nether King's Compton village hall, with him in the role of the local candidate and Roberts in that of the greased piglet. Behind him in the body of the meeting he could sense the same imminent disintegration. Several voices, male and female, were now being raised against the incursion.

'Get him out of here!'

'Freedom of speech!'

'I'm not standing for this. I want to hear what the general has to say.'

'Who *is* that man?'

'Isn't that Harold Battersby's girl?'

'He's drunk.'

'She's drunk.'

'They're both drunk.'

But over and above this cacophony of ruffled feathers, two sounds: the general's rasp risen to parade-ground strength advising of the need for Britain to 'be very vigilant, ever on guard' and Roberts's drunken shouting, 'Over Edom will I cast out my shoe: Philistia, be thou glad of me.'

And then the tent fell down.

For a second or so it was just the part over the speaker's rostrum that seemed to sway and sag while the audience watched it in alarmed fascination. Then with sudden crackling of canvas the whole structure caved in on itself and little boys and parents were a struggling shambles of confused and frightened middle class. Little boys and their mothers shrieked. Husbands and fathers bellowed conflicting commands and orders not to panic. The general shouted 'Crawl for the edge,' an order taken up by the CO and one or two others close to them. It was oddly reminiscent of the tarpaulin in the obstacle race.

Porter, who had been standing nearest to the exit, crawled out first. He stood blinking in the sunlight and gazed at the deflated marquee under which the mass of bodies heaved and struggled, emitting muffled shrieks and invocations, orders and entreaties. Quite funny actually, he thought, provided no one gets hurt. He turned back, looked across the lawn and saw two children not much older than himself. They were standing about a hundred yards away, just the other side of the ha-ha, and they were laughing. Porter knew immediately he saw them. 'Village yobs,' he said out loud, 'they did it.' And he began to run towards them. They let him get to within about twenty yards, secure on their side of the ha-ha, knowing they could be well away before he could scramble across.

'Bleeding little snob!' shouted Gavin. 'Can't catch us.'

Porter slowed to a walk. 'Yobbos!' he called back. 'Oiks! You'll go to borstal for this!'

'Yah!' Chrissie thumbed her nose. She mimicked an upper-class accent. 'I say, hadn't you better go back and find mummy and daddy, little boy?'

Then they ran off. Porter wondered whether to give further chase. He looked back at the tent and saw that most people had emerged now. Gavin and Chrissie were already halfway across the park. He would never catch them, and even if he did, what then? He shrugged his shoulders, stuffed his hands in his pockets, and retraced his footsteps. It was too bad. The village had had the last laugh after all.

* * *

Years earlier a West Hill boy had composed an end-of-term anthem for the train people. It was sung to the tune of "Abdul Albulbul Amir', a record of which, very old and an odd shade of translucent blue, was a prized item in the CO's collection of 78s. It had become a school tradition for the train people to sing it in the bus on their way to Taunton station.

That next morning, in the hangover of the marquee's collapse, it was grey and overcast as the senior train person, Peter Dunstable-Smith, called on the boys to give 'Three cheers for Mr and Mrs Burnam' before they piled into the coach and began to sing.

> 'The end of the term at the school of West Hill
> Is greeted with many a cheer.
> The car people wet
> Go off in a set
> And vanish out into the blue.'

Not very inspired words, but they never failed to make Somerset and Clarissa Burnam lachrymose, as they stood on the front steps and waved the last of their boys goodbye. The girls stood at their side and Muggins wagged his tail and barked as they watched the bus grind slowly across the gravel towards the cedar, the cattlegrid and the park beyond.

> 'The train people fine
> Go off down the line
> To Paddington, Euston and Crewe
> While the CO and staff
> Enjoy the last laugh
> And wait to begin all anew.'

Distinctly uninspired words, thought April, just turned thirteen, and safely destined for Sherborne Girls' School, but then she was still in rather a state about doggerel. The previous evening, just before he had driven off with Scatty and his mother, Stack had handed her a sealed note, not to be opened until he was clear of the grounds and therefore a free agent.

She had been hoping for something romantic or, as the boys would have put it, 'soppy', but when she opened it she found, in Stack's awkward spider's web hand:

'Tom and Mary went down to the dairy
Tom pulled out his long and hairy
Coo, said Mary, what a whopper!
Let's get down and do it proper
Three months later all went well
Six months later belly began to swell
Nine months later belly went pop
And out jumped a nigger with a nine-inch cock.'

No wonder Stack had wanted her to wait till he was out of her father's clutches. It made her feel quite ill. Disgusting boy. And yet she couldn't show it to either of her parents. They would be too shocked. And, in a perverse way, they would be as angry with her for receiving such a note as with Stack for sending it. She tore the note into tiny fragments and flushed it down the lavatory, resolved to forget all about it. But try as she might, the words kept coming back to her, and always at the least suitable moment. For months after she found herself remembering them in church. It was too bad. Goodness, she'd be glad to get to a single-sex school, well away from rude boys.

The high-pitched end-of-school song was faint now, the bus a mere Dinky toy as it wound through the park along the route O'Rourke took daily to the Plume. The Burnams watched it wistfully, still waving, until finally it disappeared over the brow of the hill. For a moment or two they continued to watch, almost as if they expected it to reappear and set the whole saga of the last few weeks in motion once again.

'I can't say,' said Clarissa, finally averting her eyes, 'that I'm sorry to see the back of them this time.'

Her husband smiled ruefully, the memories all too fresh, particularly of the dressing down he had received from General Winthrop. The general said the Girl Guides could have pitched a tent more competently. When it was found that the guy ropes had been cut with a knife he seemed disinclined to believe it, let alone apologize. The CO had revised his opinion of the world's most famous West Hillian. The parents, once it was found that there were no bones broken, had taken the whole thing in noticeably good part. Which made the general's churlishness all the worse. Of course, the parents had been mollified by the brandy O'Rourke had

223

miraculously conjured up from the Plume, but even so . . .

'Oh, don't say that, old girl.' He put an arm round his wife. 'It's not the boys' fault. They're a good lot. Look at Donald Stack. A Winchester scholar. Our first ever. He's going places.'

The farther the better, thought April furiously.

'And Porter. He's a good boy.'

'Better than the parents,' said Clarissa. 'The Commander drinks. He had a flask yesterday. And as for his wife. Did you see the way she was pawing David St Aubyn?'

The CO said he hadn't, and they turned to go indoors, back into the empty house, echoing with its ghosts of little boys past.

'I wonder what will become of them?' Clarissa always asked this at the end of term; asked it during term too, being more preoccupied with the future than her husband, who was firmly rooted in time present and time past.

The CO was thinking that, despite everything, the school had survived intact, that in many ways it had been a good term. The records would show the success of the cricket team long after the unpleasantnesses of the St Christopher's match were forgotten.

The honours board would record the awards of Stack, Porter and Fieldhouse, but there would be no written evidence of the pigs in the dingle, or the collapsing marquee, or that awful night in the Lake District. It really could have been so very much worse.

'Become of them?' he said. 'I've no idea. It's up to them. We've done our bit. They're on their own now.'